The Spirit and the Salvation of the Urban Poor

The Spirit and the Salvation of the Urban Poor

A RENEWAL APPROACH

BRANDON KERTSON

PICKWICK *Publications* · Eugene, Oregon

THE SPIRIT AND THE SALVATION OF THE URBAN POOR
A Renewal Approach

Copyright © 2019 Brandon Kertson. All rights reserved. Except for brief quotations in critical publications or reviews, no part of this book may be reproduced in any manner without prior written permission from the publisher. Write: Permissions, Wipf and Stock Publishers, 199 W. 8th Ave., Suite 3, Eugene, OR 97401.

Pickwick Publications
An Imprint of Wipf and Stock Publishers
199 W. 8th Ave., Suite 3
Eugene, OR 97401

www.wipfandstock.com

PAPERBACK ISBN: 978-1-5326-6344-4
HARDCOVER ISBN: 978-1-5326-6345-1
EBOOK ISBN: 978-1-5326-6346-8

Cataloguing-in-Publication data:

Names: Kertson, Brandon, author.

Title: The Spirit and the salvation of the urban poor : a renewal approach / Brandon Kertson.

Description: Eugene, OR : Pickwick Publications, 2019 | Includes bibliographical references.

Identifiers: ISBN 978-1-5326-6344-4 (paperback) | ISBN 978-1-5326-6345-1 (hardcover) | ISBN 978-1-5326-6346-8 (ebook)

Subjects: LCSH: Pentecostalism. | Poverty—Religious aspects—Christianity. | Holy Spirit.

Classification: BT121.2 .K47 2019 (paperback) | BT121.2 .K47 (ebook)

Manufactured in the U.S.A.   11/14/19

This book is dedicated to my family:
Kendra, Peyton, Amber, and Eden.
I love you.

Contents

Introduction: Historical Background—Renewal of the Urban Poor		1
	Definition of Terms	2
	Outline and Approach	6
1	**Urban Poverty in the United States**	10
	Introduction	10
	The Face of Poverty in the United States	13
	The Underside of Poverty in the United States	24
	Conclusion	31
2	**Urban Poverty in American Evangelical Theology**	32
	Introduction	32
	Evangelical Theology and Urban Poverty	35
	Conclusion	62
3	**Urban Poverty in Ecumenical Theology**	63
	Introduction	63
	The Social Gospel and Urban Poverty	64
	Liberation Theology and Urban Poverty	78
	Ecumenical Theology and Urban Poverty	89
	Conclusion	96
4	**Urban Poverty in North American Renewal Theology**	97
	Introduction	97
	What is Renewal Theology?	100
	Renewal Theological Responses to Urban Poverty	110
	Renewal Practical Responses to Urban Poverty	121
	Conclusion	129

5	**Pneumatological Resources for a Theology of Urban Poverty**	132
	Introduction	132
	What is Pneumatology?	134
	Challenges to Pneumatology	147
	Conclusion: A Methodology for a Pneumatology of Urban Poverty	161
6	**Pneumatology and Urban Poverty in the United States**	164
	Introduction	164
	Pneumatic Reading of Luke 4	165
	The Pneumatological Salvation of the Urban Poor	171
	Conclusion	202
Conclusion		204
Bibliography		207

Introduction

Historical Background—
Renewal of the Urban Poor

Two movements, social action and Renewal, have been prominent in the landscape of United States Christianity for the past century. The advent of the Social Gospel among pastors and theologians working with the urban poor of the early twentieth century caused social concern for the poor to begin to permeate the imagination of both academic and parochial Christianity. For instance, Walter Rauschenbusch was writing theology for the many jobless and working poor living in Hell's Kitchen, New York, which was affected by urbanization and the industrial revolution.[1] At the same time, on the other side of the country, a revival was brewing among the urban poor of Los Angeles, many of whom were dealing with similar issues as their New York counterparts. This revival would be a key site for the quick growth of the Pentecostal and Charismatic movements that together have grown into one of the largest global Christian movements.[2] These Renewal movements place a specific emphasis on the Holy Spirit but have often been labeled as quietistic concerning social issues.[3]

Both movements resonated among the urban poor in the United States yet provided very different responses to urban poverty. Both of these movements have grown and matured into very distinct expressions

---

1. For a good overview of Rauschenbusch's work see Nelson, "Walter Rauschenbusch," 442–56. Rauschenbusch's most foundational work is Rauschenbusch, *Theology for the Social Gospel*.

2. See, for instance, Pew Forum, "Global Christianity."

3. Walter Hollenweger, for instance, identifies a lack of explicit political and social involvement and attributes it to Pentecostal's anti-communist orientation. See Hollenweger, *Pentecostals*, 467–69.

within the United States. Theologies of social action among the urban poor have largely overlooked the Holy Spirit as a resource for theological responses to poverty. On the other hand, Renewal Theology has focused on the Holy Spirit with little attention to how this might apply to social issues or urban poverty.

The similarities in origin and growth of these two movements, yet their extremely different theological emphases, help to surface the question of how a theology of the Holy Spirit can or cannot help to develop a holistic theology of social action among the urban poor. The aim of this project is to explore a theology of urban poverty in the United States from a holistic pneumatological perspective. To further explain the scope of the project, we will unpack what we mean by a pneumatological theology of poverty, explain how we will take a social action approach to poverty, and briefly define what we mean by the urban poor.

DEFINITION OF TERMS

Theology

In speaking of a "theology" of poverty, the specific aim is to uncover God's own character and action toward the poor and how this would motivate a follower of God to act similarly in the world. A theology of poverty cannot focus on motivations alone. It should also shed light on possible actions that can be taken to alleviate the needs of the urban poor. Being motivated and taking action without being informed about the actual needs of the urban poor is only a reaction, not a theological response. Often within Renewal movements, social action among the urban poor has been based on reaction rather than thoughtful theological reflection and engagement based on research couple with Renewal spirituality and theology.

My desire is to explore these possible theological beliefs, motivations, and actions toward the poor, not just from a general theological perspective, but from a specifically pneumatological perspective. Christians have traditionally viewed God in a Trinitarian fashion, as Father, Son, and Holy Spirit; three equal persons who are at the same time wholly one. Each person in the Godhead has their own character and roles, which at the same time interpenetrate one another so that the character or action of one is necessarily true of all three because of their oneness. In this basic Trinitarian understanding, a pneumatological perspective should give a unique angle through which to explore poverty that looking through the lenses of the Father or the Son may not provide. My desire to limit the scope to a "pneumatological paradigm of theology" is based on a perceived gap in the current theological literature concerning poverty.

Most theological paradigms of poverty have only looked through one of two overarching lenses. Some look through a general theistic perspective, usually a theistic anthropology focusing on the dignity of humanity as created in the image of God. Most other theological paradigms of poverty begin with the perspective of the Son usually focusing on a theology of the kingdom or soteriology.[4] In proceeding from some combination of these two dominant perspectives and ignoring the Holy Spirit, these theologies have missed a whole realm of possible divine agency. Focusing on a pneumatological perspective does not deny or override work done from these previous perspectives. Rather, Pneumatology will add to and complement work done through the Father or Son. All three perspectives should necessarily overlap, but a pneumatological focus should also be unique because it is based on the unique person of the Holy Spirit. When taken with previous research, a pneumatological perspective should create a more robust theology of poverty. Our goal is pneumatological but will necessarily build on past theistic or christocentric research and so will have Trinitarian implications. If this is what we mean by a pneumatological theology, what do we mean by a social action among the urban poor?

Social Action

Social action is a rather recent term that describes deeds performed to alleviate the needs of a person or people group. Another popular term is social justice and the two terms are often used synonymously. Other terms within the same sphere include social engagement or social ministry. I prefer the term social action for three primary reasons.[5] First, social action is a more historical term that incorporates many of the earlier Roman Catholic social action movements, the Social Gospel movement, and even Liberation Theology. Second, social action is a broader term that focuses on action taken to alleviate the social and systemic causes of an issue, like urban poverty, rather than simply help an individual. A possible, yet simple, illustration is to see social engagement or social ministry as feeding a hungry person, and social action or social justice as empowering the person or reforming

---

4. These are very broad categories and may be somewhat simplistic. Certainly, every theology of poverty does not fit so cleanly into only one of these perspectives, but these two perspectives are certainly dominant as we will see in chapters 3–4.

5. This particular distinction is largely pedagogical and is taken from Petersen, *Not by Might, Nor by Power*, 246.

the systems of oppression to make sure they are not hungry again. A third reason for the term social action over social justice is that the term justice is commonly associated with equality, a definition which may not be tenable or sustainable biblically.[6] On the other hand, social action implies a generous movement toward those in need, recognizing that we are all in need at various stages and in different ways. It also recognizes that the action may not produce equality or completely solve the issue but moves toward action nonetheless. These distinctions are largely pedagogical. Their usages often overlap in both common and academic usage. Many even use the term social engagement to describe what I am calling social action. What it does point to is my desire to have social action include motivation, but also to include dealing with systemic issues that cause social ill and not just symptoms that alleviate those ills for a season or one particular person.

Finally, social action is a very broad term that can include a wide range of topics. Social issues can include such diverse topics as poverty, immigration, education reform, human trafficking, creation care, familial abuse, or gender and sexual orientation rights to name a few. Our specific focus in this dissertation is a theology of urban poverty. In its broadest sense, poverty can be seen as a common and major root issue of just about any injustice needing a social response. Gender equality, for instance, has socioeconomic implications as the majority of poor adults in America are women.[7] So poverty and social action are both broad terms that covers a great array of issues.

Poverty

By poverty we primarily mean the economic inability to meet one's basic needs, but poverty is much more complex than this. To further refine our scope, we will look at the urban poor. Urban poverty includes segregated neighborhoods in America's central cities in which a substantial majority of individual adults are either temporarily unemployed or have dropped out of the work force altogether.[8] Urban poverty is a complex issue on ev-

---

6. Wolterstorff, *Justice in Love*, 5. Jesus, in the gospels, welcomes the outcast and meets their needs on various levels, but this does not necessarily create equality. Equality cannot be a term that ends up overriding diversity and it is questionable whether equality is ever truly possible.

7. Cawthorne, "Straight Facts on Women in Poverty."

8. See Wilson, *When Work Disappears*, 18; Glaeser et al., "Why Do the Poor Live in Cities?," 1. According to Mink, 40.7 percent of all poor people live in central cities, 36.8 percent in suburbs, and 22.8 percent in rural areas (Mink and O'Connor, *Poverty in the United States*, 738).

ery level and requires a holistic response. Even how poverty is determined is much debated in academic circles.[9] One thing is clear. Regardless of the measures used, poverty continues to affect an inordinate number of individuals and families in the United States. At the time of the most recent US Census in 2010, 15.1 percent of all persons lived in poverty, defined as a lack of resources to meet one's material needs This rate is even greater for marginalized groups such as Blacks and Hispanics, children, the elderly and single women.

My own context is San Diego, CA. I grew up in San Diego and, after a decade away, moved back three years ago to work at San Diego State University as a campus minister for a Pentecostal denomination. San Diego is the eighth largest city in the United States with a population of 1.3 million people. The whole Metropolitan area of San Diego has over three million people. According to the Center on Policy Initiatives' "Poverty, Earnings and Income in the City of San Diego 2014," the poverty rate in San Diego remained at 15.7 percent of the population in 2014, relatively unchanged from the previous year's 15.8 percent, while the national poverty rate declined to 14.5 percent in 2014.[10] Like most metropolitan areas, the center of the city contains the highest rates of poverty reaching up to 47 percent in some neighborhoods. Not all of the poor in San Diego are permanently poor who moved here because of its temperate year around weather. 41.5 percent of poor adults in San Diego had jobs. Still, poverty most affected children and the elderly who are often unemployed. This rash of statistics helps to demonstrate that poverty in the urban central cities is complex, but it is these poor within my own backyard that I have in mind, particularly both working and non-working families.

This is just a basic picture of urban poverty. We will explore the topic in greater detail in our first chapter concerning poverty in the United States. Our goal is not just to paint a picture of poverty, but to develop a theological reading of urban poverty that leads to a holistic response. How will we accomplish this goal? Our general approach throughout the paper is a literary one. First, we will seek to understand poverty sociologically and theologically, identifying a pneumatological gap in current approaches to poverty. Second, we will create an epistemological framework for a response through the lenses of Renewal Theology and Pneumatology that brings a Renewal approach into conversation with other sociological, Evangelical and ecumenical standpoints. Finally, our process will be to outline a constructive and holistic Pneumatology of urban poverty utilizing the framework of the four-fold gospel which creates a four-fold set of lenses through which to

9. See Jennings, *Understanding the Nature of Poverty*.
10. Center on Policy Initiatives, "Poverty, Earnings, and Income."

view poverty holistically through our epistemological framework. In particular, we need to develop a strong Spirit-Christology as an approach through which to read the four-fold gospel since it is traditionally a christological construction. One can see this movement and approach throughout the dissertation in the following chapters.

OUTLINE AND APPROACH

In chapter 2, we will take up this question—what does poverty look like in the United States? Our central source is a body of sociological literature such as the work done by William J. Wilson on urban poverty and a number of articles exploring why poverty occurs and what it entails.[11] First, we will look at the "face of poverty" exploring in more detail the demographics and measurements used to determine poverty and what they mean. Second, we will explore the "underside of poverty," by looking at the economic, social and psychological underpinnings of poverty and their implications for those in poverty and for society as whole. Exploring both the face and the underside of poverty will help us develop the need for the holistic approach to poverty we will develop in our final chapters.

The third and fourth chapters will then survey and critique the theological literature that has focused on urban poverty, as well as engage some broader literature on poverty and social action which can be applied to our specific topic of poverty in urban America. It is here that the need for pneumatological reflection on social action as it pertains to the urban poor will be established. We will demonstrate how the large majority of current literature addresses poverty either through a theistic perspective or through the perspective of the Son. Very little if any work has been done on what the person and action of the Holy Spirit means for the poor. We will focus on what has been done already to give a framework in which to work and expand on as we seek to holistically apply Pneumatology to the topic of urban poverty.[12] Chapter 3 will focus on urban poverty in American Evangelical theology. We will see that while much of Evangelical theology has remained quietistic or focused on individual transformation with regard to poverty, a group of progressive Evangelicals, including Ronald Sider, David Gushee,

---

11. See, for instance, Wilson, *When Work Disappears*.

12. I have chosen to capitalize the term "Pneumatology" even though it is not a common practice. The term "Christology" is traditionally capitalized while Pneumatology is not, furthering the preference Christology is given in the theological world. The *SBL Handbook of Style* does not even include Pneumatology in its exhaustive examples of capitalizing terms. As a small step forward, I will capitalize both terms. See Collins, *SBL Handbook of Style*, 48.

and Jim Wallis, have been the most constructive helping us to get to a more holistic response.

In chapter 4, we will broaden our theological conversation by exploring ecumenical theologies of poverty through three groups of dialogue partners. First, we will explore the Social Gospel movement. Key in this movement is one of its greatest proponents, Walter Rauschenbusch, but also some of his major influences including Washington Gladden, Josiah Strong and Richard Ely. This movement lays many of the foundations for the continuing turn toward social salvation. Second, we will look at Liberation Theology through the lenses of both Latin American Liberation Theology and Black and Womanist Theology. Finally, we will explore an ecumenical range of responses to poverty including prophetic activism, Roman Catholicism and an example of a mainline Protestant approach. We will discover that all of these approaches in chapters 3 and 4 are useful but are also missing the pneumatological dimension. They also focus on the social but neglect the personal and so are not holistic. By making a pneumatological turn, I argue that a Renewal epistemology developed through the lens of Pneumatology provides a third way between these Evangelical and Ecumenical approaches.

After laying a foundation for a theology of social action among the urban poor on the broader levels of society and in Christianity, we will turn in chapter 5 to Renewal Theology. In this chapter, we will establish our epistemological framework via the field of Renewal Studies and its approach to theology. We will then explore how Renewal movements have historically responded, both positively and negatively, to poverty. First, we will explore how recent Renewal scholars have sought to address poverty theologically. Interestingly, many Renewal approaches still move forward from a primarily christological perspective despite its strong pneumatological emphasis. Second, we will explore how Renewal has approached poverty practically and discover that there seems to be a disconnect between its theological approach and its practical responses.

Chapter 6 explores Pneumatology and the resources it and Renewal Theology have to offer a holistic response to urban poverty. We will ask what a Pneumatology is, its scopes and challenges for responding to urban poverty. In particular, we will seek a holistic Pneumatology in which the topic of Pneumatology sets the very agenda for theology. Such a holistic Pneumatology speaks to all of life and overcomes any interior and exterior polarities. We will develop this holistic Pneumatology in a complementary manner that remains wholly Trinitarian while giving a unique and full voice to the Holy Spirit. Finally, we will outline an approach focused on a reworking of the four-fold gospel through the lens of the Holy Spirit as at the heart of a holistic pneumatological holistic response to urban poverty.

This pneumatological approach will build on the christological four-fold gospel, not subsume it, attempting to remain Trinitarian. To develop this approach, I will rely heavily on Amos Yong's pneumatological imagination to identify a possible pneumatic metaphor as a bridge between Pneumatology and poverty. Yong himself does not develop a theology of poverty but does deal with poverty in different segments of his book *In the Days of Caesar*, particularly chapter 7, when he talks about economics and explores the health and wealth gospel as a Pentecostal response to poverty.[13] In this volume, Yong uses his pneumatological imagination to identify salvation as a primary pneumatic metaphor for political theology. He then interprets this metaphor of salvation through the christological five-fold gospel rather than in a pneumatological manner.

I also want to propose the pneumatic metaphor of salvation but read it in a Renewal and pneumatological manner based on the passage Luke 4:18–19, "The Spirit of the Lord is on me because he has anointed me to proclaim good news to the poor. He has sent me to proclaim freedom for the prisoners and recovery of sight for the blind, to set the oppressed free, to proclaim the year of the Lord's favor." Jesus declares that his mission was to proclaim the gospel to the poor which includes freedom and restitution. It is often overlooked, even within Renewal, that this was a mission empowered by the Holy Spirit. When most people discuss social action toward the poor they are talking about salvation. This is not just a spiritual salvation, but a holistic salvation that includes personal, familial, ecclesial, material, social, and cosmic aspects. As Yong points out in his *The Spirit Poured out on all Flesh*, salvation is not just a function of the Son, but the Holy Spirit is involved at every level of salvation.[14] The Renewal tradition has perhaps the strongest emphasis on the Holy Spirit. Yong is right that the Pentecostal four-fold gospel serves a holistic soteriological framework that deals with salvation physically, emotionally (healing), personally (savior), communally (Spirit baptism), ecclesially (Spirit baptism), and cosmically (soon coming/eschatology).[15] Many of these spheres in which salvation works overlap, but

---

13. Yong, *In the Days of Caesar*, 257–74.

14. Yong, *Spirit Poured Out*, 91–109.

15. Yong uses the five-fold gospel because he wants to include sanctification in his discussion, even though he himself does not come from the holiness-Pentecostal tradition. I, having a background as an Assemblies of God minister, will use the four-fold gospel which is more often employed by non-holiness Pentecostals. The parentheses in this sentence are my own connections which I am making between a holistic soteriological framework and the four-fold gospel.

naming them demonstrates that the four-fold gospel has the capacity to cover a holistic vision of salvation.[16]

To complement the christological focus of the four-fold gospel within the Renewal tradition, I will develop the four-fold gospel pneumatologically demonstrating how the Holy Spirit functions is savior, baptizer, healer, and entelechy of the eschatological kingdom.[17] This is not to replace Christ in salvation, but to show the important and unique roles the Holy Spirit also plays in salvation within a Trinitarian framework and the salvation of the urban poor. To keep this balance, we will develop a complementary Spirit-Christology that allows us to read the four-fold gospel in a holistically pneumatological manner while not slipping into modalism. We do not develop this methodology fully until section 6.4 beginning on page 259 because we will spend the rest of the thesis getting to this point of establishing the need for a holistic pneumatological response and a possible Renewal framework through which to develop it.[18]

Chapter 7 will then execute the approach outlined in chapter 6 by exploring the idea of the Holy Spirit as savior of the urban poor. First, we will engage in a pneumatic reading of Luke laying a scriptural foundation for our approach.[19] We will then examine each area of the four-fold gospel describing the Holy Spirit as savior, baptizer, healer and entelechy of the eschatological kingdom and the implications of this for a holistic Pneumatology of urban poverty in the United States.

---

16. Just recently A. J. Swoboda was the first to apply the four-fold gospel to a topic of social action, creation care. We will apply it to urban poverty in a similar manner. See Swoboda, *Tongues and Trees*. Earlier, Shane Clifton also applies the four-fold gospel to social issues but does not apply it in a pneumatological way. See Clifton, "Preaching the 'Full Gospel,'" 117–34.

17. For another example of someone using a pneumatological version of the four-fold gospel (rather than five-fold gospel of holiness sects of Pentecostalism) see Tallman, "Pentecostal Ecology," 136. Tallman, however only interprets the third tenant of Spirit baptism as "Pneumatology" still speaking of salvation primarily as christological for instance rather than interpreting the whole framework through a pneumatological lens.

18. We also briefly outline the possibility of this method on page 161 in the conclusion of our section on Renewal methodology. I do not go into it fully here because we have not dealt with Pneumatology at this point.

19. Engaging constructively with Scripture is an important element of a Renewal approach to theology (as we will discover in chapter 5).

1

Urban Poverty in the United States

INTRODUCTION

John stands at the intersection of 70th Street and El Cajon Blvd in San Diego every day. I first met John when I handed him five dollars. This encounter occurred after a month of driving by him as he roamed the medians of the busy intersection with a smile on his face and carrying a cardboard sign that says, "God Bless, anything helps." This is part of John's daily routine. He collects alms that sustain him from day-to-day. After this first encounter, we have slowly built a relationship as I have bought him a few meals and spent time with him on the corner eating together.

On the outside, John wears the same tattered jean shorts and old Reebok tennis shoes each day. He then rotates between three t-shirts he owns or wears no shirt at all. He keeps these in his grocery store shopping cart along with a few other belongings most prized of which are pictures of his kids. His skin has a sun worn, leathery tan and his teeth are decaying from years of neglect. John makes between twenty-five and fifty dollars a day panhandling, all of which is under the table and goes unreported to the United States Government. John is poor by any measurement of poverty used in the United States. John was not always poor. He actually grew up in San Diego, attended San Diego State University and has two grown kids. During college, he developed a drug and alcohol addiction he could mostly control and lived as a functioning addict for many years. He had his first child when he was twenty-one years old with a girl he met at a party. They moved in together and John soon dropped out of school and began working construction all the while still addicted to cocaine and alcohol. At twenty-four, he had his second child with the same woman still working construction, but his addiction grew. He began to show up late for work and eventually started missing work altogether which led to his being let go. Getting fired sent John into a final tailspin in which he left his family, stopped working and immersed himself even more deeply into drugs and alcohol. Nearly twenty years later, John has kicked the hard drugs, but still imbibes regularly. He has tried various construction jobs held any one for long. He qualified for unemployment for a while, but his welfare benefits ran out after too many years of not working. Now, he lives on the streets doing the one thing he feels will bring in consistent income, begging at a busy intersection. He keeps in irregular contact with his kids but functionally has no home, no family, and inconsistent access to good food and shelter. John was a member of the working poor, but now he has simply given up and given in to his addictions.

Susan, her husband Jeff, and their two daughters—one and three years old—moved to San Diego two years ago from the Midwest. Susan's husband graduated with a degree in chemical engineering from a prestigious university in Ohio. Susan dropped out of the same university when she married Jeff and quickly became pregnant with their first child. After graduating, Jeff struggled to find work because of a down market. Instead, Susan and Jeff have worked at entry level jobs earning minimum wage or a little more to survive. They recently moved to San Diego hoping a bigger city and chemical engineering industry would translate into a full-time, better paying job. They have not had luck. Currently, Jeff and Susan are trying to start their own business which takes up most of Jeff's time. Susan takes care of the kids during the day, helps Jeff when she can and works as a night custodian at a local school. Even though Jeff earned his bachelor's degree years ago, Jeff and Susan are poor. Compared to John, when you first meet them you would not know they are poor. They own a car, they dress nicely, they work and go to the library for preschool story time. They live in an RV they pay for with a high interest loan and they pay monthly rent for a spot at a local RV park. Based on their limited income they qualify for Medicaid and food stamps. They are part of the working poor in San Diego but due to shame and embarrassment hide their poverty. You would not know it unless you took the time to get to know them well.

John and Susan represent two of the endless stories that make up the face of poverty in the United States. These stories are far from the totality of experiences of poverty in San Diego yet alone the nation or the world. They do serve a few purposes, however. First, they serve to demonstrate that, while it is tempting to depict the "face of poverty" in terms of demographics and trends alone, each number represents a real face and story. Each story has similarities and yet are wholly unique. Along our journey of exploring a pneumatological approach to urban poverty, I will attempt to highlight a number of the stories of those who live the life of poverty about which we are theologizing.

Second, John and Susan's stories point to a diversity of stories that exist within the United States. Statistical numbers lump all of these stories together, but going deeper reveals an underlying diversity. There is diversity in location from urban poverty, to suburban, to rural poverty. There is diversity in the racial demographics of poverty among Blacks, Hispanics, Asians, Whites and other racial and ethnic groups. There is diversity in age as poverty most harshly affects the elderly and children but does not discriminate against age. You can differentiate between the working poor, the disabled poor, the dependent poor and any number of other categories. These "diversities" demonstrate the intricacy of poverty. It is not any one ingredient, but numerous factors which lead to poverty in the United States. Poverty is a reality that faces people from every walk of life. This diversity means two things. One, it means we can never imagine our assertions fit every story. Second, since we cannot make blanket statements that apply to all the poor, it is allowed and even helpful to focus on a more specific story. Here, we will focus on urban poverty in the United States and specifically San Diego. The picture we will paint and the ideas we will suggest do not fit every person in San Diego, but they fit a wide diversity of situations that are still completely unique.

This introduces us to the final element that John and Susan's stories demonstrate. While poverty is complex and diverse, there are similarities among the varying situations and these are equally important. For instance, while the causes that lead each person into poverty are multifold and complex, the majority of stories center upon work because it provides income making lack of work a major factor of poverty. Similarly, most stories do not start in poverty but involve a gradual entrance into poverty and then moving in and out of it. It is not just the causes that are similar, but the effects. Economic effects are the most evident, but the negative effects of poverty on one's family relationship, one's mental health, and even one's physical health are equally clear. Perhaps the greatest effect that carry similarities among any story of poverty is the stigma attached to poverty within society that can lead to shame, ostracization and even banishment. Poverty is a complex story, yet also a united one.

In our discussion about poverty, we will attempt to hold these three things in tension. First, poverty is more than just numbers but people with stories, families and feelings. Second, poverty is a complex issue that cannot be oversimplified which means that any statement we make is necessarily fallible. Third, because there are also many similarities, any statement we make also has the ability to ring true for a large portion of those in poverty.

In the rest of this chapter we will explore urban poverty in the United States, but it will continue to be in the midst of these tensions demonstrating its complexity. We will start by exploring the face of poverty, what we often see on the outside through statistics, demographics and first glances. We will ask three questions: What is poverty? How is poverty determined? and Who are the poor in America? We will then narrow in more specifically on urban poverty, delineating its similarities and differences to poverty in general before finally looking at the face of urban poverty within my own context, the central city of San Diego. In the second major section of this chapter we will look at the underside of poverty, the side that is often less seen does not usually showing up in any census. We will look at three aspects of the underside of poverty: the economics of poverty, social relationship and poverty, and the psychology of poverty. This dual approach to poverty will help demonstrate our need to take a holistic approach that addresses the whole person and the complexities of poverty. This chapter will also lay the foundations of what we mean by poverty, the problems it presents and how we can begin to address it.

THE FACE OF POVERTY IN THE UNITED STATES

Poverty in the United States

"Poverty" is a concept many of us feel we can easily define and identify utilizing a simple eye test. The problem is that language and ideas in a culture are constantly in flux. The word "fantastic," for instance, at one time primarily meant something imaginary. However, in more recent English in the United States "fantastic" most often carries the meaning of something that is really excellent. This is a new nuance but one rooted in etymology. Something excellent can also be called incredible, good to be true, or imaginary. On the other hand, some words have taken on completely new meanings such as the word "bad" being used for something good, or the word "sick" being used for something awesome rather than someone who is ill.[1] Not only does the usage of a word change, but the reality behind words change. As John Iceland tells us in his book *Poverty in America: A Handbook,* views of poverty vary over time and place. What it means to be poor today is not the same as what it meant a century ago. Similarly, what constitutes poverty in the United States is very different from the developing world.[2] So, what is a definition of poverty in our context of the United States for the year 2017?

1. Emling, "These 12 Everyday Words."
2. Iceland, *Poverty in America*, 3.

At the most basic level, understanding poverty means a lack of something. In the United States, this lack is most often understood economically. For instance, a common response by the public to the question, "What is poverty" is that "being poor means not having a lot of money."[3] This is a vague definition. It must be decided how much money is "not a lot." This will be a different number depending on the economy. One example of this is that the World Bank, in determining poverty in 2008, used a global standard of income ranging between $1369 and $2190 a year for a family of three. In the United States in 2008, the poverty line for a family of three was $17,916 a year.[4] As recently as 2011, however, Edin and Schaefer demonstrated that approximately 4 percent of Americans live on less than $2/day making them poor even by global standards.[5] Factors that affect these numbers include the power of a nation's monetary unit, its average wage, standards of living, and a country's access to food and natural resources. Even within the United States where these factors can be fairly constant, the spending power the dollar carries from region to region varies greatly based on food, energy and housing costs. $17,916 goes much further in Mississippi, where the cost of living is the cheapest in the United States, compared to San Diego, the thirteenth most expensive city where the cost of living is 27 percent higher than Jackson, Mississippi.[6] Two people making the same income in these two cities will have various perceptions of their wealth. Various areas may also have varying views on what constitutes having enough in life and what constitutes being poor based on certain possessions or certain sized houses rather than using income at all.

This is only to keep poverty on an economic level of one's income, buying power, or assets to provide a certain standard of living. Some would want to reject economic criteria altogether and focus more on self-sufficiency, or even psychological factors such as the way one approaches life. While non-economic factors of poverty are important and will be discussed, their impact is more on the well-being of the individual and society which is more difficult to quantify than economic factors. Because of this difficulty, we will continue dealing primarily with economic factors which are complicated enough.

These various standards and perceptions of poverty create a need to standardize what is considered poor in the United States. Most local measurements of poverty center around the attempt to determine who needs

---

3. Iceland, *Poverty in America*, 11.
4. Ravallion, et al., "Dollar a Day Revisited."
5. Edin and Shaefer, *$2.00 a Day*, xix.
6. Cohn, "America's Most Affordable States."

governmental assistance in the form of lower taxes, housing assistance, food stamps, access to higher education, and medical care. These standards are also adopted by other agencies such as utility companies to give reduced rates to those in economic need.[7] The creation of this system by Mollie Orshansky in 1965 is well documented.[8] She based her matrix on a survey of consumption patterns for a four person, non-farm family and the assumption that such a family spends approximately one third of its annual income on food. She then determined the income required to purchase food based on the Department of Agriculture's "Economy Food Plan" and finally multiplied this number by three to determine the annual income required to sustain a family of four. This is an absolute measure of poverty because it attempts to define "a truly basic—absolute—need standard and therefore remains constant over time."[9] Relative measures are more commonly used by researchers and policy makers in Europe. Relative measures define poverty as a condition of comparative disadvantage, to be assessed against some relative shift or evolving standard of living. It may measure poverty more on how income is distributed, which is a constantly changing factor.[10] Absolute poverty methods like Orshansky's remain constant. Orshansky's number does change based on inflation, but it is based on the same standards of living from 1965.

There are advantages and disadvantages to both forms of measurement. The main advantage to an absolute poverty measurement is that it is conceptually easy to understand. It uses simple math and a simple concept that poverty is determined by the amount of money needed to feed a family of four. This makes an absolute measurement appealing to a popular audience. This simplicity also makes absolute measures useful tools for processing large amounts of data, making quick, clean and defensible decisions on issues like eligibility and in developing policy. Of course, its disadvantages also center on this simplicity. Standards of living change annually and certainly over the course of five decades. Not only do actual numbers change, but perception of what poverty means changes over time. For instance, with the new health food movement, many families spend more on food than they used to. Should this be factored into even absolute measurements solely based on food expenditures? Finally, absolute measures fail to recognize the complexity of poverty outlined above.

7. Altmeyer, "Social Welfare in the United States."

8. See for instance Jennings, *Understanding the Nature of Poverty*, 11; Orshansky, "Measure of Poverty."

9. Iceland, *Poverty in America*, 23.

10. Pearce, "Statistical Measure of Poverty," 565.

Relative measurements also have advantages and disadvantages many of which are converse to those of the absolute measurements. Social dynamics are a much more implicit assumption within relative measurements. People are considered to be "social beings who operate within relationships."[11] Recognizing this social dimension is their greatest advantage as they recognize more than just economics but includes perception and relationship to the larger society. They also allow for a more comprehensive reading of poverty beyond just one measurement. There are of course several disadvantages as well. For instance, relative measurements create a moving target which can make it difficult to create effective policy. They are also conceptually unappealing because they are denser with data and difficult to understand and agree upon. This is true even when these relative measures still primarily focus on economic factors. When they take even more alternative measurements into account, such as consumption measures, hardship measures, or social exclusion, they become even more unruly.

While the measurement of poverty in the United States is simple and somewhat clean, by failing to identify the complexity that is poverty, there are limitations. First, people who are still poor may be excluded. Perhaps their income is high, but they have endured natural disasters, family divisions, or other accidents. Second, by only paying attention to an absolute measurement of poverty, poverty is restricted to a financial phenomenon with only financial repercussions. This fails to recognize the social aspects of poverty. For instance, when a person's resources, economic or not, are significantly lower than others resources, according to Iceland, "Even if they are physically able to survive, they may not be able to participate adequately in social organizations and relationships, and are thus incapable of fully participating in society."[12] Absolute poverty, especially subsistence poverty lines, have much more meaning amid extreme hardship, but less meaning in industrialized societies where starvation is rare. Social exclusion measurements of poverty which utilize relative measurement systems are more common in Europe and academic circles in the United States for this very reason.[13] Another downfall to the simplicity of absolute measurements is that when more simplistic measurements are utilized, more simplistic solutions are offered. For instance, if one measures based on access to food, solutions will most likely center on feeding. When the absolute measurement is based on economic buying power, then financial subsidies become the center of solutions. To be fair, while most welfare solutions in the United

---

11. Iceland, *Poverty in America*, 26–27.
12. Iceland, *Poverty in America*, 27.
13. Daly and Silver, "Social Exclusion and Social Capital," 538.

States are economic, there is a diversity of resources that are subsidized, like medical care and education. Many believe health and education are basic human rights, but they are also necessary resources to become producers of wealth and move toward self-subsistence.

So, how will we define who is poor for the purpose of this thesis? I propose using a hybrid method similar to the Supplemental Poverty Measure (SPM) developed by the National Research Council of the National Academy of Sciences (NAS) and their panel on poverty and family assistance. In 1995, the NAS published the report of their congress commissioned findings, *Measuring Poverty: A New Approach*.[14] According to the developer, Kathleen Short, the SPM poverty thresholds are calculated based on how much people, "report spending on food, clothing, shelter, and utilities, plus a small additional amount to allow for other needs such as household supplies, personal care, and non-work related transportation."[15] These thresholds are further adjusted for annual variations in housing costs by state and metropolitan areas to reflect real growth expenditures on this bundle of goods. The SPM is relative because the thresholds are updated based on changes in real expenditures which rise with cost of living increases. It is only quasi-relative, however because it is still based on basic categories of consumption rather than total consumption or median income. It also more clearly defines various sources of income compared to the traditional absolute measurements currently employed by the United States government.

The SPM provides a good compromise between absolute and relative measurements of poverty. It recognizes the ongoing fluctuation of standards of living and the ever-changing perceptions of poverty but is still largely economically based so that concrete measurements can be determined. SPM poverty rates create a higher threshold for what constitutes poverty in the United States, meaning that in 2010 the poverty rate would have been approximately 19.5 percent rather than the 15 percent reported by official measurements. While the total numbers of those in poverty are changed, the percentages of various demographic groups remain largely unchanged. More people from every demographic are included with the SPM rather than demonstrating further disparity. Because of our desire to take a more holistic approach to poverty, we will use the SPM where available and the official measurements when not available. We will also strive to talk about poverty in different terms than simply economic where ever possible.

14. See Short, "Experimental Poverty Measures," 1–28.
15. Short, "Who Is Poor?," 3.

Urban Poverty in the United States

Having described what poverty looks like in the United States, we will now turn to urban poverty more specifically. We are focusing most specifically on urban poverty for three reasons. First, urban poverty makes up one of the largest demographics of the poor in the United States, compared with rural and suburban poverty. According to the 2001 United States Census, 40.7 percent of poor people live in central cities compared to 36.8 percent in suburbs and 22.8 percent in rural areas. Similarly, while 11.7 percent of all Americans were poor in 2001, 16.5 percent of people in central cities were poor compared to 8.2 percent in suburbs and 14.2 percent in rural areas who were poor.[16] The percentage of poor living in central cities went up to nearly 20 percent by 2009 and can soar even higher in certain neighborhoods.[17]

Second, we are focusing on urban poverty because it is often more concentrated making it more visible. Urban poverty is visible to the naked eye as one travels through a central city and see homeless camps set up under overpasses or in front of businesses closed for the night. It is more visible as one drives through a dilapidated section of the city where every house has bars on its windows and is overcrowded with people trying to save on rent by multiple generations of a family living together. While rural poverty is also a large and important issue, it is more spread out and further from downtown business centers, and so is often less visible. The visibility of urban poverty comes from its concentration, its causes, and its effects, but also from the attention paid to it by scholars. Much of this research started with William Julius Wilson and the Chicago School of Sociology in the 1970s and 1980s.[18] While the numbers of those in urban poverty are only marginally higher than rural poverty, the articles addressing rural poverty only makeup a fraction of articles on the poor.

Finally, we are focusing on urban poverty because of my own context in the central city of San Diego. It is an area with some suburban poverty, but very little rural poverty. We will paint this local context more specifically in the next section.

First, I want to ask two questions about the urban poor in the United States. What is the face of urban poverty, demographically speaking, in the United States? And why is poverty more concentrated in urban settings?

What is the face of urban poverty in the United States? We have already described how urban poverty compares to rural and suburban

---

16. Kahan, "Urban Poverty," 738–42.
17. DeNavas-Walt et al. cited in Iceland, *Poverty in America*, 52.
18. See, for instance, Wilson, *Truly Disadvantaged*; *When Work Disappears*.

poverty. What does it actually look like though? Historically, according to Michael Kahan, "The late nineteenth and early twentieth centuries were a peak period for urbanization and industrialization in the United States, as well as a high immigration to American cities."[19] This new urban poverty took the form of various "ghettos" settled by European immigrants, including Irish, Jewish and Italian. Even in this early period in the history of urban poverty in the United States, Kahan reports that electric trolleys and automobiles allowed the wealthy to live in new "streetcar suburbs" that were less densely settled.[20] Poverty was being identified and addressed on numerous fronts from the theology of the Social Gospel movement to the fast growth of labor unions.[21] Still, poverty was predominantly a White European phenomenon though there was certainly ethnic diversity among various European groups. According to Kahan, "World War II signaled a major shift in urban poverty as cities underwent tremendous demographic, economic and spatial transformations that profoundly shaped the character and scope of urban poverty."[22] After WWII, many Blacks and Puerto Ricans migrated to northern cities. For instance, between 1940 and 1970, five million Blacks left the South for northern and western cities.[23] At the same time that many immigrants were arriving in cities in search of high paying jobs, those who worked those jobs began moving to the suburbs and even overseas. After WWII, race remained a crucial component of urban poverty well into the twenty-first century. Poverty cannot be reduced to a stereotype of a Black underclass living in an inner-city ghetto, however. According to Kahan, since immigration laws were reformed in 1965, many poor immigrants from Mexico, the Caribbean and Southeast Asia, have "swelled ranks of the urban poor across the country."[24]

Still, when speaking about the face of poverty in the urban centers of the United States, race and ethnicity comes to the forefront. Wilson, even back in the early 1980s, noted that Blacks made up 23 percent of the population but 43 percent of the poor in central cities. He saw this as a legacy of historic discrimination against Blacks through the system of slavery and

19. Kahan, "Urban Poverty," 738.
20. Kahan, "Urban Poverty," 740.
21. We will have a whole section on the Social Gospel and its main figures—such as Walter Rauschenbusch and Washington Gladden—in the next chapter. For more information on the rise of the American Federation of Labor and its importance in addressing poverty at the turn of the century see Hallgrimsdottir and Benoit, "From Wage Slaves to Wage Workers," 1393–411.
22. Kahan, "Urban Poverty," 740–41.
23. Katz, *Price of Citizenship*, 39.
24. Kahan, "Urban Poverty," 742.

segregation. Blacks, for instance, were discriminated against far more severely than were the new White immigrants from Europe.[25] In the United States today, according to the most recent census data from 2014, 26.2 percent of Blacks are poor, 23.6 percent of Hispanics are poor, while 12.7 percent of Whites and 12 percent of Asians are poor.[26]

Besides race, one of the greatest disproportions in poverty concerns age in which 21.1 percent of those under the age of eighteen are poor while 13.5 percent of those eighteen to sixty-four and 10 percent of those sixty-five and over are poor. There have been huge strides in the poverty of the elderly, however. In 1959, the percentage of poor sixty-five and over was 35.2 percent, higher than even children (27.3 percent).[27] Now at only 10 percent, the improvement of the elderly poverty rate is due to the impact of social security and other similar programs. Poverty also affects females more than males as 16.1 percent of females are poor and 13.4 percent of males are poor. Education is also a direct factor for poverty. 28.9 percent of those with no high school diploma, 14.2 percent of those with a high school diploma but no college, 10.2 perent of those with some college and 5 percent of those with a bachelor's degree or higher are poor.

These numbers cover the entirety of the United States, urban or not. Interestingly, when these specific categories are transferred to an urban setting there is even more disparity in race and ethnicity as well as education and age. A major reason for this is that Blacks and Hispanics are usually less educated and often have more children which means more children being born into poverty. It is important that, before continuing, we reiterate there are still large amounts of people that are poor and White or poor and living in rural settings. There are more Whites who are poor simply because there are so many more Whites living in America. Poverty is complex. So, while these statistics begin to paint the face of poverty in urban America, they only tell part of the story. The final section of the chapter will focus on the effects of poverty which tells more than sheer statistics. Still, these numbers are important.

Before moving to the effects of poverty, we will answer our second question, why is poverty more concentrated in urban settings? William Julius Wilson has perhaps done the most work on urban poverty in central cities and has extensively chronicled the effects of the concentrated urban poverty that arose with suburban flight during 1970–1980s.[28] According to Wilson, concentrated urban poverty has been caused by a complex web of factors

---

25. Wilson, *Truly Disadvantaged*, 33.
26. DeNavas-Walt and Proctor, *Income and Poverty*, 12.
27. Iceland, *Poverty in America*, 40.
28. Wilson, *Truly Disadvantaged*, 46–62.

that include "shifts in the American economy, the historic flow of migrants, changes in the urban minority age structure, and population changes."[29] According to a study done by Glaeser, Kahn and Rappaport, the urbanization of poverty comes "mainly from better access to public transportation in central cities."[30] Cities and ghettos do not create poverty or keep people stuck, rather they attract poverty.[31] Those with more money have more time capital to travel into cities for work making suburbs built around the car with its extra costs, and urban settings built around public transportation. Glaeser, Kahn and Rappaport find that areas that have gained public transportation, even more suburban areas, subsequently become poorer through attraction. Center cities usually have the best public transportation and likewise have attracted poorer people. Another piece of evidence is that the poverty rate is higher for those who switch homes into urban settings than for those who have lived in urban settings for a long period of time supporting their thesis that cities attract the poor and do not make people poor.[32]

Their thesis is an open critique of previous studies like those by Wilson. Though Wilson's work provided helpful information, his theory of urban poverty only explains the separation of the non-poor and the poor, not urban poverty itself.[33] While their transport mode model is one of the most attractive for explaining why the poor come to central cities, it is still only one aspect of the explanation. For instance, Wilson mentions economic changes. Most metropolitan housing markets have older housing and older schools and those with more affluence want newer, nicer things.[34] He also mentions changes in the urban age structure. Many of the poor in urban centers have been children of large poor families and as these children grow up they continue the cycle of poverty.[35] Like most issues in urban poverty, they are complex, but these are some of the most foundational reasons poverty is more prevalent in urban settings.

Urban Poverty in San Diego

Before turning to the effects of poverty in the United States, I will describe the face of urban poverty in my local context, the central city of San Diego.

29. Wilson, *Truly Disadvantaged*, 62.
30. Glaeser et al., "Why Do the Poor Live in Cities?," 1.
31. Glaeser et al., "Why Do the Poor Live in Cities?," 2.
32. Glaeser et al., "Why Do the Poor Live in Cities?," 3–4.
33. Glaeser et al., "Why Do the Poor Live in Cities?," 6.
34. Wilson, *Truly Disadvantaged*, 34.
35. Wilson, *Truly Disadvantaged*, 36–39.

Most of our previous statements about poverty broadly apply to San Diego as well so we will be brief while pointing out the major commonalities and differences.

This dissertation will focus on the central city of San Diego as a local context for discussion because that is my own context. I grew up in San Diego and now work at San Diego State University as a campus minister. San Diego is the eighth largest city in the United States with a population of 1.3 million people. The whole Metropolitan area of San Diego has over 3 million people. The poverty rate in San Diego, according to the Center on Policy Initiatives' "Poverty, Earnings and Income in the City of San Diego 2014," remained at 15.7 percent of the population in 2014, relatively unchanged from the previous year's 15.8 percent, while the national poverty rate declined to 14.5 percent in 2014.[36] Though the percentages remained unchanged in San Diego, because of population growth, three thousand more people entered poverty bringing the city's poverty total to 212,098. This is in contrast to the most improved job market since the recession of 2008. Between 2014 and 2015 approximately forty thousand more jobs were added to the San Diego economy and the median annual income increased by $4,111 in that time. This brings up the biggest discrepancy in San Diego compared to the rest of the United States, the situation of the working poor. In San Diego, 41.5 percent of adults in poverty had jobs, not too far above the national average of 38 percent. Where things diverge even more is that 8 percent of full-time workers were under the poverty line against 3 percent nationally while 20.1 percent of part-time workers were in poverty, well above the 15.9 percent national level. This is an indictment on the San Diego job market.

San Diego is a large tourist town with above average industry in sectors like hospitality, restaurant, retail, and tourism. This provides more jobs, but they are often lower paying, part-time or seasonal jobs. This is a difficult reality to grasp especially with the affluence also present in San Diego. With a median household income of $47,076 it ranks 27th on the list of United States cities.[37] Not only is it affluent, but the cost of living is extremely high with average home price being $483,000 for which economists would suggest an annual family income of $98,534 to be able to afford such a home, over double the median income.[38] We have already seen that, according to absolute measurements, San Diego, like other urban centers, has a higher percentage of poverty than most places in the country. Because of the

---

36. Center on Policy Initiatives, "Poverty, Earnings, and Income."
37. Noss, *Household Income*, 1–3.
38. Horn, "Salary You Need."

exorbitant cost of living and the fluidity of jobs and pay, if we were to use relative measures of poverty, the poverty rate would be even higher.

The Center on Policy Initiatives is one of the few to apply such a measurement. They assert that based on cost of living and the absolute poverty measurement of the United States government, a single person in the city of San Diego would need to earn $27,655 to live at the same standard as the federal government's poverty line for a single person, $12,316. With these relative numbers, nearly 33 percent of adults and more than 40 percent of children in San Diego would be considered poor compared to the 15.7 percent under federal guidelines.[39] The Center for Policy Initiatives considers these relative numbers putting people in "near-poverty" and not the same kind of poverty indicated by the government standards. For instance, few can afford a home without spending a significant amount of their monthly income on rent or a mortgage. This means that the term "working poor" is even more relevant to the urban center of San Diego. There are also many jobless poor who would be poor regardless of where they live. Because of the high cost of living in San Diego that includes housing, energy and food prices, the poorest are even more poor by living in San Diego.

Table 1-1

Category of poverty	Nationally	San Diego
Race: Black	26.2%	24.8%
Race: Hispanic	23.6%	22.9%
Race: White	12.7%	9.3%
Race: Asian	12%	13.3%
Gender: Female	16.1%	16.8%
Gender: Male	13.4%	14.6%
Age: Under 18	21.1%	20.4%
Age: 65 and Over	10%	11.4%
Work: Adults Workers	38%	41.5%
Work: Part-time Workers	15.9%	20.1%
Work: Full-time Workers	3%	8%

In terms of the other demographics like race, age and gender, the number of San Diegans in poverty is rather representative of the national urban poverty statistics with little deviation (see Table 1-1 above). Perhaps the most notable is a higher percentage of Asians in poverty which is telling

39. Steward, "SD Income Rises."

since San Diego has a higher percentage of Asians than most other central cities.[40] In fact, compared to the national average, San Diego has slightly less Black, Hispanic, and White poor even though it has a slightly higher percentage of poor altogether. Again, this is due to the large Asian community that San Diego has. The other outlier is in the higher percentage of working adults who are poor, particularly full-time workers. This is because of the cost of living and other reasons we mentioned above. Besides these two slight outliers, San Diego is rather representative of the average central city in America when it comes to what we see on the outside. The question remains, however, is it the same when we dig deeper into the experiences of those in poverty beyond demographics?

THE UNDERSIDE OF POVERTY IN THE UNITED STATES

These deeper experiences are what we are calling the underside of poverty. The face of poverty is what we can see through the surveys, numbers, and looking at the façade of what we experience of poverty daily in the United States. As we have mentioned, poverty is much more complex than what we can see from the outside or solely economic factors. To truly understand poverty in the United States, one must understand the experiences of those who are poor. In this section, we will explore three primary areas of difficulty within urban poverty. These three areas are the economics of poverty, social relationships and poverty, and the psychology of poverty. Each category has some overlap with the others as economics naturally involves social relationships for instance, but the categories are helpful for clarity. In each of these areas we will explore how this aspect of urban poverty affects the individual and community in poverty making it undesirable and requiring a response, particularly a theological response.

The Economics of Poverty

One of the most visible areas of the underside of poverty is the economics. It is perhaps the most studied and is often the measuring stick to determine who is poor and who is not. In particular, three areas within the economics of poverty stand out. First are the dangerous positions in which people can be placed through participation in an underground economy, second is the

---

40. San Diego's population is 15 percent Asian, well ahead of its neighbor, Los Angeles (10.7 percent), and other major cities, like New York (12.7 percent) and Chicago (5.5 percent). Only San Francisco, at 33 percent Asian, is higher than San Diego.

effect of these economics on families and children, and finally the effects these factors take on our national economy.

The underground economy is an ever present, yet largely unacknowledged reality within mainstream America. When most people think of the underground economy in an urban setting they think of the criminal sphere: the mafia, money laundering, con artists, drug dealers, pimps and prostitutes. However, it also includes welfare mothers, indigents, the unemployed, and even children. The underground economy can expand even wider though. As Sudhir Alladi Venkatesh points out in his book, *Off the Books*,

> Most of us would be shocked to find that many local preachers are often intricately involved in this world. Or that the local gang leader may hold the respect of many residents, even as they decry the drugs he brings into the neighborhood. Or that a member of the underground economy is as likely to be a middle-aged mother who cooks lunches for the local hospital staff as to be a teenage criminal.[41]

In the underground economy, people work beneath the radar to earn a living and provide for their families.[42] This economy is completely different than the economy in which most of us work which utilizes receipts, bank accounts, pay checks and taxes. In this underground system, innumerable financial exchanges are unreported to the government, everything from "day care and domestic work to pimping and prostitution" is "off the books."[43] Some of these transactions are normal everyday interactions many have in the mainstream economy, such as a mechanic fixing a car, but in the underground economy the mechanic works out of an alley. Babysitting and daycare are among the most common underground economic exchange. Unlike the mainstream economy, these services occur through social ties and either barter or under the table finances rather than state licensed daycares or preschools. Other interactions include a mix of the criminal world with the more normal sectors of society. For instance, the barber may rent his back room to a prostitute or the preacher may get donations from a gang leader. Like any economy, it is an intricate balance that requires a complex web of people, commodities and interactions to keep goods and services flowing. These underground relationships are often a means of keeping the streets safe, or at least tolerable. It is providing for one's family but doing so in a way that mitigates possible risks and consequences. While social ties are extremely important, they are, with a

---

41. Venkatesh, *Off the Books*, xviii.
42. Venkatesh, *Off the Books*, 8.
43. Venkatesh, *Off the Books*, 5.

few notable exceptions, like gangs and mafia, often between individuals. Organized groups, illicit or not, tend to be the exception.

Venkatesh's study covers the underground economy of one urban neighborhood, Maquis Park, in the central city of Chicago. His study echoes Wilson's *The Truly Disadvantaged* in that the residents of Maquis Park are not just separated through their own economic structures but are socially isolated.[44] The underground economy obviously has advantages for the urban poor. They pay less for certain commodities, build the social bonds necessary for survival in a difficult environment, and have less taxable income meaning they are able to keep welfare benefits. There are also large risks that include the possibility of being strong armed or charged higher interest from people that loan them money or help broker jobs. Venkatesh, for instance, tells about the clergy of regional churches, which have members from both Maquis park and more affluent suburbs. These pastors are important brokers for domestic workers but also charge 10 percent for successful placements.[45] In settings like Maquis Park, cycles are often created in which people are dependent on government welfare, but also dependent on these brokering relationships which put them at a strong disadvantage. Still, Mark Fleisher in his article "Coping with Macro-Structural Adversity" points out that this is a form of cultural resilience that persists over time because, in the end, these exchanges are mutually supportive and beneficial in some way.[46]

Another cycle that is often created in the underground economy, of the urban poor, is a generational cycle of economic poverty. Children learn the systems of the underground economy which becomes their reality. Fleisher says that the same resilience that keeps parents engaging in these social and economic exchanges often persist over generations.[47] Children, according to Wilson in *The Truly Disadvantaged*, also see just as much present-day discrimination as any of their parents based on race and economics which also perpetuates poverty in central cities.[48] This perpetuation of the economic stresses of urban poverty is a foreboding reality given that there are more poor people in the United States under the age of eighteen than any other age group. Could this be why the number of those in urban poverty continues to rise?

---

44. Venkatesh, *Off the Books*, 18. For Wilson's work with which Venkatesh is agreeing see Wilson, *Truly Disadvantaged*.
45. Venkatesh, *Off the Books*, 27.
46. Fleisher, "Coping with Macro-Structural Adversity," 274.
47. Fleisher, "Coping with Macro-Structural Adversity," 275.
48. Wilson, *Truly Disadvantaged*, 62.

Holzer, et al., in their study on the economic costs of childhood poverty in the United States points out that the cost of this perpetuation is costly for our young people, but also for our nation.[49] According to Holzer there is a direct correlation between a child growing up in poverty and their future earnings, propensity to commit crime and quality of health. This future crime and poor health makes a large imposition on the economy costing about $500 billion per year, about 4 percent of the gross domestic product. The authors break these numbers down even more showing that childhood poverty each year "(1) reduces productivity and economic output by an amount equal to 1.3 percent of the GDP (2) raises the costs of crime by 1.3 percent of the GDP and (3) raises health expenditures and reduces the value of health by 1.2 of the GPD."[50] There are not just moral grounds for putting resources toward reducing poverty, but there are economic grounds as well. Addressing poverty helps individuals, urban communities, and our whole nation economically. It is hard to disagree with the evidence Holzer and his co-authors provide that this perpetuation of poverty for children has less to do with their families income and more to do with the "quality of family life, schools, and neighborhoods that poor children experience . . . [that become] reflected in a range of attitudes, behaviors and values that poor children develop and carry into adulthood."[51] As we have seen, much of the trauma that comes through poverty economically is directly tied to the social structures in place in urban settings. It is to these social relationships we now turn.

Social Relationships and Poverty

We have established that while the economic aspects of poverty are the most readily visible and quantifiable, there are other realities and repercussions that are less visible yet equally important to the underside of urban poverty. Still, there is an even deeper layer that hits at the heart of the true impact of poverty which are the social factors. These include the ostracization and stigmatization of the poor from the rest of society, banishment policies, and social and financial dependency on others.

Our discussion on the underground economy served to highlight some of the ostracism that occurs among the urban poor. Part of the equation is that those from more affluent sectors of society, even from the same

---

49. Holzer et al., "Economic Costs of Childhood Poverty," 41–61.

50. Holzer et al., "Economic Costs of Childhood Poverty," 41.

51. Holzer et al., "Economic Costs of Childhood Poverty," 44. They largely rely on Susan Mayer for this assertion. See Mayer, *What Money Can't Buy*.

city, do not enter poorer areas which creates natural social isolation. The rich and the poor participate in different social activities, jobs, and socialize in different areas of the city. Many in urban poverty do not travel out of their neighborhoods and other people do not travel into these "ghettos." We saw for instance in our look at Glaeser, Kahn and Rappaport's work that transportation systems are part of what attract the poor to central cities and a lack of public transportation between these cities and suburbs may also be what keeps them there and separated from the rest of society.[52] Venkatesh's example of pastors brokering relationship between the poor and non-poor shows that even when various socioeconomic groups choose to socialize at the same place, such as a house of worship, it does not mean that they interact with each other.[53] There is often, though not always, still a sense of separation, sometimes subtle and sometimes overt, between the poor and the non-poor. Even within an organization's social structures, there are structures in place that inevitably highlight the separation between economic classes such as ability to go on church retreats. This separation often occurs not because there is a real separation but because a lack of face-to-face contact causes exaggeration of the differences between the rich and the underclass creating greater isolation than there already is.[54]

Not only is there a natural ostracism and isolation, but there can be laws that force such separation. Katherine Beckett and Steve Herbert in their book *Banished: The New Social Control for Urban America* related a growing trend of banishment policies within America's central cities through which, "swaths of urban space are delimited as zones of exclusion from which the undesirables are banned. The uniformed police are marshalled to enforce and often delineate these boundaries."[55] These "off limit orders" are increasingly popular as individuals convicted of certain offenses are ordered to stay out of particular sections of a given city.[56] These laws are not titled "banishment laws." The authors want to use the term "banishment" because of the strong coercive power the state accomplishes through meting out punishment against those considered deviant through these ever-expanding forms of social and spatial segregation.[57]

Perhaps most importantly for our purpose in talking about urban poverty, Beckett and Herbert demonstrate that these banishment policies

---

52. Glaeser et al., "Why Do the Poor Live in Cities?," 1–24.
53. Venkatesh, *Off the Books*, 27.
54. Silver, "Culture, Politics, and National Discourses," 125–26.
55. Beckett and Herbert, *Banished*, 8.
56. Beckett and Herbert, *Banished*, 9.
57. Beckett and Herbert, *Banished*, 11–12.

are logical extensions of trends of segregation and control of the poor established in the civility codes of the 1980s. These antecedent civility codes came from an increased population of homeless among the urban poor and the public's concern about disorder.[58] Many of these laws are put into action for crimes such as drug use or sales, prostitution or crimes of violence such as various forms of battery. These crimes do not constitute a reality for the entirety of the urban poor, but we have already looked at how many of the urban poor do get involved in such crimes. Statistically, if one is not involved in criminal activity, then they will know someone who will still be affected by banishment policies because a loved one is not allowed to come to their house anymore. Demographically, the majority of those affected by such policies are the poor and racial minorities.[59] Interestingly, to further reiterate the connection of these laws with the urban poor, Beckett and Herbert's suggestions for alternatives to banishment center on the need to reduce *social* and *economic* inequality underlying the current urban crisis. They suggest ideas such as investments in low income housing, creation of jobs that include people with criminal records, and comprehensive medical care that includes mental health care and addiction treatments.[60]

These banishment laws, as show the possible social trauma many of the urban poor can face. Such social isolation is overt, but even the knowledge of being different and marginalized creates further isolation and perpetuates further ostracism. Even within urban communities of lower socioeconomic status, there is greater social fragmentation than rural areas, because of cultural diversity for instance. According to Sheilah Miekle's article, "The Urban Context and Poor People," the urban poor often travel in very small and fragmented circles even within their own neighborhoods.[61] Wilson, in *The Truly Disadvantaged,* also points out this social fragmentation but how it occurs even within families through divorce and getting married out of wedlock which is directly connected to the declining economic status and joblessness of Black men.[62]

Tigges, Brown and Green in their study on the social isolation of the urban poor also discuss this fragmentation. They demonstrate that poor Blacks are "less likely than other Blacks and non-poor Whites to live with another adult, to have one person outside the household with whom they

---

58. Beckett and Herbert, *Banished*, 23–24.
59. Beckett and Herbert, *Banished*, 63–67.
60. Beckett and Herbert, *Banished*, 141–50.
61. Meikle, "Urban Context and Poor People," 41.
62. Wilson, *Truly Disadvantaged*, 91.

discuss important matters, or to have a college educated person in their discussion network."⁶³ These small social networks can increase vulnerability and make it harder to recover when economic or other hardship occurs. The poor are in greater need of resources provided by social ties, but they tend to have smaller and less diverse networks.⁶⁴ All of these elements add to the isolated social identity and hardship that occurs within urban poverty. This identity is often translated to future generations through their experience of the same social norms and the projection of their parents. Early on, young people experience the same psychological strains that comes from this social ostracization.

The Psychology of Poverty

These psychological strains of poverty encompass the final area within its underside. These economic and social hardships do more than hurt individuals and families economically or socially, they create psychological trauma. There are two ways to approach this subject, one is to analyze the psychological trauma caused by poverty. The second is to recognize that many are in poverty because of psychological trauma.

Goodman, Saxe and Harvey, in their article "Homelessness as Psychological Trauma" argue that "homelessness itself is a risk factor for emotional disorder and psychological trauma."⁶⁵ They define psychological trauma as "a set of responses to extraordinary, emotionally overwhelming, and personally uncontrollable life events."⁶⁶ As we have seen, the stories of those in urban poverty are full of uncontrollable life events. Many of those in poverty move in and out of it through loss of jobs, natural disaster, and familial problems, all of which can cause psychological trauma. For those who are in perpetual poverty, especially in an urban setting, they are more likely to encounter extraordinary events such as sexual abuse or other violent crimes. Each person's reactions to traumatic events vary widely depending on their social networks, environment, and the specific event. Some reactions can include "substance abuse, self-mutilation, intolerance of intimacy, a general sense of helplessness, and a sense of isolation and existential separateness from others."⁶⁷ According to research, approximately 53 percent of surveyed poor single women and mothers

---

63. Tigges et al., "Social Isolation of the Urban Poor," 53.
64. Tigges et al., "Social Isolation of the Urban Poor," 55.
65. Goodman et al., "Homelessness as Psychological Trauma," 1220.
66. Goodman et al., "Homelessness as Psychological Trauma," 1219.
67. Goodman et al., "Homelessness as Psychological Trauma," 1219.

in St. Louis, had full-blown cases of PTSD. Goodman, Saxe and Harvey, for instance, focus on social disaffiliation and learned helplessness as key responses from the psychological trauma the poor experience which keep them experiencing further poverty and psychological trauma. It can become a vicious cycle in which the trauma is partly caused by their poverty, but then also contributes to continued poverty. The poor are more likely to report physical abuse and sexual abuse both as children before they experienced poverty and as adults while poor. Psychological trauma is brought to one's new experiences of poverty which is then exacerbated by that poverty often leading to further alcohol and substance abuse, social disaffiliation and learned helplessness.[68]

Julius Wilson also draws out how one has to pay attention to the psychological trauma that comes with both historic and contemporary discrimination.[69] Historic discrimination, Wilson holds is even more important than contemporary.[70] Historical discrimination causes a psychological trauma that is passed on through intimate social relationships from a very early age. Finally, historical discrimination also has direct implications on possible contemporary psychological trauma.

CONCLUSION

In this chapter, we have explored the nature of urban poverty in the United States. We have seen that poverty is a complex phenomenon affecting a great number of people from every possible background. Urban poverty has especially affected racial minorities, women and children. While our definition of poverty is primarily economic, we have seen the complexity of the causes and effects of poverty in the United States on individuals, families, communities and our nation. It is this complexity that makes urban poverty so difficult to solve. Any theology hoping to address poverty must be dynamic, fluid and holistic in order to take into account this complexity. It cannot offer easy answers but must address the face and the underside of poverty. It must address the economic, but also the physical, social and psychological. It must address the individuals, families and communities in poverty, but also systems which cause and perpetuate poverty. Before turning to such theological responses and solutions, we will explore previous theological approaches to urban poverty in Evangelical theology, Ecumenical theology and Renewal Theology. It is to urban poverty in American Evangelical theology that we now turn.

68. Goodman et al., "Homelessness as Psychological Trauma," 1222.
69. Wilson, *Truly Disadvantaged*, 30.
70. Wilson, *Truly Disadvantaged*, 32.

2

Urban Poverty in American Evangelical Theology

INTRODUCTION

Having explored what poverty means through the lenses of various sociological approaches to urban poverty in the United States and seen the need for a holistic approach to address its complexities, we will now turn to theological responses to poverty in the United States. While poverty is a sociological phenomenon, we have seen that it also involves other aspects of a person including the spiritual. Because of this multi-faceted nature of poverty, it is important to approach it from several disciplines, but our primary task is a theological one. We will explore two specific theological avenues in the next two chapters that can help lay the ground work and provide helpful dialogue partners for our own constructive work later. The first group of dialogue partners we will explore in this chapter includes modern Evangelical scholars in the United States who have discussed urban poverty in their theological work. The second group includes ecumenical theologies beyond Evangelicals that we will explore in the next chapter. Before beginning to analyze Evangelical theologies of poverty, it will be helpful to establish two primary reasons that American Evangelicals provide good dialogue partners for our work.

First, Evangelicals are the closest ecclesial neighbors to my own Pentecostal background through which I will be engaging Renewal Theology in the constructive part of this thesis. Some see Pentecostalism as a subset of Evangelicalism, but it is probably better seen as its own movement that began running parallel with Evangelicalism during the twentieth century.[1] While

---

1. Evangelicalism itself goes back to sixteenth-century Europe and saw particular

it has many similarities, there are also significant differences, particularly on a global scale. Some, most famously Donald Dayton, trace the antecedents of Pentecostalism to Methodist and holiness roots in England and then the United States in the nineteenth century.[2] Many future Methodist, holiness, and Pentecostal denominations have maintained theological and historical ties with Evangelicalism including their participation in the National Association of Evangelicals (NAE) after World War II. Pentecostalism also has all four of the theological markers identified by David Bebbington as at the core of Evangelical theology: conversion, biblicism, activism (primarily in the form of evangelism and missions), and crucicentrism.[3] Finally, Pentecostalism also had some of the anti-liberal inclinations that some believe led to many of their, and to many of Evangelicalism's, theological identifiers.[4]

While this evidence may seem to point to Pentecostalism in the United States being a subset of American Evangelicalism, there are also historical and theological reasons why this should not be considered the case.[5] Walter J. Hollenweger, traces very different roots for many Pentecostals in the United States that are separate from Methodist or holiness roots.[6] Pentecostalism was always a rather isolationist movement, preaching separation from the rest of the world and even Christianity at times.[7] It was separate from the doctrinal formation that was occurring in Evangelicalism as it developed in some of the more conservative seminaries in the United States such as the Princeton school. Before their involvement in in the NAE there was also a somewhat tenuous nature to the relationship between Pentecostals and other Evangelical denominations. This may have been due to a mix of factors such as the pauper beginnings of Pentecostalism, its somewhat unruly

---

growth in America through the Great Awakenings of the nineteenth century. For more on the history of Evangelicalism see Noll, *Rise of Evangelicalism*; Bebbington, *Evangelicalism in Modern Britain*.

2. See Dayton, *Theological Roots of Pentecostalism*.

3. Bebbington, *Evangelicalism in Modern Britain*, 2. While Pentecostals have a clear crucicentrism it does differ from Evangelicalism's in that it focuses more on the atonement metaphor than the forensic metaphor.

4. Anderson, "Varieties, Taxonomies, and Definitions," 15.

5. Even this distinction of American Pentecostalism is a broad one as Black Pentecostalism, southern Pentecostalism, etc., all had different relationships with Evangelicalism throughout this history. See Hollenweger below for instance.

6. Hollenweger, *Pentecostals*, 14–28.

7. William Seymour, the primary leader of the Azusa Street revival from which many classical Pentecostal denominations in the United States trace their roots, held that only those baptized in the Holy Spirit with speaking in tongues would participate in the marriage supper of the lamb, a doctrine that would certainly be seen as separationist. See Jacobsen, *Reader in Pentecostal Theology*, 49.

and emotional nature, and theological divides on issues such as spiritual gifts and the nature of revelation. As Pentecostalism matured it began to experience more upward mobility that also changed its acceptance and respectability among other Protestant denominations.

A second, more historical, problem with calling Renewal a subset of Evangelicalism is that Renewal is much bigger than Evangelicalism. The Charismatic Renewal, over against early Pentecostals who formed their own self-standing denominations, arose out of and stayed within their current denominations. Many of these denominations were Evangelical, but they also included Roman Catholic Charismatic, Episcopalian Charismatic, and Lutheran Charismatic groups that are not usually included in Evangelical ranks. Then there are neo-Pentecostal churches and denominations across the globe who know nothing of American Evangelicalism. So, while classical Pentecostalism may or may not fit within various Evangelical paradigms as we broaden our framework to include this large vision of Renewal, it has outgrown Evangelicalism. It is for these reasons that we will compare and contrast Evangelicals and Pentecostals as entities that are separate enough that we can put them into conversation with one another.

As we discuss Evangelical and Ecumenical theology each in its respective chapter, we will be focusing on three topics. First, we will discuss the nature of poverty, including its causes and effects, according to each group. In the last chapter, we talked about what poverty looks like and the effects it has on both those in poverty and our society as a whole, in essence why poverty is a problem. In this chapter, we will also focus on what causes poverty but from a theological perspective. Starting with causes is important because it points us toward the nature of poverty. Such a question can have a number of responses from a number of different disciplines. Theologians often draw from sociological, psychological and philosophical resources in their own analyses, so these will be reflected here, but built into these discussions are theological reasons and underpinnings which we will draw out. Second, we will explore theological responses to poverty within these movements. These responses involve theological themes that underlie the causes of poverty, the theological paradigms through which poverty is assessed, and theologically driven solutions to poverty. Finally, we will end each section with an overview of the practical responses to poverty for each group. Some of these will naturally come up in the previous sections, but we will focus specifically on what each group says should be done about poverty based on their view of the nature and theological responses to poverty because any theological approach to poverty should include practical responses.

EVANGELICAL THEOLOGY AND URBAN POVERTY

The Rock Church is the largest church in San Diego. It is an Evangelical haven for over fifteen thousand people from various ethnic and socioeconomic backgrounds.[8] Though it is diverse, much like the city of San Diego, its parishioners are predominantly middle class. Like many megachurches, the "Rock" is built partly on the charismatic shoulders of its leader, Miles McPherson. Even before starting the church, McPherson was a well-known figure, leading annual evangelistic crusades in the city with thousands in attendance. The crusades, and now the church, employed methods common to Evangelicals such as rock music, trendy dress, and a focus on a simple gospel message to invite its many visitors into a born-again experience. The Rock has also publicly taken strongly conservative stances, in line with the larger Evangelical movement in the United States, on a number of social issues such as gay marriage.[9] The Rock reaps both the benefits and common criticisms of being heavily linked with modern American Evangelicalism. It is not just perception. The Rock fits all four Evangelical descriptors put forth by Bebbington above. While their main focus is evangelism, the Rock also employs a number of socially focused ministries. One of these is their "Rock Thrift Shops" which they have opened in two locations over the past five years. Over this time, they have given out over thirty-eight hundred vouchers for free clothing and/or furniture items to the poor. This fits with their stated purpose to "bring hope and healing to the San Diego community and beyond by providing: a welcoming, affordable retail experience to its shoppers; donations to those in emergency or crisis situations; and a place to gather and experience the love of Jesus."[10]

One man, David, tells the story of how he went to the Rock directly after being released from prison. He hoped to get a job quickly and begin to start a new life, but without any money, one of David's greatest needs was professional looking clothing to wear for job interviews. He visited the Rock Church and a greeter set him up with vouchers for free clothing from the Rock Thrift Store. According to David, this act of generosity empowered him to obtain a job that paid him thirty-two dollars an hour helping

---

8. As I mentioned in our introduction and second chapter, we do not want our theology to be completely disconnected from what is occurring on the ground of these movements. For this reason, I try to start each chapter with a minor case study from my own context demonstrating what we will unpack theologically. In this case, the Rock Church in San Diego is largely representative of what we will be discussing concerning Evangelical approaches to poverty in the United States.

9. Long, "Miles McPherson."

10. "About the Rock Thrift Store."

to get him out of poverty, eventually remarry, and even reconcile with his estranged children. David now volunteers at the Rock in two other socially inclined ministries, "5 loaves, 2 fish," a ministry that helps feed the poor, and "The Most Excellent Way," a ministry that helps people to overcome chemical dependency.[11] David's is one story of many the Rock tells of lives that have been changed through their social initiatives focused on homeless ministry, human trafficking, prison ministry and orphanages abroad, just to name a few.[12] The Rock is one of a number of Evangelical churches in San Diego which has become more socially conscious seeking to help the poor in their urban setting.

Overall, the Rock church is probably typical of other modern Evangelical churches in San Diego and the United States. It has a number of socially oriented ministries, but the motivations for these ministries is often evangelizing the individual and building up the local ministry rather than necessarily enacting social change. What the Rock participates in is what William Pinson calls "social ministry." Pinson defines social ministry as an "effort to help persons in special need and those hurt by adverse social conditions, such as the poor, the neglected child or the sick. It is an attempt to help those who are hurt rather than to deal with social causes of their hurt."[13] It is charity work rather than work geared toward systemic change. Many critics would rather see Evangelicals engaging in social action, which Pinson says, "Endeavors to correct harmful social conditions, such as war, an unjust and exploitative economic system, or a corrupt political system. It is distinguished from social ministry in that it is directed primarily to the social cause of human hurt rather than to persons who are hurt."[14]

Evangelicals have received criticism concerning the type of activism they employ and their motivations for employing it. Specifically, they do not employ a strong social activism in line with a holistic gospel. They are accused of being more motivated by saving the person's soul than the entire person. This has not always been the case. Brantley Gasaway holds that it was early in the twentieth century that an individualist ethic began to displace early Evangelicalism's commitment to progressive social reform.[15] This shift, which David Moberg famously termed "the Great Reversal," came through an increased belief in spiritual and moral transformation of

---

11. Kaun, "Generosity Multiplied."
12. "Ministries."
13. Pinson, *Applying the Gospel*, 13.
14. Pinson, *Applying the Gospel*, 13.
15. Gasaway, *Progressive Evangelicals*, 7.

individuals as the ultimate source of social transformation.[16] This emphasis came as a reaction against liberal modernists who accepted biblical criticism and the Social Gospel movement. Evangelicals rejected liberalism believing that its theology belittled personal conversion. According to Gasaway, by the 1920s, this rejection had caused any social reform pulse within Evangelicalism to atrophy.[17] This weakening social conscious continued even as Evangelicals saw their greatest numerical growth in the 1960s. By this golden era, this reversal was well cemented into being a major part of the Evangelical identity.[18]

Gasaway and Moberg are not the only scholars to identify the lack of social concern within United States Evangelicalism in the twentieth century. Many see this shift to a more individualized religion that focuses on personal growth and development as a substitute for a solution that moves toward social reform.[19] In what follows, we will explore Evangelical Christianity's theology of poverty. This theology will include what Evangelicals see as the causes of poverty and how they respond to poverty both theologically and practically. We will see that while some criticisms may be warranted, many Evangelicals see their "social ministry" as an equal, if not more legitimate, form of social action than their liberal counterparts. Beyond this different interpretation of what constitutes effective social change among Evangelicals, there are other branches of Evangelicalism, those Gasaway calls progressive Evangelicals, which are clearly engaging in social ministry, but also social action birthed out of a legitimate social concern. Evangelicals cannot be pigeonholed but have a diversity of approaches worth investigating.

Richard J. Mouw tells us to pay attention to Evangelical theology. Even though it may be misguided in some areas, they have a unique finger on the pulse of North American undercurrents, especially as it relates to economic realities. Evangelicals have had great success reaching United States culture because of it. Any theology of the poor that tries to be North American must pay attention to Evangelicalism.[20]

16. Moberg, *Great Reversal*, 1–17.

17. Gasaway, *Progressive Evangelicals*, 8.

18. It was during the 1960s they formed the National Association of Evangelicals and benefited from world renowned leaders like Billy Graham. Even during this time there were outliers within Evangelicalism, such as Ronald J. Sider, who focused on social issues alongside of more traditional Evangelical themes like conversion and the centrality of the Bible. We will analyze many of these more progressive Evangelicals later in the chapter.

19. We will see the more communal nature of Pentecostalism, particularly as seen in the doctrine of Spirit baptism and the creation of a Spirit empowered community, as a natural critique of modernity and Evangelicalism's individualistic focus.

20. Mouw, "Thinking About the Poor," 32.

Causes of Urban Poverty

Responses and solutions to poverty cannot be fully imagined unless the causes of urban poverty are determined. At best, one will only be alleviating symptoms rather than finding long-term solutions to the root issues of the problem. In our second chapter, we looked at sociological theories about causes of poverty and saw that only a multidimensional answer is appropriate for such a complex issue. In general, we saw two categories of possible causes for poverty, structural causes and personal causes. Our sociological sources focused more on structural causes, such as transportation issues or historical discrimination. Some still see personal causes as at the core of poverty, however, as seems to be the norm of more conservative, western, and Evangelical theological interpretations. Still, some Evangelicals have spoken of structural or societal causes, particularly progressive Evangelicals. David Gushee, for instance, speaks of how the sexual character of our civil society is a structural cause of poverty because of its part in perpetuating out of wedlock births.[21]

Stephen V. Monsma, in his article "Evangelicals and Poverty," sees three categories of possible causes. The first is that poverty is a natural result from the cyclical nature of a free market economy. A second set of causes include structural features of our economy such as discriminatory practices in employment. Finally, he also mentions personal reasons including mental health, lack of education and drug abuse.[22] We will start with structural or societal causes. Second, we will investigate the personal causes most identified by Evangelical theologians. In both of these areas we will compare and contrast them with the sociological views already discussed. Finally, we will ask the question of whether or not these theological perspectives on the causes of poverty have room for, or even dictate, the idea of possible spiritual causes to poverty.

Potential structural causes of poverty are endless as poverty and society are complex, but a few often come to the forefront in Evangelical theological writings. We already mentioned David Gushee's article on sex and society found in his own edited volume. His proposal is that a major cause of poverty is single parent families, many of which are caused by out of wedlock births or divorce. On the surface, this would seem to be a personal cause to poverty, the result of personal decision. According to Gushee, however, many of these single parent families can be traced to being a result of a deteriorated social ethic in the United States. He sees this stemming from

---

21. Gushee, "Rebuilding Marriage and the Family," 512.
22. Monsma, "Evangelicals and Poverty," 42.

a lack of coherent and appropriate sexual socialization. The various sectors in society—from family, religion, and education to entertainment—all communicate vastly different views of sexuality. Gushee traces the beginnings of this breakdown to the sexual revolution of the 1960s and its new sexual ethic. He identifies this new ethic as a "sex-with-mutual consent" ethic as opposed to the "sex-within-marriage" ethic of Judeo-Christianity, both of which compete with the modern "sex-within-loving-relationship ethic" that is currently challenging both for dominance.[23] For Gushee, these varying sexual ethics create a vacuum in which no sexual ethic is accepted by a majority of the culture. Instead, people move in and out of whichever ethic suits them best at the moment.

Another societal issue leading to births out of wedlock is the growing legitimacy of unmarried mothers and of divorce.[24] Gushee strives to provide a holistic solution to what he calls "marital permanence." His solutions include personal responsibilities, a Christian civil social strategy, and public policy options.[25] There is not a direct correlation between births out of wedlock or children in single parent homes and poverty. Not all poor are from such situations, nor are all single parent households poor. There are, however, enough correlations between single mother homes and poverty that it must be considered among one of the many possible causes.

It is not surprising that Evangelicals, even more progressive ones like Gushee, focus on the decline of marriage as an important cause of poverty in the United States. It is only one chapter in his edited volume, but Evangelicals have given a large amount of focus to marriage in other areas. They have focused heavily throughout the nation on fighting to preserve what they call the sanctity of marriage between a man and a woman against marriage equality proponents who promote same sex marriage. Many Evangelicals see the nuclear family as the building block of society and society's ills as the direct result of the weakening of the nuclear family.[26] This creates a vicious cycle in which newly accepted societal norms concerning sex and marriage have deteriorated the family. This corrosion perpetuates society to make worse decisions which causes further corrosion negatively affecting the family. It is not surprising that one of the few expositions on the causes of poverty in the Evangelical literature I surveyed involved the family. While Gushee's solutions are focused on divorce they also have ramifications for

---

23. Gushee, "Rebuilding Marriage and the Family," 514.
24. Gushee, "Rebuilding Marriage and the Family," 515.5.
25. Gushee, "Rebuilding Marriage and the Family," 518.
26. For further comments on the Evangelical focus on the family, see Bendroth, "Evangelicals, Family, and Modernity," 56–69.

poverty, specifically in those cases in which it is related to single female households and should be considered in a holistic approach to overcoming urban poverty in the United States. Gushee does not believe, however, that secular organizations can be expected to suddenly communicate a countercultural message on sex and family making the only choice for Christians to focus on "strengthening the fundamentally countercultural religious and moral vision and practice" within its churches.[27]

Another chapter in Gushee's edited volume focuses on the possible causes of poverty in the United States. George N. Monsma posits that "two of the major causes in increasing inequality are changes in the distribution of earning among workers and changes in family composition and work patterns."[28] It is interesting again that, even in a new area of discourse, another Evangelical finds the roots of this societal ill in family life. In family life Monsma, like Gushee, includes single parent families and their limited earning power as part of the cause of unequal income distribution. Not only is it having one income, but single and minority mothers often earn less than other individuals at similar jobs. The breakdown of the family is not the only cause of poverty according to Monsma, he cites the demand for labor shifting away from low-skilled workers to higher skilled workers faster than the supply of higher-skilled jobs have grown. He also cites technological changes and increases in foreign trade as providing lower cost labor options and either eliminating jobs or making them in less demand meaning lower wages.[29] While Monsma gives more politico-economic structural causes, his proposed responses to income inequality which can help overcome poverty focus the most on strengthening the family. The few larger economic solutions he mentions—increasing the Earned Income Tax Credit and the minimum wage—are limited and only helpful if done in conjunction with one another and with other moral societal reforms among the family.[30]

Finally, Ronald J. Sider, one of the patriarchs of progressive Evangelicals who most thoroughly deals with urban poverty pays the most attention to various structural causes of poverty. Many of the causes he outlines are echoes from what we saw in the sociological literature on the decreasing number of low-skill, well-paying jobs or jobs being moved overseas and replaced by technology.[31] Other reasons that Sider mentions for growing

---

27. Gushee, "Rebuilding Marriage and the Family," 520.
28. Monsma, "Income Distribution in the United States," 175.
29. Monsma, "Income Distribution in the United States," 177.
30. Monsma, "Income Distribution in the United States," 85.
31. Sider, *Just Generosity*, 43. The same possible structural causes are also mentioned by Monsma.

inequality include the falling real value of the minimum wage, drop in welfare payments, declining unions, a growing trend in part-time workers over full-time workers and institutional racism all as part of the possible causes of poverty.[32] He also mentions personal causes that are intertwined with these structural causes, like "personal and misguided behavior patterns."[33] In particular, Sider focuses on marriage and out of wedlock births, but focuses more on the personal choices made in these instances over against Gushee's discussion of societal causes. But Sider also recognizes that there are even greater causes besides structural or personal such as sudden catastrophes and permanent disabilities which cannot be controlled or deterred, only handled as they come.

Other scholars outside of Evangelicalism see income distribution and falling spending power and opportunities for jobs as a moral issue of greed or discrimination. These roots of the economic causes are not mentioned in the Evangelical literature. Evangelicals do mention such root causes when it concerns personal choice and the family unit such as seeing sexual morals as a factor concerning income distribution. Other personal choices mentioned by Evangelicals can include sloth and laziness or drug and alcohol usage that makes one unfit to work. Kurt Hendel for instance, in his historical study on early German Protestant usage of the poor chest as a way to provide for the poor, latches on to the fact that these Protestants only used this collected money for those they deemed the "worthy poor." The worthy poor were those "people of faith with honorable reputations in addition to having obvious financial needs. Widows, orphans, young women without families, workers and artisans who simply could not earn enough to support their families, and people who became ill and could not work were counted among the honorable poor."[34] So again, you have a distinction based on morals and personal choices. In this case. the distinction is whether someone is worthy to be helped. This a line of thinking puts a higher emphasis on the morals of poverty and personal choice seeing it as a worse kind of poverty that is irredeemable. Hendel more meticulously describes and spends time on the personal causes to poverty than the structural causes. But in his paradigm, it is only those poor who are poor because of structural issues such as a poor economy, death, or war that are deserving of help. This implicitly moralizes the social and structural factors of poverty while also minimizing them by seeing them as more happenstance than patterns that can be fixed or overcome. This leads to solutions like a poor chest which ends up

---

32. Sider, *Just Generosity*, 45–46.
33. Sider, *Just Generosity*, 47.
34. Hendel, "Care of the Poor," 530.

helping with the symptoms through a social ministry of financial handouts, rather than addressing root causes structurally. Being a religious institution who focused more on morals, the German Protestant Church probably did offer to provide spiritual help to the unworthy poor they refused to help financially. This paradigm of "help" fails to recognize, however, that even those causes of poverty that seem to be beyond one's control can often be within the control of a community through the way it structures its culture, policies, norms and values.

Is this because Evangelicals are so fixated on issues of personal sin that it has become a blind spot, causing them to turn a blind eye to structural sin, or is this something they can offer to the conversation? While Evangelicals have a unique perspective on the morality of poverty, many of them, especially the more progressive Evangelicals, see structural causes as a nearly equal part of the equation of what causes poverty with in the United States. This may actually bring more balance to this complex matrix than those who over focus on structural issues. It helps one to get beyond just possible policy changes and think about the very norms and values of the culture that have caused such policies and trends that need to be fixed in the first place. It recognizes that there are spiritual issues at stake in what causes poverty and underlies the sociological. Where Evangelicals stray slightly is in over-dichotomizing the spiritual and the sociological rather than seeing them as an intertwined reality. Racial discrimination is a spiritual issue that stems from a person's heart and indeed is found in the very *Zeitgeist* of our nation as much as it has become a failure of American society on a structural and policy level. This is why I find Amos Yong's many tongues perspective on the need for wide and diverse voices helpful because we need all perspectives, they all lack something and each also brings something unique and needed to the table.[35] Having explored possible causes of poverty within Evangelical theology, let us now turn to how Evangelical theologians seek to respond to urban poverty, first theologically then practically.

Theological Responses to Urban Poverty

In this section, we seek to further survey the actual responses that Evangelicals pose to the problem of urban poverty. The writing is not overly voluminous adding to possible criticisms that Evangelicals are behind on the topic. In fact, the discussion takes two general tones, some scholars recognize the shortfall within the Evangelical response making their work more negative as they seek to provide a corrective reconstruction to fix a

---

35. Yong, *In the Days of Caesar*, 93–103.

lacking or broken perspective concerning the urban poor. The other tone involves Evangelicals trying to construct a theology of the poor from their own theological locus, Evangelicalism in the United States. Both are helpful in our synthesis and critique of Evangelical theologies. We should really be talking about Evangelical theologies as opposed to an Evangelical theology to better represent the diversity that is present within this one movement. To proceed, we will incorporate both voices, starting with those critiquing Evangelical theologies from within and then moving toward those voices which have spoken more constructively.

Perhaps one of the greatest critiques of Evangelical theologies of poverty from within is from Richard J. Mouw, a heavy hitter in Evangelical theology having been the president of a prominent Evangelical seminary on the West Coast, Fuller Theological Seminary. Within Evangelicalism, Mouw and Fuller Seminary have been perceived to be on the progressive side of Evangelicalism. Mouw's self-identification and his theological work, however, have planted himself firmly within the Evangelical realm. In his article, "Thinking about the Poor: What Evangelicals Can Learn from the Bishops," Mouw engages in an ecumenical conversation between Evangelicals and the United States Roman Catholic bishops in their work on economics. Mouw's work in this brief yet insightful article covers the majority of Evangelical lack and so will help create our structure for this section while we intersperse other pertinent scholars' views who agree with Mouw before we turn to those who disagree.

Before going into his formal critique of specific areas within Evangelical theology, Mouw criticizes the whole enterprise saying, "Evangelicals need some preparation simply to get to the stage where they are ready to receive theological teaching on the subject of economics because Evangelicals in contemporary North America have not nurtured their communal theological-economic memories."[36] He goes on to say that they have been content to work with the bare minimum of theological articulation regarding economic matters, usually employing proof texts.[37] Mouw recognizes that this is not true of all Evangelicals, particularly those in the progressive camp led by *Sojourners*, the *Other Side* and Ron Sider's Evangelicals for Social Action, but wants to focus on the dominant view. We saw this same lack of attention to economic realities by Evangelicals in our overview of Evangelical views on the causes of poverty. Mouw sees this lack as a deficiency in paradigm altogether because Evangelicals simply have not thought in economic terms. This is one thing Evangelicals can learn from other theological

---

36. Mouw, "Thinking About the Poor," 23.
37. Mouw, "Thinking About the Poor," 24.

traditions such the Roman Catholic bishops who do have structures for thinking economically. The discussion goes both ways of course with Evangelicals having some emphases from which others can learn.

According to Mouw, Evangelicals give special emphasis to the creation and fall motif when dealing with wealth, poverty and economic justice, but utilize this motif differently than Roman Catholicism.[38] In other traditions, this motif is often used to account for sinful distortions of the divine purposes in the world which have led to thinking of the poor as victims of exclusion and powerlessness. Evangelicals see this in more individualist terms, however. They believe that the soul of each person is distorted through the fall and in need of restoration. This places the solution more in the realm of salvation and evangelism than social action. This unique interpretation of the creation–fall motif also gives rise to three other areas in which Evangelical theologies of poverty are unique according to Mouw.

The first is the Evangelical formulation of indolence. We have discussed indolence already in terms of one's personal choice causing their own poverty. A personal cause requires only a personal solution rather than a shifting of structures or policies. Mouw is correct that there is a "significant strand in the Bible that emphasizes a connection between poverty and personal indolence."[39] Evangelicals' Biblicist interpretation of this strand creates cliché-ridden, shallow responses when taken as the only possible formulation of poverty. Lydia Bean in her article "Compassionate Conservatives?" also points out this underlying theme of indolence that is more present in American Evangelicalism compared to Evangelical churches she studied in Canada. Both sets of Evangelical churches she studies in the United States and in Canada have similar social ministries solving personal need. The Evangelical churches in the United States vehemently reject the welfare system as a viable option for helping solve poverty while Canadian Evangelicals embrace it, however. In Canada, acts of personal compassion are seen as in line with the welfare state and part of a larger national collective memory of support for the poor.[40] American Evangelicalism has an added theology of the undeserving poor because of this idea of indolence that makes them weary of blanket welfare systems that might reward those underserving of help.

Bean also attributes the difference in American Evangelicalism, over against Canadian, to an individualistic anti-structuralism which lives itself out in a rejection of not just the welfare state, but other structural solutions

---

38. Mouw, "Thinking About the Poor," 27.
39. Mouw, "Thinking About the Poor," 29.
40. Bean, "Compassionate Conservatives?," 169.

as well as a disparaging of the Social Gospel in the churches she studied.[41] This coincides with Mouw's second theological factor, "the strong volitionalism of Evangelical religious thought."[42] This volitionalistic individualism even influences the choice of Scriptures about poverty used by Evangelicals emphasizing those focusing on indolence. Coupled together, this means that indolence is not caused by structural norms or oppressions that cause defeat or a victimization of the poor but are only a result of personal choice and decisions. This combination is problematic in light of other evidence we have seen since urban poverty is specifically loci based and follows certain demographic trends which make it extremely unlikely such a large group of individuals would all make the same choices that would lead to a life of poverty without some kind of structural powers at play. Mouw is correct that we should not ignore personal choice or indolence as factors in poverty, but they also fall short of explaining poverty.

The final underlying theological factor that plays into Evangelical views on poverty, per Mouw is an "either-now-or-never assessment of the way God deals with unfortunate situations."[43] This can be seen in Evangelicals thinking either that poverty is not as bad or complex as many think, or it is so bad and the world so broken there is nothing we could ever do about it. In either case, poverty should not be an emphasis, especially not over evangelism, global missions, or personal holiness. Of course, this now-or-never approach is applied selectively to poverty rather than say evangelism. Regardless, it ultimately leads to an inadequate theology of poverty.

These factors—indolence, volitionalism and an either-now-or-never mentality—should not be overlooked even though they are not comprehensive. Ultimately, Mouw does not appear to believe Evangelicals in the United States have the theological resources on their own to address something economically centered, especially urban poverty. Their current formulation leads to a paternalistic approach, that must be transcended to an approach that emphasizes more solidarity with the poor and oppressed like the Roman Catholic bishops to whom Mouw is comparing Evangelicalism.

William Cook, in his article "Evangelical Reflections on the Church of the Poor," is another Evangelical who sees shortcomings in American Evangelical theology. He also sees the Roman Catholic Church as a helpful and challenging conversation partner for Evangelicals. They challenge Evangelical hermeneutics in light of the poor, their comfortable way of

---

41. Bean, "Compassionate Conservatives?," 172.
42. Mouw, "Thinking About the Poor," 29.
43. Mouw, "Thinking About the Poor," 30.

understanding institutional Christianity, and their missiology as well.[44] Cook particularly focuses on the base ecclesial communities of Latin American Liberation Theology from which we can learn that sin is social and horizontal between humans, not just personal and vertical between an individual and God. Also, LALT's focus on solidarity and a God who suffers with the poor is a resource that can help take Evangelicals beyond social ministry and almsgiving to solidarity with the oppressed.[45] Julijana Mladenovska-Tešija, in her article "Crucified as a Necessity," sees Jürgen Moltmann as an equally helpful conversation partner to aid Evangelicals in deepening their commitment to the poor through the church's involvement and solidarity with those who suffer.[46] This need for a movement from individuality to solidarity and from anti-structuralism to social responsibility is a common theme in the writings of Evangelicals critiquing their own movement using language and resources outside Evangelicalism. In the next chapter, we will analyze some of these major ecumenical resources.

We have already seen how the criticisms of Evangelical theologies of poverty still bear some fruitful dialogue and positive additions to the discussion. Many see very few resources for such dialogue from the Evangelical perspective, however. Joel Hunter, for instance, tells the story of how when he was named the president of the Christian Coalition in 2005, a conservative, evangelically driven political advocacy group, he desired to expand the coalition's agenda to include the poor. In response, a board member declared to him that "those issues are fine, but they are just not what we do."[47] Hunter's story tells both sides of the current Evangelical predicament. There are those, like Hunter, who want to change the Evangelical response to the poor, but many who do not. Stephen Monsma holds that there has been a shift going on in Evangelicalism and that the movement is not as uniform as it appears to outsiders. He cites a 2007 Pew survey that 57 percent of White Evangelicals agreed with the statement, "The government should do more to help needy Americans, even if it means going deeper into dept."[48] He also cites a 2004 survey by *Religion and Ethics Newsweekly* that 65 percent of White Evangelicals reported they were either very worried or somewhat worried "there is a growing inequality between the rich and poor in this country."[49]

---

44. Cook, "Evangelical Reflections" 51.
45. Cook, "Evangelical Reflections," 53.
46. Mladenovska-Tešija, "Crucified as a Necessity," 17.
47. Hunter, *New Kind of Conservative*, 21.
48. Monsma, "Evangelicals and Poverty," 46.
49. Monsma, "Evangelicals and Poverty," 46.

Brantley Gasaway systematically chronicles the emergence of what he calls progressive Evangelicals who have begun to pursue social justice including solutions to poverty. Gasaway identifies the beginning of this shift occurring with the formation of *Freedom Now* magazine which eventually became *The Other Side* a reference to providing an Evangelical theological alternative.[50] This magazine did not begin by giving a systematic theology for public life, it wrote what emerged within the course of its publisher's activism. There were even shifts within the publication itself as it moved toward using the language of justice more than the language of love as the foundation of social concern.[51] Later, progressive Evangelical leaders would spend more time articulating and even systematizing theological frameworks for their public and political practice. For example, Jim Wallis only wrote systematically years after he founded his own magazine *Transformation* which would later become *Sojourners*.[52] The most systematic outworking of an Evangelical public theology on the poor comes in a series of works by Ron Sider who founded the organization, Evangelicals for Social Action. Unlike Wallis, Sider was an academic and longtime professor of theology, holistic ministry, and public policy at Palmer Theological Seminary.[53] According to Gasaway, Sider's book, *The Scandal of Evangelical Politics* culminated Sider's "decades-long efforts to develop a public theology, for he saw the need for a biblically grounded, sophisticated Evangelical political philosophy that could guide hundreds of millions of Evangelicals around the world to love their neighbors more effectively through wise political engagement."[54] While these authors attempted to progress beyond Evangelicalism, they still contested liberal philosophers like John Locke or John Rawls who gave primacy to individual liberties and rights that did not affirm the equal importance of communal responsibilities and the common good. Also, Evangelicals held on to religion as an important element for a just political order over against liberal philosophers who sought the limitation or privatization of religion to seek consensus among the religiously diverse.[55]

So, what were the hallmarks of this progressive Evangelical theology as it applies to urban poverty? First, because of Evangelicalism's emphasis on the Bible, we will start by overviewing some of the major biblical arguments

50. Gasaway, *Progressive Evangelicals*, 29.

51. Gasaway, *Progressive Evangelicals*, 30.

52. Wallis's primary works include: *Soul of Politics*; *Faith Works*; *God's Politics*.

53. Besides his edited volumes, Sider's primary monographs that contain work on poverty include: *Rich Christians in an Age of Hunger*; *Evangelism and Social Action*; *Just Generosity*; *Scandal of the Evangelical Conscience*; *Just Politics*.

54. Gasaway, *Progressive Evangelicals*, 55.

55. Gasaway, *Progressive Evangelicals*, 54, 56.

of Evangelicals as these form the foundation for any theological reflection done within the movement. Second, we will rely on Richard Mouw's contention that theologies of social action, including Evangelical theologies, tend to fall into three categories, creation-fall motifs, incarnational theology, or eschatological concerns. We will allow these three categories to structure our discussion of constructive theological contributions in Evangelicalism.

Brantley Gasaway, in his work on progressive Evangelicals, identifies four biblical paradigms that as foundation of an Evangelical theology of social justice, all of which also apply to poverty.[56] The first paradigm comes from mosaic legislation. Particularly useful from here are edicts on tithing, gleaning and loaning which protected the poor from economic inequalities. The second Evangelical biblical paradigm came from Jesus's transformation of economic attitudes and relationships among his followers. Jesus asked his disciples to renounce their possessions to share resources freely with the community and the poor. This would also include Jesus's teachings like the Sermon on the Mount. A third area of biblical resource Gasaway identified is the idealized communitarian practices based on Acts 2 and 4. Believers shared everything in common even selling their own possessions to help take care of the poor and disenfranchised among them through redistribution. They also had common meals in which everyone was treated equally. A final biblical paradigm that Evangelicals have utilized is Paul's collection for the impoverished Jerusalem church which extended economic sharing from within the local community across ethnic and geographic lines.

Ron Sider in his book, *Just Generosity,* probably did the most to flesh out these biblical themes. He did not want to take an approach of proof texting he saw Evangelicals often falling into, however.[57] So, while he heavily utilized the paradigms Gasaway mentioned above, Sider also asked four questions he saw as particularly important for attempting to construct a biblical approach to poverty in the United States. The first question Sider asked was, "What is the relevant foundational framework for approaching the issue of poverty?"[58] In response, Sider outlines a creation Lordship framework in which God is sovereign owner of everything including the Lord of all economics. Because God created out of nothing material work and history are finite, good and full of meaning. This includes humans who are created in the imago dei and fashioned for community. Persons possess inestimable dignity and value that should transcend any economic process

---

56. Gasaway, *Progressive Evangelicals*, 200–208.

57. For a similar concern about Evangelical hermeneutics on the topic of poverty, see Halteman, "Market System," 74–75.

58. Sider, *Just Generosity*, 60–65.

or system. For instance, the right to private property cannot undermine general welfare because of both the social nature of humans and the fact that only God is an absolute owner. According to Sider, persons are not just socioeconomic material machines; they are also spiritual enjoying God-given rights and responsibilities. Each person is a body-soul unity made for relationship with God, neighbor and Earth.[59]

The second question that Sider asks is whether, according to the Bible, justice requires only honest courts and fair procedures or if it also insists on specific outcomes? Sider sees biblical teaching as pointing to outcomes being equally as important as the procedures. The greatest argument that Sider gives for this is the biblical connection between love and justice. This creates a dynamic restorative character for justice that cares as much about the person and their outcome as whether things are fair.[60] The person themselves being restored is just as important as justice being restored and justice is not done unless it becomes personal.

A third question Sider asks is concerning the biblical definition of equity. For Sider, this equity includes equality of opportunity and access to productive resources rather than how much one has. Because humans have free choice, and free choice has consequences, the various choices one makes will have repercussions concerning one's actual resources. Here, he draws primarily on the first of Gasaway's biblical themes, the mosaic law and which demands justice by requiring every person or family to have access to productive resources and if they have lost this access the opportunity to restore it every so often.[61]

Finally, Sider asks the question, who should care for the poor? Should it be the government? Families? The church? Sider sees the primary biblical principle being one in which the local community has an obligation to generously care for those who cannot care for themselves.[62] Here again he draws on the Levitical code concerning tithes for the orphans and widows, zero interest loans for the poor and the releasing of slaves. He also draws heavily on creation motifs concerning how even the poor have been created in God's image and deserve dignity and the same opportunity afforded to every other person. Ultimately, Sider believes all three of these entities must work hand in hand if they are in a position to help those less fortunate than themselves. Still, Sider and other progressive Evangelicals hold a particular place for social groups such as churches and families seeing them as the

---

59. Sider, *Just Generosity*, 116.
60. Sider, *Just Generosity*, 68.
61. Sider, *Just Generosity*, 76–79.
62. Sider, *Just Generosity*, 83.

foundation of society. In his final suggestions for a comprehensive strategy concerning a just society for the poor, Sider holds that "because the Trinitarian God created persons for mutual interdependence in community, society must be organized in ways that nurture the common good. Since persons reach their potential only in a multilayered community of diverse intuitions, society must promote policies that strengthen all institutions to play their full proper role."[63] This is a holistic vision in which everyone helps because the human person and society are complex. Family is particularly important and should be an emphasis in policy and a focus for social institutions if poverty is to be addressed from a biblical perspective.

Because Scripture requires justice and not just charity, these progressive Evangelicals taught that Christians must exercise political influence in order to promote "redistributive public policies that alleviate poverty and moderate inequalities."[64] Paul Markham, in his chapter in Gushee's *A New Evangelical Manifesto*, promotes what he calls "prophetic politics" which involves being a public witness, not just for personal salvation, but for engaging in the hard work of addressing problems and systems that affect a wide range of people. This combines the Evangelical foundation of conversion with efforts to transform society. Since politics refers to the basic process of humans working together to achieve a desired goal, the question is not whether Evangelicals will be politically active, but how.[65]

These biblical perspectives are an important aspect of an Evangelical theology of poverty. They are something we will come back to in our own construction of a holistic Pneumatology of poverty especially as we dialogue with Pentecostalism, another tradition that places a high emphasis on the authority of Scripture. These biblical perspectives are also important because they lay the biblical foundation for the three theological motifs Richard Mouw mentions are at the heart of a theology of the poor: the creation-fall motif, the incarnational motif, and the eschatological motif. It is to these theological constructions we now turn.

Mouw holds that the creation-fall motif is the most expressed theme within Evangelical theologies of poverty, His belief holds true throughout the literature. Stephen Monsma, for instance, outlines an Evangelical approach based on God creating human beings in his image. According to Monsma, since humanity has been created in God's image, it is a Christian duty to have a deep concern for the poor just as God is shown through some 2000 references to the poor in the Bible to have this same concern.

---

63. Sider, *Just Generosity*, 116.
64. Gasaway, *Progressive Evangelicals*, 209.
65. Markham, "Theology That 'Works,'" 43–45.

Monsma wants to go beyond only an individualistic concern by also pointing out the "underlying God-given purpose of government to seek justice in our world."[66] Government should have a role in taking care of the poor but it should be limited to empowerment and should not include charity or paternalism. Finally, responsibility toward the poor should go beyond individuals or governments to incorporate civil society because families, service clubs, religious congregations etc., grow out of the inherent social nature of human beings who are created in God's image.

Stephen Mott also sees creation as providing the primary biblical paradigm for economic justice that would help the urban poor. For Mott, because the world is created out of nothing by a loving, almighty creator, the material world is both finite and good.[67] The world and its inhabitants are not divine, but this does mean that the physical condition of a person is core to our nature as humans. Because humans are created in God's image, they contain inestimable dignity and value that transcends any one economic process or system. This means that any economic system is subservient to the dignity of the human person. For Mott, bodies are good, persons are free and communal, and this means that economic injustice is a "family problem" since we are all God's offspring.[68]

James Halteman is another Evangelical scholar who, in the same volume by Gushee, attempts to look at the economy through an Evangelical Christian worldview based on similar biblical themes of human dignity. For Halteman, the world was created with shalom the way it was supposed to be, and this is a dream God still has for his people even though human sinfulness precludes an ideal social order in the present. This "shalom dream" of God includes sufficiency for each person and harmony in all relationship because humans were created with dignity and for relationship since they were created in God's image.[69] Practically then, social organizations seeking to help the poor should be built on sharing relationships of trust with others that provide security and support since this is the purpose for which we were created. Similarly, these organizations and initiatives to help the poor should be evaluated based on their contribution to this shalom, not just short-term personal pleasure.

Nicholas Wolterstorff is an Evangelical philosopher who has written extensively on the theme of love and justice, two common themes within the realm of ethics and social action. While not speaking specifically to

66. Monsma, "Evangelicals and Poverty," 47.
67. Mott, "Economic Justice," 18.
68. Mott, "Economic Justice," 20.
69. Halteman, "Market System," 74–75.

these progressive Evangelical's work, Wolterstorff provides an important correction to creation motif as outlined by his fellow Evangelicals. He holds that while the being created in the image of God can help to ground the idea of human rights, it cannot do it on its own. It is only the relation to God of being loved by God that fully does the work of giving the human being worth. God's care for human beings is evoked by God's attachment to them.[70] This is an important contribution. We saw earlier, Monsma's comment that progressive Evangelicals such as in the magazine *The Other Side* shifted their language more and more to the language of justice than the language of love. For Wolterstorff, one cannot have a true understanding justice without understanding God's love. The reverse is equally true that justice is a part of God's love. This is an important tension to continually hold together when theologizing about urban poverty. Justice is certainly needed, but if love is not what drives this justice it may fall short of true justice if justice if it is even possible.

The second motif Mouw mentions is the incarnational motif which focuses on the Son of God becoming flesh in the person of Jesus of Nazareth. David Lipscomb was an influential minister within the nineteenth-century restorationist movement and the Church of Christ (Disciples of Christ) denomination. Anthony Duvvant outlines David Lipscomb's early Evangelical theology and proposes it as a possible resource for modern Evangelicals to emulate. Lipscomb's theology is specifically christological in nature. According to Duvvant, it focused strongly on solidarity with the poor and being the church of the poor which are themes also present in LALT which is similarly christologically focused.[71] This comparison by Duvvant is rather anachronistic, but Lispcomb does have a number of parallels to LALT. For Lipscomb, Jesus's proclamations in the gospel concerning the poor shows that God may be found in the poor. Also, the idea of kenosis, that Jesus humbled himself and took on human flesh, the lowliest of forms as a baby born to a family of low socio-economic status provides theological foundations to develop and live out a theology of the poor. Through this incarnational theology, Lipscomb developed a missionary practice in which the poor would evangelize and help the poor rather than relying on the rich to preach to the poor. This is because, for Lipscomb, the poor, and preaching to the poor, best embodies the spirit of the church as established by Christ. Lipscomb was not fully in line with LALT or even progressive Evangelicals as he did not believe the church should engage in political action to try and

---

70. Wolterstorff, *Justice in Love*, 153.
71. Dunnavant, "David Lipscomb," 30.

change the social order.[72] This is because he saw the church as sufficient for any transformation society needed.

William Kostlevy does a similar historical study, but of Benjamin Titus Roberts who Kostlevy sees as utilizing a similar "preferential option for the poor" in the early Free Methodist Church of the late nineteenth century. The Free Methodists became one of the earliest members of the National Association of Evangelicals (NAE). Like Lipscomb who was also compared to Latin American Liberation Theology, Roberts's group of Free Methodists took a more christological and incarnational perspective seeing Jesus's preaching to the poor and helping set them free as the center of Jesus's gospel.[73] Even when mentioning the Spirit, it is the Spirit of Christ and the fact that this Spirit's action is centered on sympathy with the poor.[74] Roberts goes so far as to say that the proof of Jesus's messiahship was that he preached to the poor and lived among the poor.

Again, Kostlevy's analysis, along with Dunnavant's, seems somewhat anachronistic especially since LALT was also on a completely different continent and had wholly unique antecedents. Both analyses also claim to be "Evangelical" but only focus on two figures from nineteenth-century Evangelicalism. Lipscomb and Roberts probably do not truly represent the Evangelicalism of their day, yet alone modern Evangelicalism which continues to be criticized for its lack of social action among the poor. Even Ron Sider, one of the modern forefathers of a theology of poverty purports a kind of Evangelical theology of liberation. Still, he is appreciative yet equally critical of LALT.[75] In his *Rich Christians in the Age of Hunger*, Sider sees God as on the side of the oppressed and opposing the rich and powerful as a fundamental expression of God's compassion and justice. He also tries to get away from personal choice and blames poverty on unjust economic systems that enable the oppressive actions of rich individuals and exacerbates inequality.

These examples demonstrate two important ideas. First, no matter what period or movement, even with Evangelicalism, there can always be found those talking about and acting toward of the poor. Gasaway echoes this reality that modern progressive Evangelicals are not an historical anomaly. Gasaway reports that Evangelicals across denominational lines, particularly those in the North, participated in progressive and sometimes radical campaigns to combat social problems such as "expanding literacy, enhancing education, championing temperance, advocating prison reforms,

---

72. Dunnavant, "David Lipscomb," 42–45.
73. Kostlevy, "Benjamin Titus Roberts," 60.
74. Kostlevy, "Benjamin Titus Roberts," 62.
75. Gasaway, *Progressive Evangelicals*, 203–4.

promoting peace, alleviating poverty, and opposing slavery."[76] There was especially an increase in social activism with the growth of the doctrine of entire sanctification. Popularized by Charles Finney, this doctrine urged Christians to pursue a perfect personal life, but also a perfected society. Other holiness movements and leaders such as Phoebe Palmer urged hundreds of churches to develop urban ministries offering food, clothing, housing, employment assistance and medical aid.[77] That there are always some segments of movements who seek justice for the poor is to be expected as there are clear biblical themes concerning the poor that some movements are bound to find, reflect upon and act on. There will also be similarities among these various groups, particularly with a movement like LALT who has theologized so comprehensively on the topic. Second, these two specific examples demonstrate that the incarnational theme, while used less than the creation-fall motif, has been a consistent theme within various sectors and periods of Evangelicalism including some of the earliest movements.

Having considered some of the historical Evangelical uses of the incarnational theme, perhaps the modern Evangelical who takes up this theme the most is William Pinson in his book *Applying the Gospel: Suggestions for Christian Social Action in a Local Church*. In his opening chapter on the biblical mandate for social action, Pinson mentions human nature and the created order as realities which God creates and sustains and we should do likewise.[78] Pinson spends the most time on the life and teachings of Jesus, however. He begins with the idea of the incarnation through which we see God's concern for the totality of life, both the physical and the spiritual. It is in the incarnation we most fully see the merging of spiritual and physical in the God-man. Jesus's willingness to take on flesh shows that God does not disdain the physical but embraces it. During his life, Jesus's mission and his role as Messiah included physical and spiritual needs as seen in his own messianic proclamation in Luke 4. Rarely do you see Jesus giving handouts to people, rather Jesus helped them to help themselves through empowerment.[79] Pinson also mentions love being central to Jesus's teachings and the love-based theme of servanthood showing us that we should help care for the total needs of a person. Finally, Jesus's view of judgment is also intricately connected to social concern and the idea of the kingdom of God in Jesus's teachings encompasses both the social and the personal. This means that our social action should do the same, not just focus on the personal.

76. Gasaway, *Progressive Evangelicals*, 5.
77. Gasaway, *Progressive Evangelicals*, 6.
78. Pinson, *Applying the Gospel*, 15.
79. Pinson, *Applying the Gospel*, 17–18.

Interestingly, Pinson is one of the only Evangelicals to mention the role of the Holy Spirit in social action. Per Pinson,

> In the early church the Holy Spirit helped break down the barriers of prejudice which separated Christians from one another. The book of Acts, which is a record of the acts of the Spirit, shows God's care for all persons without respect of race or nationality or class. Jesus promised the power of the Spirit would enable the disciples to be witnesses unto him in all parts of the earth (Acts 1:8). At Pentecost, the Spirit came upon persons without distinction as to race or nationality (Acts 2:1–11). The Holy Spirit showed his concern for Samaritans, Black persons, Roman soldiers and other Gentiles. . . . Jesus indicated that the Holy Spirit would reveal truth to Christians (John 16:13–15, 25–26). That is a comforting promise for those grappling with the complexities of modern social problems.[80]

It is not as thorough an analysis of the role of the Holy Spirit in social action as I hope to provide later in this thesis. It does, however show how the Holy Spirit creates a community void of various social discriminators such as race, gender, and class all of which are indicators of urban poverty. If the Holy Spirit empowers the believer to break down these barriers and to know the truth concerning God's heart of reconciliation and community, then one would think many more spirit-empowered believers would be taking up the cause of the poor. This part of Pinson's work does not fit cleanly into the incarnation paradigm. In fact, it somewhat transcends all three categories to include the creation motif, the incarnational motif and the eschatological motif. This will be a major part of our contention in our final chapters which will outline a holistic pneumatological theology of urban poverty; the contention that a pneumatological approach both ties together the previous motifs and transcends them, adding to each in a manner that has not been done before.

Interestingly, William Pinson is also one of the only Evangelical scholars who even comes close to developing an eschatological motif, the third motif Mouw believes makes up Evangelical approaches to poverty in the United States. Mouw holds that this motif argues that, in the present age, God is at work preparing the world for a new and exciting future in which a very different economic order will be obtained.[81] While this new economic order is an eschatological hope, God is at work preparing this reality. While Evangelicals often think eschatologically, Hal Lindsay and the Left Behind

80. Pinson, *Applying the Gospel*, 22.
81. Mouw, "Thinking About the Poor," 25.

phenomena being obvious examples, they are reticent to apply this motif to the poor because it has the possibility of romanticizing the poor as a generic class that would receive special treatment now and in the eschaton.[82] For Evangelicals, this cancels out their emphasis on personal salvation. They would rather envision those who, in their experience of poverty, consciously yearn for the coming of a divine savior experiencing such an eschatological hope, not just the poor in general. Pinson is one Evangelical who does pick up this eschatological theme, however, particularly as it relates to judgment. For Pinson, the second coming of Jesus is one in which the Son of man comes as King and will judge the world based on how people deal with social needs according to Matthew 25. Pinson also draws from other New Testament eschatologies including Paul, Peter, and James who all in some way connect Christ's second coming with the idea that Christians should continuously engage in doing good works including helping the poor.[83]

One other Evangelical scholar who works from an eschatological motif is John Mason in his article "The Good City." Mason sees the city in the Bible as occupying a central part of the biblical narrative. He holds that in the biblical tradition the city promised greater security, but that "the exact reverse too often exists today, when the central city represents harm and movement to the surrounding region offers greater hope for safety and opportunity."[84] Like many Evangelicals, he focuses primarily on civil organizations such as the family and churches as the best avenues through which we can help lead society into acting upon legitimate forms of metropolitan responsibility. He sees four categories of possible improvement: place-based initiatives designed to bring economic revival to the inner city, mobility strategies assisting those who live within the inner city to find jobs and/or housing, income redistribution measures, and restructured government.[85]

In each of these categories, Mason believes that the model we see in biblical Israel puts the onus primarily at the local level, particularly the family. He sees the principle of voluntarism as central, but this does not negate the possible strategic nature of the government standing ready to assure an adequate level and appropriate forms of assistance.[86] While Mason's methods and solutions remain thoroughly Evangelical, being focused on

---

82. The influence of such dispensationalist thinking many in fact be another reason why Evangelicals have not fully engaged in caring for the poor. This word will end soon anyway, so there is little reason to worry about the poor now, we should rather care about souls.

83. Pinson, *Applying the Gospel*, 17.

84. Mason, "Good City," 344.

85. Mason, "Good City," 363.

86. Mason, "Good City," 379.

individual responsibility and voluntarism, it is his unique concern for the city, especially as seen in the biblical authors' eschatological vision that resounds as a rallying cry for those wishing to address urban poverty. Mason is correct that if the city is the center of the eschatological vision seen in Revelation 21 for instance, we should be more concerned for the proper structures and moral meaning of city and metropolitan life in our current day.

While the eschatological theme as applied to poverty is not a strong one in Evangelicalism beyond Pinson and Mason, it is among some of the more prominent theologies on poverty, particularly Latin American Liberation Theology. This is a surprising gap for Evangelicals as there are some rich resources within eschatology to give hope to the poor, inspire the church to take care of the poor, and even for how to engage in such social action in an urban setting, all of which we shall take up in our own analysis in later chapters from a pneumatological perspective. These three motifs, as developed in Evangelical theology, are void of Pneumatology. The creation-fall is most connected with a deistic approach in which God is generally seen as creator and sustainer of creation. The incarnational and eschatological motifs are most commonly connected with the Son, who came in flesh and will also come again in the eschaton. What is missing is the Holy Spirit who was ever-present in each of these motifs, but rarely if ever mentioned. This point ties all three motifs together while also adding other themes that are often overlooked.

Practical Responses to Urban Poverty

These theological motifs and theses by various Evangelical scholars beg the question, what do Evangelicals believe should be done about poverty in our world. A number of scholars have chronicled what Evangelicals have already done and others give proposals about what should be done, both will be examined briefly here to conclude our examination of Evangelical theologies of the poor.

Lydia Bean echoes the negative perspective we have already seen that many Evangelical churches give to charity but do not do much affecting the structures of poverty.[87] Kurt Hendel gives a prime example of such charity in his article, "The Care of the Poor: An Evangelical Perspective." Hendel holds that Evangelical Christians who are empowered by the gospel will naturally respond to those in need, they should begin at home with those they know

---

87. Bean, "Compassionate Conservatives?," 164.

and with whom they have relationship.[88] He also proposes, however, a communal poor relief system such as the poor chest mentioned earlier. Regular offerings would be taken up specifically for the poor, and money would be solicited from local governments and organizations for the poor chest. Hendel's proposal amounts to a church ran and locally controlled welfare system. For Hendel, there should be a distinction between the worthy poor and other poor to discern who should benefit from such a system.

William Kostlevy gives another account of what Evangelicals have done that amounts to charity rather than structural response. Kostlevy's study of the early Free Methodists reveals that they have consistently been involved in the lives of economically dispossessed seeing their forefather Wesley's ministry among the poor as defining their own ministry and providing a relevant paradigm for the reconstruction of society. From its inception, the Free Methodist church understood its mission as two-fold, "to maintain the Bible standard of Christianity and to preach the gospel to the poor."[89] They did this largely through preaching to the poor and empowering the poor to change their own lives and to help change the lives of other poor in their midst. This change occurs through spiritual reformation with financial assistance to keep people solvent when needed.

Many modern proposals go beyond just simple charity to include more structural solutions, but they are not cohesive from author to author depending on their emphasis and the context. Because of this diversity, there is no particularly logical way to order them. Most seem to agree, however that partnership between the government, churches and non-profits is always necessary.[90] Sider takes this idea furthest saying that there is danger if people conclude the government can or should slash social programs because religious institutions will take care of the problem. He sees an absolute need to work together because even though the relationship of these three spheres are complex, people are equally complex. People are both spiritual and material beings. Both unjust social structures and bad moral choices create social problems. Solutions therefore require inner, moral, spiritual change and outward, socioeconomic and structural change.[91] For Sider, this can include government reforms such as an increase of the child tax credit which has benefited many families or providing universal healthcare so that a lack of adequate healthcare does not cripple one's access to opportunity.

88. Hendel, "Care of the Poor," 547.

89. Kostlevy, "Benjamin Titus Roberts," 44–46.

90. A number of progressive Evangelicals make statements similar to this, including Gushee, *Toward a Just and Caring Society*, 46; Sider, *Just Generosity*, 25; Monsma, "Evangelicals and Poverty," 53.

91. Sider, *Just Generosity*, 25–26.

He also proposes a job for everyone who can work because opportunity is the best solution for poverty and the right of every person.[92] Both involve policy changes at the governmental level, but Sider also envisions spiritual reform that can be provided by civil institutions, like the church, who focus on empowering individuals and families to make better choices and become more productive in life. Other non-profits besides churches can help in empowerment also. Beyond organizations, families are an important part of the civil solution proposed by Evangelicals. These smaller units work together with organizations to create norms for society. Stephen Monsma similarly calls for a strengthening of civic society because it is these institutions that deal with and strengthen both social structures and personal responsibility to help overcome poverty through offering emotional support, mentoring and training to those in poverty.

Timothy Slaper adds a similar vision but from a different perspective. He begins by denying relative measures of poverty since the poor will always be with us and someone will always be poorer than another.[93] At first this begins to sound like the either-now-or-never paradigm Mouw mentions, but Slaper is one of the few Evangelicals who even talks about measurements of poverty to begin with. Slaper's proposal does not end up in an "either-now-or-never" frame of mind. It is because he wants to begin with the end in mind, God's justice and shalom in the world, that he does not want to resign to a relative form of measurement in which someone will always be poor. Shalom, for Slaper, is a peace that speaks to the presence of justice, it means wholeness, health and harmony of community.[94] Such a vision elicits the importance of communal and interpersonal relationships and the role of institutions and social structures in fostering fruitfulness, harmony and justice. Slaper uses health as an example on which to build his case for shalom. Health is the proper functioning of mind, body, spirit and emotion.[95] Such wholeness enables fully human social relationships contributing to the human flourishing that God intended. So, a particular congregation should (1) care for health impaired members within their own congregation (2) preach a holistic concept of health, and (3) have outreach and advocacy for the uninsured in their communities. Slaper's proposal of the shalom and flourishing is helpful for getting to the core of the problem and solution of urban poverty in the United states and will be a theme we will rely heavily upon in our own construction.

92. Sider, *Just Generosity*, 135.
93. Slaper, "Redefining Progress," 210.
94. Slaper, "Redefining Progress," 218.
95. Slaper, "Redefining Progress," 234.

Nicholas Wolterstorff presents the idea of agapic love that provides another layer to Slaper's idea of shalom. Agapic love seeks to secure for someone the good of being treated as befits her worth.[96] Self-love is the model for this in the biblical paradigm, it gives us the parameters of what good means. We want for others the same good we want for ourselves. To seek good for someone involves enhancing their wellbeing or flourishing, a love in which that person's rights are honored. How does one do this? Wolterstorff proposes the term care, not for someone who needs aid or assistance, but literally to care about someone.[97] Such a care does not just desire well-being but actively seeks to promote it. How does one promote it? For Wolterstorff it involves (1) intending success for someone, what he calls benefactions, (2) acknowledging that the good is already there for someone, (3) and investment—invested in the good of their endurance, in the good of their flourishing.[98]

Andi Thomas Sullivan in his article on "Those Suffering From Preventable Diseases" helps provide some of further theological grounding for Slaper's idea of shalom through health and Wolterstorff's idea of agapic love as care and benefaction focused on flourishing. Sullivan proposes healthcare, particularly preventative healthcare, as a central part of the gospel and what it means to be an Evangelical. For Sullivan, loving my neighbor means living out Jesus's words: "I was sick and you took care of me." Jesus did not just preach this but he lived it out spending most of his time teaching, feeding and healing. Sullivan himself has taken part in trying to raise money to provide bed nets to help fight malaria.[99]

These proposals have numerous strengths, particularly their holistic and biblical centered approach. One can see the potential for developing helpful solutions even as Slaper applies it to health, a continual issue for the urban poor. Slaper's own proposal focuses on the civil structure of the church as the primary initiator. If coupled with some of the other proposals that emphasize a three-pronged approach including government, it may be even stronger. While Slaper and Sullivan's proposals only focus on health addressed through civil structures, their work helps demonstrate that, because poverty is complex, there are numerous avenues through which any one organization can approach the problem and still make a huge difference while not focusing specifically on poverty or public policy. Still, there must be some approach that focuses more specifically

---

96. Wolterstorff, *Justice in Love*, 93.
97. Wolterstorff, *Justice in Love*, 101.
98. Wolterstorff, *Justice in Love*, 142–43.
99. Sullivan, "Those Suffering From Preventable Diseases," 85.

on poverty while utilizing methods like these that also deal with repercussions of poverty such as health.

Having seen multiple proposals of how Evangelicals can begin to address the complex problem of urban poverty in the United States, we will end with the proposal of William Pinson as a possible method for Evangelicals to put into practice a theology of poverty. First, according to Pinson, a community must stimulate concern through education about a particular issue, overcoming possible resistances by answering questions and likely disagreements. After this period of developing proper concern, a community should establish guidelines for how they will address the issue. For any Evangelical church, Pinson proposes eleven guidelines that include the project being distinctly Christian, biblically based, balanced, flexible, comprehensive, realistic, preventive as well as corrective, unselfish, humble, compassionate, and cooperative.[100] These are a helpful guide to any organization wishing to engage in a project seeking to help the poor in their own urban setting. Finally, Pinson recommends developing a specific sub-organization within the church, such as a Christian life committee, to focus on the project and ensure the workforce necessary to get the work done. Once the problem is identified and an organization is developed, they will want to locate specific resources, evaluate possible methods of bringing social change while also determining their own priorities, plan for specific action using the above guidelines, let the program run its course and then make sure that it always reviews and revises everything that is happening on the ground.[101]

Such guidelines as proposed by Pinson may seem rather elementary and pastoral. Having been in pastoral work myself, I know that one of the biggest hurdles is developing a feasible plan to execute the passions a person or congregation may have. It is helpful to see that while Evangelicals have often been accused of quietism, that an Evangelical has made such a practical proposal to help organize and administrate proposals that often remain on the theological level. Most of Pinson's ideas here are not specifically Evangelical but apply to any organization and would be helpful for anyone if the first two guidelines of being distinctly Christian and biblically based are removed. Still, these two are what makes Pinson's proposal specifically Evangelical. My hope is that in thinking of the Holy Spirit we will think well theologically and even more robustly than many Evangelicals have done, while also attempting to remain wholly practical as Pinson has here.

---

100. Pinson flushes out each of these more fully in his book, Pinson, *Applying the Gospel*, 43–45.

101. Pinson, *Applying the Gospel*, 72–74.

CONCLUSION

Having reviewed Evangelical perspectives on poverty, we have seen some of the shortcomings but also some of the possibilities for a more robust theology of poverty. In particular, our overview of Evangelical theologies of poverty has shown the challenges and promise of a movement often accused of quietism even if it is within the more progressive realms of Evangelicalism. This gives us hope, Renewal can also be redeemed from quietistic charges. Some of the challenges have included the fact that most Evangelicals focus too much on the spiritual and the moral and not on the whole person. Evangelicalism also focuses on a christological salvation of the poor and there is a clear pneumatological gap present that we will seek to address in chapters six and seven. Evangelicalism also focuses too much on the individual without recognizing the societal causes and implications of poverty. They focus too much on the spiritual and do not develop a holistic response to poverty to match the complexity we saw in chapter 2. Still, there is promise, because some of these weaknesses also become Evangelicalism's strengths. Evangelicalism provides a corrective of ecumenical theologies of poverty in that they recognize the moral, spiritual and individual elements of poverty that ecumenical theologies sometimes neglect. We will try to hold these poles we see in chapters 3 and 4 together in our final constructive chapter that seeks a holistic response. In the next chapter, we will perform a similar task of surveying the theological literature on poverty, but as it applies to ecumenical theologies in North America.

3

Urban Poverty in Ecumenical Theology

INTRODUCTION

Back in 2014, I volunteered at the Project Homeless Connect in downtown San Diego. It is a one-day resource fair that helps connect the homeless in San Diego to a vast array of services available to the homeless. It was one of the first times I personally saw the various sectors of our city come together to address urban poverty. The government was represented through the San Diego Housing Commission and the San Diego Police Department Homeless Outreach Team. Local business was represented by non-religious non-profits including the YMCA, YWCA, and Family Health Centers of San Diego. Religious organizations were represented through Father Joe's Village, a Roman Catholic ministry, the San Diego Rescue Mission and the Interfaith Shelter Network. These were just a few of the many involved from these three sectors. I helped check in over twelve hundred homeless people that came to the event for resources. As I asked each person what they were looking for that day they each had different needs and different organizations that could help meet those needs. Jim needed a job and wanted to connect with local employment agencies. Mary had a job but could not get housing with her bad credit and so needed immediate help through the Interfaith Shelter Network and long-term help from the San Diego Housing Commission to secure low-income housing. Carlos felt anxious and alone and needed spiritual and psychological help. Each person had different needs and one organization, one church, one government agency could not provide all of these needs. It took all these groups working together. It took each voice asking what we could do to address poverty. It also took an individualized approach of asking what each person needed.

No one movement, school, or perspective—sociological, theological or otherwise—has the final word on poverty. It is for this reason we have proposed exploring a variety of voices concerning urban poverty, particularly from a theological perspective. In the last chapter, we looked at one of the central religious movements in the United States, Evangelicalism, we saw it is not a cohesive movement, but a cacophony of voices. Some have been more quietistic concerning poverty and some, like progressive Evangelicals, have addressed poverty head on. In this chapter, we will turn our attention to several ecumenical voices from the United States and the Americas to gain a broader perspective of the resources available through which we can develop our own theology of poverty.

In many ways, "ecumenical" in this chapter functions as a catch-all word for everything that is not Evangelical or Renewal and therefore analyzed in chapters 3 and 5 of this work. However, as with any body of work so large, we must identify some criteria dictating what we will engage and not engage. First, we are obviously looking for sources that deal with poverty in an important and constructive way. This is necessary since, as we have discussed, Evangelicalism and Renewal are quieter about poverty. Whenever a movement like Renewal Theology attempts to venture into a new area like a theology of poverty, it is necessary to begin with already present voices to provide it with the required language and starting ideas to begin the conversation as it develops its own resources. These exterior voices provide a kind of sounding board. Second, to be ecumenical, these movements must be engaged in the larger discussion on poverty in two ways. They must be engaged with the larger theological literature, but they should also be heavily engaged and respected by others working on the issue of poverty. Their centrality to the discussion in this way will mean they have worthy resources to offer. We will analyze the Social Gospel movement, Liberation Theology, and a small sampling of other voices including prophetic activism, Roman Catholicism, and an example of mainline Protestantism. We will demonstrate that each has an important contribution to a theology of poverty while also lacking something we hope a holistic pneumatological perspective will address. We will engage these three movements in a chronological order as they provide context for those movements that follow.

THE SOCIAL GOSPEL AND URBAN POVERTY

In 1940, Charles Howard Hopkins saw the Social Gospel Movement as "America's most unique contribution to the great ongoing stream of

Christianity."[1] It arose in the Gilded Age of 1877–1920 during which there was a rapid of industrialization and economic growth. As the name "Gilded Age" insinuates, however, this growth largely fed the pockets of the top 1 percent. Poverty also grew, particularly among the millions of immigrants flooding into the country.[2] This great disparity amid seeming progress caused many to call into question society and its structures. In particular, a group of Protestant pastors and scholars began to address American society and its ills from a theological perspective, a perspective they termed "the Social Gospel."

The Social Gospel was primarily an urban, northeastern, White, male endeavor.[3] Most of its early iterations were pastoral, based on need and responding through programs to help parishioners and sermons to inspire vision that would support to these programs. Later, these figures would theologize in more systematic ways. Often seen as the father of the Social Gospel, Walter Rauschenbusch embodies this paradigm.

Rauschenbusch was born in Rochester, New York to a German family. He went to Rochester Seminary but also studied economics at the University of Berlin. The theology and higher criticism he learned in these environments, while they never left him, underwent a drastic transformation during his time pastoring the poorest of the poor. In particular, he worked with German immigrants at the Second German Baptist Church in Hell's Kitchen, New York between 1885–1897.[4] It was in these fires that Rauschenbusch developed his Social Gospel, but he would not write about it systematically until his *Theology for the Social Gospel* came out some twenty years later in 1917.

Others like Washington Gladden in Columbus, Ohio followed similar trajectories but in their own urban contexts. Others like Josiah Strong and Richard Ely, both of whom Rauschenbusch saw as model pioneers of Christian social thought in America, never pastored.[5] Strong and Ely wrote solely from more academic perspectives while still championing the cause of the poor worker and calling for economic justice and social solidarity.[6]

The Social Gospel was one of the first American movements to specifically address poverty from a theological perspective. It was also the most

---

1. Hopkins, *Rise of the Social Gospel*, 3.
2. Nichols and Unger, *Companion to the Gilded Age*, 7.
3. Luker, "Interpreting the Social Gospel," 1.
4. Shriver Jr., "Introduction," xiii.
5. We will primarily utilize Walter Rauschenbusch, the father of the Social Gospel, because of our limited space but bring in these other voices where applicable.
6. Edwards, "Manifest Destiny," 81.

comprehensive treatment and has had a lasting impact on numerous American theological movements. While few since World War II see themselves as "Social Gospelers" in the same sense as the figures we will explore, their theology has many of the same underpinnings and themes. Anyone dealing with poverty and social issues in America will in some way, whether directly or indirectly, dialogue with the themes brought up by the Social Gospel movement. Like our previous chapter on Evangelicalism, we will proceed in three areas, the causes of poverty, theological responses to poverty and practical responses to poverty within the Social Gospel movement.

Causes of Urban Poverty

First, we will explore what the Social Gospel movement sees as the causes of urban poverty in the United States. Many of these writers theologized nearly one hundred years ago, so the question must be asked whether the causes of urban poverty would be the same today as they were then? While poverty will not look the same, the topic is still worth exploring for two reasons. First, exploring what the Social Gospel movement believed the causes of poverty to be sheds light on how they formulated their theological responses and how the movement views the nature of poverty. Second, we will find that many of the proposed causes of poverty are similar to today. While the numbers have changed, some of the names and players have changed, the structures, systems, and issues that were central are still very much relevant.

The Social Gospelers identify three primary areas that caused poverty in their urban settings. These three areas overlap with one another, but still do not cover the entirety of the issue. Rauschenbusch, in his *The Social Principles of Jesus*, calls these three areas "recalcitrant forces (which) have to be brought into obedience to God's law: the desire for power, the love of property, and unsocial religion."[7] For Rauschenbusch, these forces cannot be solved only by education, but must be overcome by the reign of God as they actively seek to resist and work toward the "true social order."[8] In his *Theology of the Social Gospel*, he identifies three different forms of sin, which I see as parallel to these three forces: sensuousness, selfishness and godlessness.[9] While Rauschenbusch does not pair his three societal "recalcitrant forces" with the three sins himself, it is evident as one explores them

---

7. Rauschenbusch, *Social Principles of Jesus*, 151.

8. While Rauschenbusch says it is not just a matter of education, it should be noted, education and writing was his primary way of combatting these injustices.

9. Rauschenbusch, *Theology for the Social Gospel*, 47. It is I who make this connection between two different schema Rauschenbusch uses.

that there is a close connection between each respective category. Below, we will treat each set—desire for power/sensuousness, love of property/selfishness, unsocial religion/godlessness—as a unit which speaks to the same issue from a different perspective, the first an external societal force and the second an interior personal force.

Sensuousness, according to Rauschenbusch, is a sin against one's "higher self."[10] While he does not connect sensuousness and the desire for power, one can see how they parallel each other as sensuousness feeds off the feeling of power and draws one down morally, even while one feels they are climbing the power ladder. While power affects individuals and their desire for power is an affront against one's own "higher self," it is not just an individual problem, but something built within the very fabric of our world through the fall. Sometimes it can be such a strong force that one does not even mean to hurt others by their power, but it is a natural byproduct. This is due to the nature of the fall which is "active in every new life" as a variable which it is our duty to diminish in "each young life and for every new generation."[11] The power of the fall is social. It runs through generations not just biologically, but through social assimilation.[12] While this double view of the transmission of sin, through both the biological and the social, may seem grim, it also gives hope because if it is not just biological but social, we can stop sin socially. Through a more social gospel, people's hearts can be changed, and they can find solidarity with one another that would trump this desire for power. This is necessary because the nature of power is that when "one man sins, others suffer, and when one social class sins, other classes are involved in the suffering which follows on that sin. The more powerful an individual or class is, the more they can unload unjust suffering on the weaker class."[13] The problem with power is that it comes at the expense of others and we often cannot control except for the power of the gospel.

The second major cause of urban poverty, according to Rauschenbusch, is the love of property. I connect this with the idea of selfishness

---

10. Rauschenbusch's view of the "higher self" is in line with common liberal theology. For Rauschenbusch, this higher self is an idyllic self not currently being lived because of these sinful forces. The higher self is the pre-fall self. It is the self one was created to be by God in which a person is able to experience the true "goodness" God created him to experience. See Rauschenbusch, *Theology for the Social Gospel*, 45–47.

11. Rauschenbusch, *Theology for the Social Gospel*, 5, 43.

12. Rauschenbusch, *Theology for the Social Gospel*, 61.

13. Rauschenbusch, *Theology for the Social Gospel*, 182. The Social Gospel writers did not live in an era of gender inclusiveness. I have left their patriarchal language intact when quoted directly from the text.

because the idea of this love of property incorporates the accumulation of wealth and possession in a way that leaves out the poor. This is selfishness. One can see how there is a natural overlap between the love of poverty and the desire for power. Power is often associated with the accumulation of possessions and property. According to Trawick in his article "Called to a New Ethic," he says that "the problem of sin takes up much of Rauschenbusch's attention in the book (*A Theology for the Social Gospel*). For Rauschenbusch, the essential nature of sin is selfishness."[14] While sensuousness and the desire for power is a betrayal against one's own self, selfishness and the love of property and possessions is a sin against other human beings. Richard Ely in his book *Social Aspects of Christianity and Other Essays* writes a good deal about the problem of selfishness and its perpetuation of poverty. In regard to property, loans and finances, Ely holds that the American church should recover the Mosaic economic legislation of charging no interest to the poor, but because of greed, the church has often passed over this teaching.[15] He also holds that a major perpetuation of the problem of poverty is people spending extravagantly on elevating themselves, but not using their wealth to elevate others.[16] Even the common problem of gambling is an example of selfishness and people putting their own economic gain ahead of the welfare of others. For Ely, the proper theological response to this selfishness is to recover the centrality of the cross which teaches us a life of renunciation and sacrifice.[17]

Finally, the third cause of poverty most talked about by Social Gospel proponents was the problem of unsocial religion or godlessness. While not equating the two, again we can see an easy connection as unsocial religiousness, while still religion, would have been ultimately godlessness because it fails to live out the kingdom of God in the world. Rauschenbusch says it this way in *The Social Principles of Jesus*, "Christian morality finds its highest dignity and its constant corrective in making the kingdom of God the supreme aim to which all minor aims must contribute and from which they gain their moral quality. The church substituted itself for the kingdom of God, and thereby put the advancement of a tangible and very human organization in the place of the moral uplifting of humanity." For Rauschenbusch, the church put itself and its own gains, selfishness and power, ahead of the good of humanity. The church has been "unsocial" and focused on organization rather than people. In this way, it is missing out on its God-given

---

14. Trawick, "Called to a New Ethic," 149.
15. Ely, *Social Aspects of Christianity*, 14.
16. Ely, *Social Aspects of Christianity*, 31.
17. Ely, *Social Aspects of Christianity*, 37.

purpose and has become godless. Josiah Strong, in his book *Our Country*, sees this as particularly apparent in the Roman Catholic Church or what he calls "Romanism," which was rapidly growing in the United States.[18] For Strong, the Roman Catholic Church stood against much of what he saw as American religion such as sovereignty, liberty of conscience and freedom of the press. These freedoms are controlled by the Pope in Roman Catholicism, according to Strong. In particular, he mentions Roman Catholicism's attitudes toward free institutions, especially schools, as having a harmful effect on the poor by removing access to free education. He also sees the type of education they provide as not fostering an environment of free thinking and enterprise which has helped to make the United States so successful.[19]

A final argument, and perhaps the strongest, concerning a lack of social religion in the United States, is Rauschenbusch's assertion that Jesus, in his God consciousness, rose above three temptations often besetting other religious spirits.[20] The first temptation was mysticism which Rauschenbusch associated with a desire to escape from the world. Such an escape would not care about the poor or their social problems but only more spiritual things. This is like Rauschenbusch's third temptation Jesus overcame which was asceticism and other worldliness. In this he sees the church going away from society which would contradict one of Rauschenbusch's primary responses to poverty, solidarity. It is this temptation toward other-worldliness that has created the social situation of poverty in the first place. The second temptation Jesus overcame was pessimism, one that said the social problems of the world cannot be solved. Instead Jesus approached these problems head on by preaching the gospel to the poor and living in solidarity with the poor.[21] This cause of poverty, a lack of social religion, is especially interesting because it was not mentioned at all within Evangelical theology, at least not explicitly. But it makes sense that if the gospel and Christianity are believed to be an answer to poverty that a lack of socially engaged religion may also be part of the cause. It might be easy to see this cause as a lack of religiosity by those who are not Christian, but the Social Gospelers place the blame equally on the church for not living out the social nature of the gospel and buying into the world's desire for power, possessions and individuality.

18. Strong, *Our Country*, 59–60.

19. Strong, *Our Country*, 74.

20. Rauschenbusch's Christology is a classical liberal approach in which he sees he focuses on the Jesus of history as fully-human but not necessarily fully-divine. Rather he sees Jesus having a kind of God consciousness through a close connection with God that we are able to obtain and live out. See Rauschenbusch, *Theology for the Social Gospel*, 125.

21. Rauschenbusch, *Theology for the Social Gospel*, 155–57.

Many of the Social Gospel theologians cite other more "practical" causes of poverty such as the industrial revolution, lack of good wages, deterioration of the family through alcohol and gambling, and a lack of affordable housing or jobs.[22] These can all fall under one of the three more theologically driven attitudes which underlie the causes of poverty. These three allude to the Social Gospel's definition of poverty as well. For them, poverty is a lack of possessions and spending power as seen in their concern about property and selfishness. It is not just a lack of resources, but what that privation signifies. It is the powerlessness that comes with this lack of resources, particularly when it occurs at the hands of those greedy enough for power that they exploit others and perpetuate cycles of lack and powerlessness. Finally, poverty is also the phenomenon of being outcast, on the outskirts of society, and lacking solidarity with the rest of the human community. Poverty is a composite of all three of these factors that rob the poor of dignity and humanity.

Ultimately, the Social Gospel blames poverty on the systems of society and those in power over them, whether it be large corporations, the government, or religious institutions. It is problematic, however that while they speak repeatedly of social class, they seem to leave the conversation at critiquing the upper classes, rather than critiquing the entire class system itself as something fallacious. Also, compared to what we saw with Evangelicals, Social Gospelers have very little mention of personal responsibility as a cause of poverty. Perhaps it was because the systems causing poverty were so much more overt during their time than they are today? Or perhaps they had a greater understanding and emphasis on the social nature of humanity? These authors are probably missing out on a part of the equation by not emphasizing personal responsibility more, but it does open a different realm of theological solutions than we saw in our exploration of Evangelicals.

Theological Responses to Urban Poverty

We have already hinted at some of the theological responses that the Social Gospel's perspective implies in its causes of poverty and injustice. These responses include solidarity, self-sacrifice and a reinterpretation of religion. These three responses correlate almost directly with the three causes mentioned above. We will get to these more practical responses in the next section, but there are greater theological themes that underpin these causes and responses that are necessary to explore to understand how and why the

---

22. See, for instance, Rauschenbusch, *Christianity and the Social*, 177–234; Hopkins, *Rise of the Social Gospel*, 24.

Social Gospel and its advocates would respond to poverty in these ways. These three theological themes, which buttress their response to poverty, include the dignity and worth of humankind as beings created in the image of God, the moral example of Jesus in the strain of the prophetic vision, and the kingdom of God initiated by Jesus as a new social order.

While not talked about the most, the idea of the value of human life is a starting point for the Social Gospel because, without it, there would be no need for social concern in the first place. According to Rauschenbusch in his *Social Principles of Jesus*, "Man is a child of God and that dignity gives some calm and assurance amid the worries of life."[23] It gives calm because it means that God is actively at work through his kingdom, the true social order, to bring about the highest good for humanity.[24] This dignity does not start with some intrinsic worth within humanity, but the intrinsic worth of God because "God is the common basis of all our life. Our human personalities may seem distinct, but their roots run down into the eternal life of God. . . . The pervading life of God is the ground of the spiritual oneness of the race and of our hope for its closer fellowship in the future."[25] Our human individual and collective worth is based on God as being the source because all humanity has been created in the image of God. It is also a continual reason for God's care for humanity, his loving creation of each one of us. Finally, it is also the reason we should care for one another because each of us has worth, but we also have an inherent connection in our spiritual and created lineage. This theme is not just based on creation stories but reiterated by Jesus himself and his own regard for human life. According to Rauschenbusch, that regard was so strong that it "determined all his (Jesus') view points and activities. He affirmed the humane instinct consciously and intelligently and raised it to the dignity of a social principle."[26] Jesus affirmed the dignity of humanity through the way he lived, through the way he interacted with others, and through his institution of the kingdom as a new social order for the benefit of all humanity.

This example of Jesus upholding the dignity and worth of humanity is the second theological theme we will explore among the responses of the

23. Rauschenbusch, *Social Principles of Jesus*, 49.

24. The kingdom of God as the true social order is a kind of utopian society, a sphere in which humanity can live out its highest good without disruption. It stands in contrast to the social stratification and suffering humans are experiencing in this current kingdom. See Rauschenbusch, *Theology for the Social Gospel*, 133–37.

25. Rauschenbusch, *Theology for the Social Gospel*, 186. Rauschenbusch uses the term personality here as the exterior manifestations of our true selves that make us appear different, but for him our true persons are all the same and all rooted in the divine.

26. Rauschenbusch, *Social Principles of Jesus*, 8–9.

Social Gospel to poverty in their urban settings. From a modern Evangelical perspective, it would be easy to think of the incarnation as a strong statement for the dignity of humanity. Jesus's birth into relative poverty is seen as a statement of Jesus's and God's care for the poor. For Social Gospelers, however, they want to focus more on the character of Jesus rather than on his nature. Rauschenbusch says, "The Social Gospel is not primarily interested in the metaphysical question; its christological interest is all for a real personality who could set a great historical process in motion."[27] This becomes a major critique of the Social Gospel and a point of controversy for more conservative Christians because of the denial, or at least the downplaying, of Jesus's divinity in a metaphysical sense.[28] But despite the omission of divinity, Rauschenbusch sees Jesus as integral to the initiation of the new social order that is the kingdom of God. He says, "The fundamental first step in the salvation of mankind was the achievement of the *personality* of Jesus. Within him the kingdom of God got its first foothold in humanity. It was by virtue of his personality that he became the initiator of the kingdom of God. His personality was an achievement, not an effortless inheritance."[29] Extrapolated to our own responsibility, this personality, or what we might call personhood is something that we also can achieve in our character as we follow Jesus's moral example and participate in the kingdom of God that Jesus initiates.

The personhood of Jesus is particularly lived out in his mission to care for the poor following the Old Testament prophetic tradition. Rauschenbusch cites Jesus's turning to the passage in Isaiah (Luke 4) and his response to John in prison (Luke 7) that "the helpless were receiving help and the poor were listening to the glad news," as evidence that Jesus's "fundamental sympathies were with the poor and oppressed."[30] It was not just Rauschenbusch that emphasized Jesus's care for the poor as central to the gospel. Kostlevy in his attempt to situate the origins of the Free Methodist Movement firmly within the Social Gospel tradition holds that from its inception in 1860, it "maintained the Bible standard of Christianity to preach the gospel to the poor."[31] Kostlevy, in demonstrating that Free Methodism developed similar concerns as the Social Gospel tradition at the same time cited from the *Free Methodist Discipline* saying that, "this preaching of the

---

27. Rauschenbusch, *Theology for the Social Gospel*, 150.

28. See, for instance, Tony Campolo's response to Walter Rauschenbusch in the 2008 edition of *Christianity and the Social Crisis* in which he brings this up as a major concern. His other biggest concern is Rauschenbusch's failure to grasp the radical sinfulness of the human race (Campolo and Rauschenbusch, "Response," 77).

29. Rauschenbusch, *Theology for the Social Gospel*, 151.

30. Rauschenbusch, *Christianity and the Social Crisis*, 66.

31. Kostlevy, "Culture, Class, and Gender," 164–65.

gospel to the poor was the crown proof that Jesus was the one that should come. In this respect, the church must follow in the footsteps of Jesus. She must see to it that the gospel is preached to the poor."[32] Richard Ely holds that the primary message of Christ was the exaltation of humanity in which he specifically includes the poor being exalted out of their impoverished state.[33] Jesus's care of the poor was central to figures like Rauschenbusch and Ely and movements like the Free Methodist Church and the National Council of Congregational Churches. His actions were an example to follow that became the embodiment of a new Social Gospel standard for American politics and social action among the poor.

It is not just in the life of Jesus that Social Gospelers find a theological response to poverty, but also in his death. We already looked at how Richard Ely saw in the cross, an example of living a life of renunciation for others.[34] This is not just spiritual renunciation but giving up luxuries, selfishness and materialism for the betterment of the poor and humanity. Rauschenbusch similarly saw all of Jesus's life events as being able to be interpreted through his death which helped to finally establish the kingdom of God, establishing his work of solidarity and reconciliation between God and person and within humanity.[35] This death was the single most clear act of prophetic suffering for the sake of others by which every other act must be interpreted. Any acts performed today must follow this model of sacrifice for and solidarity with humanity.

One final area of theological response to urban poverty, and perhaps the most central is the idea of the kingdom of God. Indeed, it was this very kingdom which Jesus came to establish. According to Rauschenbusch,

> The kingdom of God is divine in its origin, progress and consummation. It was initiated by Jesus Christ in whom the prophetic spirit came to its consummation, it is sustained by the Holy Spirit and it will be brought to its fulfillment by the power of God in its own time. The kingdom of God, therefore is miraculous all the way, and is the continuous revelation of the power, the righteousness, and the love of God.[36]

The kingdom of God is Rauschenbusch's vision of the highest good, the perfect social order. He makes the concept so all-encompassing that it becomes a universal concept for anything he wants to see happen positively in the

32. Kostlevy, "Culture, Class, and Gender," 165.
33. Ely, *Social Aspects of Christianity*, 60.
34. Ely, *Social Aspects of Christianity*, 37.
35. Rauschenbusch, *Theology for the Social Gospel*, 150, 266.
36. Rauschenbusch, *Theology for the Social Gospel*, 139.

world. For instance, Rauschenbusch says that the kingdom of God cannot be connected with any singular social theory, but it means

> Justice, freedom, fraternity, labor, joy. Let each social system and movement show us what it can contribute, and we will weigh its claim. Mother who feeds, farmer who feeds the people, the teacher that trains them, etc. . . . they are all contributing to the kingdom, provided they view their work so, and are trying to put an evolutionary plus into it which will fit the total nearer to the divine will. The kingdom is the supreme task, and all small tasks are part of it.[37]

Any task, if it adds to the higher good of humanity, is part of the kingdom of God. One's work ethic is a big emphasis for the Social Gospel because it naturally builds toward a better society and the common good. This becomes a kind of sacramentalism in which, according to Ely, all things become sacred whether connected with a person's business or his religion.[38]

A final aspect of this kingdom is the this-worldly nature of the kingdom. Rauschenbusch rejects any kind of apocalyptic eschatology, instead putting forth a realized eschatology focused on building the kingdom of God in this world.[39] Ely echoes this sentiment saying that "Christianity is primarily concerned with this world and it is the mission of Christianity to bring to pass here a kingdom of righteousness and to rescue from the evil one and redeem all our social responsibilities.[40] This "worldliness" is in many ways, a conflation of the transcendent and the immanent as well as the future *Parousia* with the current kingdom. We will see that Renewal in the next chapter offers a critique of this view still seeing these realities as connected and interplaying with one another, yet separate.

Practical Responses to Urban Poverty

So how do these theological responses to the causes and problems of poverty already explored in the Social Gospel paradigm live themselves out in practical responses? What is to be done about poverty according to the Social Gospel? Three primary areas we have already mentioned—solidarity, self-sacrifice and a reformation of religion—are worth brief comment

---

37. Rauschenbusch, *Social Principles of Jesus*, 85.
38. Ely, *Social Aspects of Christianity*, 57.
39. Rauschenbusch, *Theology for the Social Gospel*, 208–239.
40. Ely, *Social Aspects of Christianity*, 53.

here. We will keep it brief because these ideas have already been explored, to some extent, above.

According to Rauschenbusch, the central Christian conviction is the "worth of manhood and the solidarity of mankind."[41] This conviction is rooted in the idea that humanity must overcome individualism, perpetuated by puritanism and modernity, and care about the social and the poor to lift society up toward the ideal of the kingdom. According to Robert Trawick, the way that one can live in solidarity with the other according to Social Gospel theologians, especially Rauschenbusch, is through reclaiming the notion of human work, but not just as an individual, rather as one whose work perpetuates the betterment of humanity and lifts up society as a whole.[42] This concept of solidarity through work is connected with the kingdom of God which Rauschenbusch describes as a commonwealth of labor. Love is the kingdom's guiding virtue because one cannot actively love another without serving their needs. Applied more specifically to poverty, work becomes a response in two ways. First, work helps in a natural social uplift though a trickle-down effect especially if one works a job that specifically helps the poor.[43] Second, empowering the poor to work helps both the poor and society to overcome their powerlessness and lack of resources.

A second practical response to poverty within the Social Gospel movement is the idea of self-sacrifice. According to *The Social Principles of Jesus*, social redemption is wrought by vicarious suffering. It was a principle lived out by the prophets, Jesus and the disciples.[44] This sacrifice was seen particularly in Jesus going to the cross through which the kingdom of God is established. It was a road of suffering and self-sacrifice for the betterment of humanity. It was also seen in the first Jesus community sharing everything in common and taking care of each other's needs. We already saw how Ely saw self-sacrifice as the only response to overcome the selfishness which helped lead to the poor being oppressed and many of the social ills facing America. This self-sacrifice is also an act of solidarity because it is choosing not to live for oneself but to live for the betterment of one's fellow person. This includes practices like donating to food kitchens, benevolence

---

41. Rauschenbusch, *Christianizing the Social Order*, ix.

42. Trawick, *Perspectives on the Social Gospel*, 140.

43. The "trickle-down effect" finds its roots in the Veblen-Jhering model of economics developed during this same period of the late nineteenth century, but in Germany, though it was not called the trickle-down effect and has been significantly developed since then into what one may recognize today. See McCracken, "Culture and Consumption," 71–84.

44. Rauschenbusch, *Social Principles of Jesus*, 167.

funds and the establishment of "poor houses" to help those fighting poverty.[45] Practically today, many see government run social programs, such as social security or unemployment, as a necessary sacrifice the rich can make to help the poor.[46]

A final practical response by the Social Gospel movement was religious reformation. This is an interesting phenomenon because religion was seen both as one of the causes of poverty, but also part of its solution. It can only be a solution when it is reformed religion that cares for the poor, the orphan and the widow. This reformation is necessary in two ways, first proper religion changes the individual person and lifts them out of poverty or transforms their heart to be a change agent socially. In *Christianity and the Social Crisis,* Rauschenbusch puts it this way,

> The greatest contribution which any man can make to the social movement is the contribution of a regenerated personality, of a will which sets justice above policy and profit, and of an intellect emancipated from falsehood. Such a man will, in some measure, incarnate the principles of a higher social order in his attitude to all questions and in all his relations to men, and will be a wellspring of regenerating influences.[47]

True religion also has the power to affect change in the entire human race. Again, Rauschenbusch says, "There are two great entities in human life—the human soul and humanity—and religion is to save both. The soul is to seek righteousness and eternal life; the race is to seek righteousness and the kingdom of God. The social preacher is apt to overlook the one. But the Evangelical preacher has long overlooked the other."[48] Overlooking the individual has been a common criticism of the Social gospel movement and Rauschenbusch here readily admits as much. He holds that there needs to be a balance of how salvation works and how religion brings about the kingdom of God in the world. One way the Social Gospel movement did this practically was the 'Men and Religion' Forward movement in 1922. According to Susan Curtis, "All the major denominations joined together to recruit men for the cause of Christian reform. Making the kingdom of God the focus of their message they challenged men and boys to devote their lives to its establishment on earth."[49] Even here, the primary response was

---

45. Wagner, *Poorhouse,* 1–18.

46. Many of these did not come into existence in their modern form until after WWI—such as Social Security, under Franklin D. Roosevelt, in 1935.

47. Rauschenbusch, *Christianity and the Social Crisis,* 287.

48. Rauschenbusch, *Christianity and the Social Crisis,* 298.

49. Curtis, *Consuming Faith,* 4.

education which was a major emphasis of the Social Gospel and often a common critique that it was more intellectual than practical.[50]

Evaluation

The Social Gospel's theological responses focus on three primary areas of the dignity of humankind, the person of Jesus and his moral example, and the kingdom of God, initiated by Jesus and focused on building an idyllic society on earth in which the good of humankind is achieved. In light of our thesis, it is worth mentioning there is very little about the Holy Spirit beyond the Spirit giving inspiration to humanity. The Holy Spirit also helps to fulfill the kingdom set out by Jesus and to help humanity bring solidarity as seen when the Spirit fell at Pentecost. Regarding this dearth of reference to the Holy Spirit, Rauschenbusch says that because the Spirit deals with intimate and mystic experiences of the soul, it does not seem to belong to the field of the Social Gospel.[51]

The problem is that this is exactly what the Social Gospel seems to be missing, an explanation of how people are empowered to change and overcome the sin that has filled the world. Jesus was a man of the Spirit. It was not just his humanity, but his Spirit-empowerment which enabled him to live out the kingdom on earth. This view of the Holy Spirit empowering Jesus would even fit into the Social Gospel's Christology of Jesus as a moral example and not necessarily the second person of the Trinity, though I would not make this move. If they are hesitant to confirm the deity of Jesus, however, then it makes sense that they would also downplay the Holy Spirit. Both become problematic for their this-world agenda and the dichotomy they have created. This also connects with the common criticism of the Social Gospel movement, that it does not seem to take seriously the sinfulness of humanity and so does not have much need for the Holy Spirit to bring redemption to the human heart. Another possible criticism of the Social gospel is its over emphasis on the social without recognizing it is made of individuals and smaller social units that also need reformation.

While these are worthwhile criticisms, there are a lot of strong points that the Social Gospel adds to a theology of poverty. I have sought to bring these out in the information that I have included and engaged with throughout this section. The idea of the social nature of the gospel is important because, as we saw in our second chapter, there are several social factors and not just individualistic causes that affect poverty. The establishment of

50. See, for instance, Luker's criticism in Luker, "Interpreting the Social Gospel," 1.
51. Rauschenbusch, *Theology for the Social Gospel*, 188.

the kingdom of God is also an important argument within the Social Gospel movement that should be paid attention to. While the Social Gospel vision of the kingdom of God is limited through its breadth and lack of definition, it is moving in the right direction but a Trinitarian vision of the kingdom that is also holistic would help to refine it.

LIBERATION THEOLOGY AND URBAN POVERTY

Another integral movement addressing urban poverty in the United States is Liberation Theology. Like all movements, Liberation Theology cannot be spoken of as a monochromatic endeavor. There are several clear-cut branches of Liberation Theology including Latin American Liberation Theology, Black Liberation Theology, Womanist Theology, Chicano/a Liberation Theology, Feminist Theology, etc.[52] Even among these, some groups, such as many within Feminist Theology, do not want to identify with "Liberation Theology" because of its male dominated origins and focus. Other movements like post-structuralism seem like they may fit into this category but want to move well beyond where Liberation Theology "proper" has gone.[53]

While recognizing these difficulties in talking about Liberation Theology, we will specifically be focusing on two movements that have traditionally fallen into the Liberation Theology category. We will look at Latin American Liberation Theology and Black Liberation Theology because they focus the most on poverty and often in an urban setting. We will explore their views on poverty and the marginalized as well as the resources they help provide to a theology of poverty. As with most of the other theologies of poverty we have explored, there is little talk of the Holy Spirit, but many of the themes considered can give us the foundation on which to launch our own thoughts from a more concretely holistic and pneumatological perspective.

Latin American Liberation Theology and Urban Poverty

Latin American Liberation Theology (LALT) had its peak in the middle of the twentieth century. It did not emerge as an intellectual exercise but as an attempt to give language to the irrupting voices of the poor and oppressed, their grievances, struggles, and fight for survival. One of the founding theologians of LALT, Gustavo Gutiérrez, describes the movement as a

---

52. See for instance, Cadorette, *Liberation Theology*; Floyd-Thomas and Pinn, *Liberation Theologies*.

53. Moore, *Poststructural-Ism and the New Testament*, 120–27.

theological reflection based on the gospel and on the experiences of men and women committed to the process of liberation. It asks, "How can we present the gospel to the poor, hungry and exploited?"[54]

Numerous international events helped provide the context of LALT's advent such as several political revolutions in Latin American countries like Cuba and the increasing importance of Marxism on a global scale. Its inception was also influenced by religious developments including the 1948 World Council of Churches which proposed the category of enculturation as a way to repair some of the damage done by missionaries. Another important event was the Second Vatican Council. The council opened the door for liturgy in the vernacular. This move affirmed the local and contextual as important for theology and helped in the rejection of the idea that the only legitimate Christian expressions resembled European ones. The council also affirmed other traditions as having kernels of divine truth which opened theology to broader perspectives. These events did not necessarily cause LALT, in some ways LALT helped to make these events what they were, but they were part of a synergistic context which helped give rise and voice to the dominant themes within the movement that sought to help the poor in Latin America.

While LALT does not have its roots in the United States, it has been central to thinking about poverty and social justice globally. It is a common conversation partner in the academic world both for its positive contributions and as a foil to critique and build from. This is true particularly of other Liberation theologies, but broader groups as well, particularly those dealing with poverty. LALT has in fact been a major dialogue partner for Latino/a theologies in the United States including Latino Pentecostals. Finally, more than any other movement we will examine, LALT has an emphasis on the Holy Spirit. While it is not a primary emphasis, it far outweighs any other movement, particularly in the work of José Comblin. We will return to Comblin and LALT's views of the Holy Spirit later in chapter 6. Here we will look at the movement's method which reveals their perspective on poverty. We will outline three major themes that comprise the foundation of this method: the preferential option of the poor, the hermeneutical circle, and theology as praxis.

We already described how Liberation Theology is committed to presenting the gospel to the poor. They are also committed to defining the gospel from the perspective of the poor. Concerning poverty, there is not a single answer, but the methodological decision of the hermeneutical privilege of the poor, or what Gutiérrez calls the "preferential option for the poor," that

---

54. Gutiérrez, *Theology of Liberation*, xiii.

underlies all of LALT's method.⁵⁵ At its most local level, this preferential option for the poor meant the creation of new critical spaces from which the poor could think and reflect about their condition of poverty, organize themselves as a human collective and think about strategic approaches to challenge the present structures of oppression. This represented a radical shift in the orientation of the church in Latin America especially as many Roman Catholic priests took up the cause of the poor. One mode for this theological reflection among the poor was Base Ecclesial Communities that attempted to read Scripture in light of the local context and the plight of the poor.⁵⁶ Since there is an emphasis on the poor, this theology also focuses on those problems which cause poverty. This means that theology must incorporate other areas and disciplines within the historical including economics, politics, and social sciences. These sectors now fall within the scope of theology and the Christian life. Because LALT makes a strong affirmation of the human person, the agency of the poor, human responsibility and divine-human interaction and relation, they move to develop a stronger anthropology and interdisciplinary work through which to reflect theologically on these issues. There is a resistance to spiritualizing the oppression of the poor and an insistence on dealing with the ideological, social and political structures that cause this oppression.

Since the dominant church had not properly addressed poverty, there was a need to redefine the ecclesial structures (as seen in the Base Ecclesial Communities), but also the very method of theological inquiry itself. Juan Luis Segundo, in his book *The Liberation of Theology*, writes about the hermeneutical circle as a methodological tool to help do theology from the perspective of the poor.⁵⁷ Segundo's hermeneutical circle rejects the "naïve belief" that the Bible can be applied to human realities in a vacuum immune to ideological tendencies and struggles of the present day. Rather than starting with this idealized version of Scripture and then applying it to human activities without contextualization, Segundo instead holds that our methods of interpreting the Bible need to repeatedly be changed by the ongoing variations in our present-day reality.⁵⁸ It must first arise out of questions of the present that are rich and basic, but these questions must change the way we customarily interpret the Bible otherwise the circle is terminated. First, reality is experienced, and this experience leads us to a suspicion of our ideologies. Second, we are to apply these suspicions to larger ideological

---

55. See Gutiérrez, *Theology of Liberation*, xxv; Vigil, "Option for the Poor," 13.
56. Boff, "Church," 125ff.
57. Segundo, *Liberation of Theology*, 7–9.
58. Segundo, *Liberation of Theology*, 8.

superstructures such as theology. Third, this changes our theological presuppositions and specifically how we read the Bible. Finally, this gives us a new way of interpreting our faith based on experience as well as a new way to interpret experience itself. This circle will then start again as new experiences cause us to question this new ideological perspective.[59] Segundo goes on to show how many other movements break this circle somewhere and so do not truly allow their theologies to respond to the realities of the poor in the present. It is the poor's true and raw experience of the world that should cause us to question our present ideologies and ways of reading Scripture that have led to the oppression of the poor.

This idea of the hermeneutical circle, combined with the preferential option for the poor, help to provide our third theme in Latin American Liberation theological method, theology as praxis. We see this in Segundo's hermeneutical circle which starts with lived experience before thinking theologically about these experiences. Clodovis Boff, author of *Theology and Praxis*, utilizes the hermeneutical circle as a primary way to do theology as praxis as opposed to theology just being theory.[60] Boff does not call for praxis instead of theological theory, nor does he call for the two to work together in a correlative relationship, but rather dialogically as they inform one another equally. Praxis informs theory, which in turn informs praxis and how one lives in the world. Likewise, living in the world necessarily informs theory, and the circle continues. For Boff, praxis takes priority even though he admits one cannot have praxis without some form of theory, even if that theory is implicit or not articulated.[61] This is because praxis forms the basis of all theology. We cannot have theological reflection unless it is based on an experience. It is not just that praxis informs theology, however, but praxis is theology. Living in the world, and specifically living for the liberation of the poor, is theological and spiritual in and of itself, even prior to its influence on ideological and theological reflection.[62]

Many criticize LALT for not going far enough in its definition of poverty. Diana Hayes, a Black Womanist theologian, criticizes LALT for pigeonholing the idea of oppression and not extending it to include gender and race.[63] Robert Warrior, a first nations theologian, critiques LALT for not talking enough about first nations poverty and the loss of land through

59. Segundo, *Liberation of Theology*, 10.
60. Boff, *Theology and Praxis*, 135–39.
61. Boff, *Theology and Praxis*, 150–51.
62. This is demonstrated in Sobrino, *Spirituality of Liberation*, 1–5. See also Sobrino, "Spirituality and the Following of Jesus," 680.
63. Hayes, *Standing in the Shoes*, 6, 80.

genocide.[64] LALT tended to focus more on males who were still a part of the dominant culture, but just poor. As we saw in our second chapter, poverty most often affects those marginalized in areas such as race, gender and age. Other criticisms, such as those of Sallie McFague and James Cone, talk about the necessity of metaphor in how we talk about God and about making a stronger emphasis on personal sin as a major part of oppression.[65] Such critiques help show that LALT has at times gone too far toward the historical while neglecting the spiritual and personal underlying the historical. For these groups, their critique is that these polarities cannot be separated so easily.

Certainly, Latin American Liberation Theology's methodology is not perfect, but it takes essential steps toward a theology of poverty. The preferential option for the poor, the hermeneutical circle and theology as praxis are important going forward toward a constructive Pneumatology of the poor. In fact, we will see how the Holy Spirit, and the experience of the Spirit in the world, is an important starting point for a theology of poverty that is focused on experience and praxis. The idea of Base Ecclesial Communities as communities of empowerment and doing theology for the local community will also be something that we will draw in as we talk about the Holy Spirit as the former of communities. We will return to LALT in our section on the Holy Spirit to see more of how they develop a theology of poverty, particularly from the perspective of the Spirit. But this discussion has opened a new door to explore another sector of Liberation Theology, Black and Womanist Theology.

Black and Womanist Theology and Urban Poverty

Cornel West in his book, *Prophesy Deliverance*, gives a helpful overview of the history of Black Theology and its Liberation trends. West identifies the first stage of Black Liberation Theology (BLT) as its primordial roots which critique the institution of slavery based on the Black slave experience prior to the emancipation proclamation of 1863.[66] After slavery, it shifted to its second stage he calls "Black Theology of Liberation as Critique of Institutional racism."[67] This period included fighting against Jim Crow laws and theology by figures like W. E. B. Du Bois, whose book *The Souls of Black*

---

64. Warrior, "Canaanites, Cowboys, and Indians," 1–8.

65. McFague, *Body of God*, 141–50. See also Cone, *Black Theology of Liberation*, 116–18.

66. West, *Prophesy Deliverance!*, 101.

67. West, *Prophesy Deliverance!*, 102.

Folk, showed in vivid imagery what the social, political and intellectual life of Black people was like in the post-civil war United States.[68] It was not until after this period in 1969 when James Cone published his *Black Theology and Power*, that BLT entered into the more academic realms of theology, but this third stage began by critiquing White, North American Theology, especially its "silence on racial justice and the White racism within mainstream establishment, churches and religious agencies."[69] Of course there was theology before this time in Du Bois and other figures, but it was Cone's work which was the first fully fledged academic Liberation Theology, Black or otherwise, in the United States.[70] Still, this period of theology was narrow in its focus and it was not until the fourth stage that Black theologians began to do theology on their own terms. They began to critique United States capitalism because of its part in causing poverty and oppression among the Black community in the United States, particularly in urban cities. During this period after 1977, Cone began to write articles like "Black Theology and the Black Church: Where do We Go from Here?" In this article, Cone saw the root problem as "human sinfulness which nurtures monopolistic capitalism, aided by racism and abetted by sexism. Our crisis is spiritual, material and moral."[71] West's own work in *Prophesy Deliverance* attempts to transcend even this by engaging BLT's prophetic Christian tradition with the Councilist stream of Marxism.[72]

A number of women, such as Katie Cannon and Diana Hayes have taken BLT even further through the Womanist stream that sees not just the Black race as affected by poverty, but women as often the most oppressed even among Blacks.[73] Still, a major thread throughout all of BLT is the plight of the poor. While BLT is often focused specifically on the Black community, many of its arguments apply to poverty on a broader scale, especially in an urban setting where most of the poor are minorities. Du Bois, Cone, West,

---

68. Du Bois, *Souls of Black Folk*.

69. West, *Prophesy Deliverance!*, 104. See also Cone, *Black Theology and Black Power*.

70. Other figures like Bishop Henry McNeal Turn, Marcus Garvey, Benjamin Mays, Howard Thurman, and Martin Luther King Jr.

71. Cone, "Black Theology and the Black Church," 150.

72. West, *Prophesy Deliverance!*, 137. For West, Councilism is to Marxism what Liberation Theology is to Christianity: a promotion and practice of the moral core of the perspective against overwhelming odds for success. It's normative commitment to prefigurativism, along with an adamant anticapitalistic and anti-imperialist stance make it especially attractive to West. For more on Councilism and the Worker's Councils, see Gorter et al., *Non-Leninist Marxism*.

73. Cannon, *Katie's Canon*. See also Hayes, *Standing in the Shoes*.

and Hayes will be our primary sources as we seek to explore the causes, theological responses and practical responses of BLT.

At its core, Black theologians like Cornel West, in his book with Tavis Smiley, *The Rich and the Rest of Us,* want to define poverty as a shortage of money. They want to avoid the idea that poverty means something is wrong with you, your character, habits, lifestyle or choices. They know that the reason one does not have money is more nuanced than this, but they put most of the guilt on society for either not paying working people enough or not having work for them at all.[74] Three primary areas come up in the BLT's literature we will now examine: lack of opportunity, inequity even when the opportunity is there, and stigmatizing language concerning the poor.

At its core, poverty among Black urban communities has become a poverty of opportunity. The problem of a lack of opportunity, according to Smiley and West, is close to becoming a permanent reality in the United States. This is because poverty becomes cyclical when a lack of opportunity makes people hold on tighter to the resources they do have, but this hurts the economy and makes people even more poor.[75] Opportunity affects numerous areas in American society, especially since the economic downturn of 2008. There is also a lack of opportunity in education because of rising education costs. A final area where Smiley and West see poverty of opportunity is in the prison system where many are incarcerated for small crimes. This imprisonment not only hurts the individual, but that person's family, giving them less wealth and opportunity.[76]

A second area that causes poverty according to Black Theology is inequity. Often prosperity in the United States comes at the expense of its poor. Smiley and West cite the Reagan era's surrender in the war on poverty and initiating the war on welfare. While it was a period in which many saw the nation as wealthier, statistics show the poverty rate grew, particularly in cities. This also left a legacy of devastating conditions for the poor that has yet to be reversed.[77] Like opportunity, inequity goes well beyond just money to include inequity in education, health care, job training, housing and land.[78]

A final cause of poverty is language and stigmatization against the poor. According to West in *Prophesy Deliverance*, "The two basic challenges presently confronting Afro-Americans are self-image and self-determination

---

74. Smiley and West, *Rich and the Rest of Us,* 22.
75. Smiley and West, *Rich and the Rest of Us,* 45–48.
76. Smiley and West, *Rich and the Rest of Us,* 128.
77. Smiley and West, *Rich and the Rest of Us,* 63.
78. Smiley and West, *Rich and the Rest of Us,* 105. See also Gebara, *Longing for Running Water,* 5.

... how humans attempt to define who and what one is ... and the political struggle to gain significance over the major institutions that regulate people's lives."[79] The language of labeling gives the poor not just a lack of resources, but a poverty mentality that creates a lack of vision. It becomes a form of manipulation and of keeping power at the expense of the poor they demean through "cynical and manipulative vocabulary."[80] It is not just calling the impoverished "poor" but trivializing people's poverty, pain and suffering. This can include talking about how poverty will never be solved or will always be with us, language often used by Christianity, to continue to beat down and oppress the poor.

As with most of the theologies of poverty, the theological responses often parallel the views of what causes poverty. We will look at three theological responses that continue to be used among a diversity of responses within the BLT literature. These include self-determination which is a response to poverty of opportunity and inequity, the historical and physical relevance of the Gospel, which responds to inequity and views that poverty is trivial, and writing one's own story which responds to the stigmatization of the poor.

James Cone, in his book *God of the Oppressed*, holds that "Black Theology must reject any conception of God which stifles Black determination or which pictures God as the God of all people.... God identifies with the oppressed so their experience becomes God's experience."[81] For Cone, liberation is freedom to relate to God as one is; to relate to self and community as God created one to be not under outside influence. At the center of the idea of why the oppressed should experience self-determination and freedom is the understanding of human dignity for everyone regardless of age, race, or socioeconomic status. Du Bois holds that such dignity allows one to be oneself and denounce conforming to the dominant culture or its expectations.[82] This is what Smiley and West call a culture of affirmation. It involves the poor affirming their own worth, but can also involves the rich first acknowledging the poor and then cultivating compassion based on the person's worth and dignity.[83] Such dignity is so central to Black Theology that West defines the Black prophetic tradition as "the universal commitment, the dignity and sanctity of persons and the commitment to live and die in the struggle for freedom and democracy."[84] Affirming this dignity

---

79. West, *Prophesy Deliverance!*, 22.
80. Smiley and West, *Rich and the Rest of Us*, 67.
81. Cone, *God of the Oppressed*, 134.
82. Du Bois, *Souls of Black Folk*, 3–5.
83. Smiley and West, *Rich and the Rest of Us*, 72, 119.
84. Smiley and West, *Rich and the Rest of Us*, 125.

and sanctity is constitutional of love and is the center of a gospel response to poverty. Salvation and love are not just for the individual, but they are for the community as well. There has been a movement of tolerance lately within the United States. It affirms people with disabilities, different sexual orientations and even different races, but such affirmation has not crossed over socioeconomic lines in the dignity with which we treat the poor.

The second area of theological response is concerning the historical relevance of the gospel. The oppression of Blacks, while it has spiritual implications, primarily takes place in present physical and economic sufferings and so the salvation offered must do likewise.[85] If read correctly, Black theologians see historical and physical salvation is at the center of the Christian story. Scripture must be reread through Black experience to uncover these realities. Likewise, Black history must be reread through the gospel, a kind of hermeneutical circle. According to Cone, Black experience must be read in light of Scripture and particularly Jesus Christ.[86] Katie Canon likewise finds a source for Black Theology in Scripture through Israel's and Jesus's experiences as Black people in Egypt.[87] West turns primarily to Prophetic Christian thought which calls for the care of the poor and which he believes Jesus, in his Luke 4 proclamation of the gospel to the poor, situates himself within.[88] Hayes also emphasizes the historicity of the gospel for Black Theology, holding that the "Black gospel emerges from the experience of slavery, colonialism, Jim Crow segregation, second-class citizenship and the continuing denial of our humanity. Black Catholic Theology is holistic, seeing no separation between the sacred and secular."[89] The gospel must then be rooted in the historical Jesus and the good news of the coming kingdom of God, a kingdom based on love and community, a "'kin-dom' in which all would be welcomed regardless of race, gender, or class."[90]

This desire for historicity is also part of Cornel West's turn toward progressive Marxism. Marxism critiques Christianity's dialectic between human nature and human history and their belief in a "transcendent God who seems to work most effectively beyond history rather than in history."[91] The gospel must have these historical outworkings for it to truly be the gospel.

---

85. West, *Prophesy Deliverance!*, 15.
86. Cone, *God of the Oppressed*, 28.
87. Cannon, *Katie's Canon*, 31–49.
88. West, *Prophesy Deliverance!*, 15.
89. Hayes, *Standing in the Shoes*, 118.
90. Hayes, *Standing in the Shoes*, 154.
91. West, *Prophesy Deliverance!*, 95.

This is the kind of community Jesus was trying to build and which responds to Black experiences of poverty in the physical and historical world.

The gospel must not only respond to the Black experience but also come out of the Black experience and that is our third theological response within BLT, the importance of writing one's own story in order to keep Black identity intact. From the beginning, there was a backlash to having their story told by their oppressors which led to a large number of autobiographies by figures like Equiano, Fredrick Douglas, Harriet Jacobs and W. E. B. Du Bois. This was the beginning of contextual theology for Blacks because it gave them control over their own destiny. A second way this has been done is through recovering theologically rich texts, songs, and traditions that may not have even been considered theological. Du Bois encourages this recovery of Black people's "natural religiosity, and preserving this African soul."[92] James Cone does something similar in his book *The Spirituals and the Blues* which explored theological themes like Christology, theodicy, suffering and eschatology through these historical expressions of groaning.[93]

This contextualization of theology from a people's lived experience is not new with BLT but stems from American pragmatic philosophy that says philosophy, and in turn theology, is bound to culture, society and history.[94] For Black Theology this looks like embracing what West calls the humanist tradition of Afro-American response which "extols the distinctiveness of Afro-American culture and personality (while also accenting) the universal human content of Afro-American cultural forms."[95] The universal human content is an important part of this equation because it recognizes that, while the Black experience of poverty is distinct and needs to have its own accounts, these accounts will naturally inform other communities' experiences of poverty and oppression. Hays calls this being an "organic intellectual," one who emerges from a particular community and is sent forth by that community to garner knowledge and skills, but then to return to the people to work with and for them to bring about their empowerment.[96]

So, what do these theological responses to poverty within BLT look like practically? Smiley and West make it clear that it cannot just look like charitable giving because anyone can give charitably while maintaining lifestyle choices which continue to oppress the poor. They would rather see people

92. Du Bois, *Souls of Black Folk*, 142.

93. Cone, *Spirituals and the Blues*, 16–18.

94. West, *Prophesy Deliverance!*, 20. See the works of Charles Peirce, William James, George Mead, and John Dewey.

95. West, *Prophesy Deliverance!*, 71.

96. Hayes, *Standing in the Shoes*, 155.

fighting for just distribution and equal opportunity through challenging the government to restructure tax laws that benefit the richest of the rich.[97] Equality in taxes are one way to fight, but job opportunities would probably be the next greatest need. Other ways to fight for just distribution include grassroots movements like the occupy movement which sought change through solidarity and standing up to the powers that be through non-violent protest. Other more organized communities must also be formed to fight, such as the National Black United Front or the National Black Independent Political Party.[98] Response must take place not just on the personal level but also on the social and structural level. Though it should be remembered that throughout their discussion of these causes, they do emphasize the personal sinfulness of humanity. They do not, however, propose any solutions for how personal sinfulness affects poverty, something that should be addressed.

Another area of practical response is in changing language. This response begins with the need for a new understanding of poverty and of racism in the United States, a vision that sees a way forward rather than an impasse. It is not just about helping the poorest of the poor, but helping the citizens who find themselves "living in America's great middle and are now struggling for resources to find their way."[99] Such a redefinition and change of language can create a culture of what Smiley and West call "uninhibited innovation" which can lay the foundation for an equitable economy by creating jobs, rebuilding communities, and strengthening families. But it begins with a new understanding and redefinition of what poverty is and is not in America.[100] It also begins with the self-determination and writing of one's own story that was emphasized in the theological responses of BLT, because it is only though the telling of stories and the growth of understanding that vision will change.

Evaluation

Liberation Theology, both LALT and BLT, provides an array of rich resources for a theology of poverty because it is one of the few theological traditions that has made poverty its emphasis This poverty is much more complex than just a socioeconomic reality, it encompasses race, gender and other social dimensions as well. Still, both movements speak about poverty primarily in economic terms as a lack of financial resources that stems from other privations such as opportunity. Perhaps its greatest strengths are its

---

97. Smiley and West, *Rich and the Rest of Us*, 133.
98. Smiley and West, *Rich and the Rest of Us*, 144–45.
99. Smiley and West, *Rich and the Rest of Us*, 149.
100. Smiley and West, *Rich and the Rest of Us*, 139.

methodological resources such as the option for the poor, its emphasis on praxis, doing theology contextually within and for a certain community, and being open to a revision of our understanding of the biblical text and the world through the hermeneutical circle. Black Theology takes this a step further wanting to address poverty through affirming the person not just through emphasis, but through new language and vision. Such a new vision is necessary when addressing poverty, especially when it comes to urban poverty which has been extremely stigmatized and stereotyped in the media even today.

Perhaps the greatest weakness of both movements is their over correction toward the historical. While it is necessary that the gospel address the physical and the historical, the gospel is something that should address the whole person and one of these cannot be *a priori*. There must a balance between the individual and the corporate and between the physical and the spiritual. Addressing each aspect of the person is necessary to overcome poverty because poverty affects the whole person. For many, once they find themselves impoverished just receiving opportunity or money will not solve their poverty fully.

Another strength is the emphasis on community and community organizing within these movements. I would take it even a step further, however, that it is not just the community of poverty, or the community of Blacks, but that micro-communities within these are equally important. Because poverty is so complex, each person's situation is different and requires different responses on the local level. Each community, family and person must tell their own story because it is in telling their own story that they can name and begin to overcome their oppression. Base Ecclesial Communities move in this direction, but a pneumatological paradigm would help address the whole person while also doing it within community. Failure to address Pneumatology is a critique that we have leveled against every movement we have studied. We will look at Jose Comblin's Pneumatology of liberation in chapter 6 but see that it is also lacking some important elements and perspectives that would add to a theology of poverty.

ECUMENICAL THEOLOGY AND URBAN POVERTY

In this final section of our chapter on urban poverty in ecumenical theology, we briefly explore just a few more perspectives that fit into this broad category. We will focus on just three more voices that will move us forward toward our goal of a pneumatological theology of urban poverty. First, we will explore prophetic activism as outlined by Helene Slessarev-Jamir because it gives us the broadest picture into other theological work on urban poverty we have not explored. Second, we will focus on a brief engagement with Roman Catholicism in the United States. Finally, we will look at one example of a mainline Protestant through the work of Susan Holman, senior writer at the Global Health Education and Learning Incubator at Harvard University.

Prophetic Activism and Urban Poverty

Prophetic activism is not a self-identifying movement, but more of a category created by Helene Slessarev-Jamir, professor at Claremont School of Theology, to include groups for which religion is used to frame progressive politics that prophetically call for justice, peace and the healing of the world.[101] She is concerned with the larger category of justice, but speaks specifically of poverty as a root cause and symptom of these injustices. We will use her work to provide a brief glimpse into current religious responses to urban poverty, both theological and practical, outside the purview of what we have explored so far.

By the word "prophetic," Slessarev-Jamir specifically means "a religious understanding of politics defined by its inclusiveness, its concern for the other, for those who are marginalized."[102] Most often these movements are found in more liberal Christian traditions, though congregations like Saddleback Church, an Evangelical, Southern Baptist church in Southern California, show, through the remarkable range of social issues they have engaged, that there are always exceptions to the rules. Similarly, she notes, how suburban United Methodist churches can be as politically conservative as most Evangelicals. So, theological conservatism or liberalism cannot be the only factors in determining prophetic activism, geographic and socio-economic location are equally important.[103]

This leads to an important distinction she makes between "borderlands" and "cosmopolitans." Each category describes not just a geographic location but a set of identities such as immigrant, low-wage, service worker, ex-felon, lesbian or gay couple, which are most commonly present in the borderlands space. Cosmopolitan, on the other hand, describes those in a position of privilege but who identify with people on the margins.[104] There are borderland cities which embody these geographic locations where many live in the borderland and where urban poverty is most prevalent. While

---

101. Slessarev-Jamir, *Prophetic Activism*, 3–4.
102. Slessarev-Jamir, *Prophetic Activism*, 4.
103. Slessarev-Jamir, *Prophetic Activism*, 20–21.
104. Slessarev-Jamir, *Prophetic Activism*, 22.

urban poverty takes place in the borderlands, theological and practical responses can occur from either sector. Religious justice organizations, in fact, often act as a bridge between these two social locations.[105] This is because, for Slessarev-Jamir, religion has the power to evoke solidarity among humanity because of the sacred bonds humanity naturally shares. She also evokes the theology underlying humanity's dignity which gives everyone the warrant to access basic human rights. All the groups Slessarev-Jamir explores are not even religious, some are secular, but part of her argument is that there is such a strong tradition of social justice within Christianity and the Abrahamic religions, that even secular institutions adopt religious frameworks to explain their motivations and responses to urban poverty.

Slessarev-Jamir sees many of the same causes at play as previous theologies we have explored sees the globalization of capital and production as the greatest exacerbation of income inequality that leads to impoverishment in urban settings.[106] In response, present-day prophetic activism uses both words and actions. It uses words through hearing and telling the stories of human misery and oppression occurring in our country's borderlands. They often connect these stories to similar stories in the biblical prophetic tradition to show the needed response in today's world.[107] These stories are central to action. They give the poor a voice that empowers them to act on their own behalf, stand in solidarity with one another and allows others, like cosmopolitans, to understand the poor and also stand in better solidarity. Knowing these stories also allows one to tailor their response to what is causing poverty an. Concerning action, prophetic activists prefer non-violent resistance as a method to call for and affect change on a larger scale, again, much as the biblical prophets did. They seek political change through protest, lobbying and voting. They provide several services and resources which empower the poor from help with citizenship, to housing, or lawyers. Finally, she emphasizes congregation-based community organizing as one of the most powerful forms of prophetic activism.[108] These are small communities that often focus on their own community but make big change.

Theologically, Slessarev-Jamir does not talk much about christological or pneumatological responses but primarily focuses on a theistic vision of God as reflected in the Old Testament prophets. She sees prophetic activism as relying heavily on creation motifs, but also adds an element of exploring the righteousness of God which is "not just a value; it is God's part of human

---

105. Slessarev-Jamir, *Prophetic Activism*, 29.
106. Slessarev-Jamir, *Prophetic Activism*, 5.
107. Slessarev-Jamir, *Prophetic Activism*, 38.
108. Slessarev-Jamir, *Prophetic Activism*, 67.

life. God's stake in human history."[109] Prophetic action becomes a visible sign of God's presence and power in the world as well as future realities that can be achieved more wholly.

According to Slessarev-Jamir, Roman Catholic parishes comprised one-third of all congregations engaged in prophetic activism. This one-third is also possibly the most powerful third because of the size and resources of local Roman Catholic congregations.[110] Another third of these, however include various Protestant denominations, mostly mainline. The final third involved in congregational prophetic activism including African American Protestants, Jewish synagogues and Islamic mosques. Even though there seems to be a larger percentage of Roman Catholics addressing urban poverty, it was not until Leo XIII's encyclical *Rerum Nevarum* that the Roman Catholic Church developed its modern social teaching. This encyclical insisted that the role of the state is to promote social justice through the protection of rights while the church must also speak out on social issues to educate and help bring harmony between the classes. Leo XIII also held that workers should not be treated as slaves, because they too are created in God's image.[111] Pope Pius XI's encyclical forty years later *Quadragesimo Anno* seeks a reconstruction of the social order by encouraging a living wage and extoling social justice as a personal virtue. Such reconstruction comes only though just individuals and just institutions.[112] These encyclicals and their theological statements helped open up the way for figures like Caesar Chavez to hunger strike, taking only water and Eucharist wafers for twenty-five days after which he broke the fast by taking the Eucharist.[113] Rituals like the Eucharist and prayer are important and powerful symbols of solidarity, salvation and social change for Roman Catholics.

Besides these encyclicals, the Medellín conference in Latin America and the rise of LALT was important in impacting responses to urban poverty in the United States. LALT's call to become the church of the poor resonated deeply with many priests and lay people who reoriented their praxis toward transformative work among the poor. One hub of Roman Catholic social action among the urban poor was in San Antonio where in 1969 fifty priests formed PADRES (Padres Asociados para Derechos Religiosos, Educativos y

109. Slessarev-Jamir, *Prophetic Activism*, 43.

110. Slessarev-Jamir, *Prophetic Activism*, 69–70. The United States Catholic Conference of Bishops awards roughly $10 million annually to a wide variety of community-based justice organizations, consistently making it the single largest source of support to congregational-based community organizing.

111. Burgess, "Christianity," 55.

112. Burgess, "Christianity," 55.

113. DeYoung, "Christianity," 69.

Sociales—Association of Fathers for religious, education and social rights). This organization was formed to "empower Chicanos by integrating Latin American forms of popular religion into the Roman Catholic Church and by promoting civic engagement with discrimination and social justice."[114] Virgilio Elizondo was one of the founders of this movement as well as an attender of the 1968 Medellín conference at which Liberation Theology was first presented. He pushed for an understanding among Roman Catholics in the United States of income inequality as primarily a social sin and called for the church to take the side of the poor.

Even before this movement and the rise of LALT, however, was the Catholic Worker Movement founded by Dorothy Day and Peter Maurin in 1933 during the Great Depression. It was a newspaper and a movement, both of which sought to catalyze a radical renewal of Roman Catholicism and the larger society.[115] Today there are 185 Roman Catholic worker communities around the world. They focus primarily on practicing simple living and serving as places for hospitality among poor workers. Beyond the Catholic Worker Movement, the Roman Catholic Church is one of the foremost funders of local social action. Their Catholic Campaign for Human Development (CCHD) organized groups of White and minority poor to develop economic strength and political power. The CCHD also educates people about poverty which leads to a greater sense of solidarity.[116] It embodies its own mission by giving preference to funding organizations run by the poor and organizations seeking to empower the poor and change unjust social structures rather than just do charity.

Theologically, Roman Catholicism in the United States' starting point for social justice among the urban poor is the grace of God which can be found in the transforming power of the gospel on individuals and communities. Also central is the idea of *Koinonia* as lived by the early Christians. Their concern for the poor, widows and strangers is an extension of their worship and shows the norm of the kingdom of God which cares for those who have less.[117] This again emphasizes the congregational community that prophetic activism explored as a response to poverty, a reason why Roman Catholicism was so central to Slessarev-Jamir's work. Another interesting part of the Roman Catholic response to poverty has been its dialogue with Pentecostalism on the topic. We will explore this more fully in our sixth chapter on Pneumatology.

---

114. Slessarev-Jamir, *Prophetic Activism*, 78.
115. Slessarev-Jamir, "Christianity," 71.
116. Slessarev-Jamir, "Christianity," 73.
117. Kärkkäinen, "Evangelization," 17.

Mainline Protestants and Urban Poverty

To conclude this chapter, I will briefly look at Susan Holman's work in her book, *God Knows There's Need*, as an example of a response to poverty in mainline Protestant denominations.[118] Holman considers three primary paradigms through which to engage the poor theologically.

First, she discusses "sensing the poor" as the "initial process in any rhetoric about physical and social needs."[119] It is in this sensing that personal perception is either created or awakened as one experiences the other through the physical senses. Experiencing poverty with our own bodies is important because it brings it into dialogue with our perception of our own needs and creates empathy.[120] Eventually this will expand from sensing one person or situation to a global awareness of the injustice of the world. We have seen this idea of storytelling as prevalent in our discussion of ecumenical perspectives on poverty. It is necessary to discover and respond to the plight of the poor and to give the poor empowerment and self-actualization over their story and situation.

Second, Holman considers the concept of "sharing the world" which can only follow the initial sensory encounter. She speaks of "sharing" and not "giving," because real justice, relief and cosmic healing are never one-way activities but engagements in reciprocity and "relating to one another equally at the level of creation."[121] Sharing the world begins with friendship and relationship with those in poverty which creates a platform to hear the voices of the poor and reach the other.[122] Here she draws out eschatological themes. She believes that most relief programs are founded on some ideal of global wholeness or cosmic, eschatological unity as the goal of their work and mission. This vision causes one to share the world with the poor through a range of actions including relief, philanthropy and political action. Holman sees finances as at the center of one's response to poverty, but a holistic view of finances that include "where I purchase, what I purchase, what I keep . . . and what I give. . . . Giving is powerful. Giving can change the world, but not just giving to the poor. Sharing the world calls for a powerful

---

118. Holman is by no means the only voice within mainline Protestantism, but her contribution is important and certainly in line with, and somewhat representative of, other approaches by mainline Protestant scholars.

119. Holman, *God Knows There's Need*, 15.

120. Holman, *God Knows There's Need*, 25.

121. Holman, *God Knows There's Need*, 19–20.

122. Holman, *God Knows There's Need*, 43.

recognition of mutual commonality of interdependence, working together as members of a body."[123]

Finally, Holman sees embodying the sacred kingdom as the final step of responding to the needs of the poor. This goes deeper than just social action in that it merges the physical response with the spiritual, recognizing that both matter and spiritual are important. The divine is embodied in Christ, our bodies are important, but they are also redeemed into something more important than their present state.[124] The body in its brokenness is brought into direct relation with the divine urban vision for the world. At the center of this for Holman is liturgy which uses the body to serve both the divine and the community. Liturgy is service and worship that is grounded in the material world into which God himself breaks in and responds to our need.[125]

Evaluation

In this final section of ecumenical responses to poverty in the United States, we have explored prophetic activism, Roman Catholicism and an example of mainline Protestantism. Prophetic activism's emphasis on community organizing within small and local communities reiterates what we saw in Evangelicalism's emphasis on civic life. It shows the breadth of responses within the United States, and even globally, that take on a religious and theological form. Still, much of the theological response centered around creation mandates and the christological kingdom situated within the prophetic tradition. There is no mention of either the Holy Spirit or of Pentecostalism within this range of theological and practical responses.

Roman Catholicism has a similar shortfall, though we will see when dialoguing with Pentecostalism that they do have resources for such a discussion. Still, Roman Catholicism in the United States has been one of the most, if not the most, effective organizations at addressing poverty, religious or otherwise. This may be because of its long history of social action and longevity of being dedicated to addressing the causes of urban poverty. It may also be because of the lived experience of poverty among early Roman Catholics as they largely began among poor immigrant classes, themselves oppressed in the United States.[126] This lived experience gives them a "borderlands" loci while also having cosmopolitan type resources to help.

123. Holman, *God Knows There's Need*, 139, 146.
124. Holman, *God Knows There's Need*, 22.
125. Holman, *God Knows There's Need*, 159.
126. Slessarev-Jamir, *Prophetic Activism*, 71.

This lived experience is also what Susan Holman adds to the conversation in her idea of "sensing need" having to come before any response can even be given. She echoes the Roman Catholic emphasis on ritual and sacrament as important, but for her it is because of how worship embodies a hope for poverty through painting another possible reality, yet in a way that the divine is still central. This merging of body and spirit and this balance that Holman strives for is something we will keep at the center of our own pneumatological response. Renewal will also add to this discussion in the next chapter.

CONCLUSION

Having now reviewed views on poverty through sociological, Evangelical and ecumenical lenses, we have seen the great strides that have been made in creating a theological response to poverty. We have also seen the pneumatological gap that exists within these theologies and the fact that most theologies of poverty focus on either the exterior versus the interior or the individual versus the social falling short of a holistic approach. We now turn toward a Pneumatology of poverty incorporating what we have already explored but doing so through a pneumatological lens that will reveal new insights and practices to address urban poverty. The final section of this dissertation will include three chapters that move us toward this pneumatological perspective. Chapter 5 will be on the topic of Renewal Theology, a theological movement that has Pneumatology at the heart of its theology and practice. Chapter 6 will examine contributions to Pneumatology from other sources that would be helpful in constructing a holistic Pneumatology of urban poverty. Finally, our last chapter will construct such a theology based on a pneumatic interpretation of the four-fold gospel.

4

Urban Poverty in North American Renewal Theology

INTRODUCTION

Wilfredo "Choco" De Jesús is the pastor of one of the fastest growing churches in urban Chicago.[1] New Life Covenant, a church within the Pentecostal denomination, the Assemblies of God, has grown from fifty people when Pastor Choco took over in the year 2000 and now has over seventeen thousand people in weekly attendance. Part of what makes Pastor Choco unique as a Pentecostal pastor in America is his emphasis on social justice and poverty. He is also the Vice President of Social Justice for, the National Hispanic Christian Leadership Conference.[2] He earned this position not just through having a large church but through how the church has grown. It has not been just typical Evangelical or Pentecostal evangelization methods focused solely on spiritual needs. New Life Covenant reaches out to the most down and out people of their city—to the poor, the homeless, the prostitute, the "gang banger." According to De Jesús, "We reach the people nobody else cares about. We care about the whole person. We don't just care about their souls but their well-being. Still part of that is their souls, if that (their soul) isn't right, nothing will be right." One of the biggest groups that De Jesús reaches out to is underprivileged children. The church has adopted every single elementary school in their section of Chicago providing their

---

1. This information, unless otherwise noted, and the story about "Judy's family" was obtained by the author in a personal interview with Wilfredo De Jesús, Anaheim, CA, June 1, 2016.

2. Warren, "Wilfredo De Jesús."

children with school supplies and free tutoring. "We don't just want to give a hand out, we want to change the person's situation, their whole reality."

De Jesús told me of one story about a single-mother family living on welfare. "Judy" came with her three children to the church's backpack giveaway at the beginning of the school year. She could barely feed or clothe her children because most of her income went to paying rent in their low-income housing complex.[3] "She was trying to do it right, but it just wasn't working," said De Jesús. New Life Covenant helped immediately through clothes and groceries from their food pantry. They also found Judy a new job that paid better. "I saw their family this Sunday and they thanked me, but the light in her kids' eyes was enough. I told her 'You're welcome, but that is simply what the gospel does, it changes lives.'"

Pastor Choco is part of an emerging generation of Renewal leaders challenging the trends and outside criticisms of Renewal in the United States as quietistic. This criticism has been prevalent. Hollenweger, in his book, *The Pentecostals*, for instance, while recognizing the social significance of Pentecostalism, describes a lack of explicit political and social involvement due to their anti-communist orientation.[4] A review of a periodical like *Apostolic Faith* magazine from the early years of the Azusa Street Revival would also show very little, if any, interest in social concern. On the other hand, authors like Cecil M. Robeck have shown the social concern of pivotal leaders in the founding of Pentecostalism including Frank Bartleman, William Seymour and A. J. Tomlinson.[5] Despite recent works that clearly show that this early social consciousness has not been lost to all Pentecostals, criticism remains because the history of social action among Pentecostals is clearly checkered.[6]

Similar quietistic criticism has been leveled against the Charismatic Renewal that began among many mainline denominations and soon included a wave of new denominations and independent churches around the globe.[7] Nigel Scotland, for instance, expresses his hope that "Charismatics

---

3. "Judy" is a pseudonym for the actual person De Jesús told me about. I have changed her name to protect her identity.

4. Hollenweger, *Pentecostals*, 467–69.

5. Robeck Jr., "Social Concern," 98–103.

6. See Petersen, *Not by Might, Nor by Power*. For a more recent overview of social action among some current Charismatic groups, see Miller and Yamamori, *Global Pentecostalism*.

7. While some delineate between a second and third wave of the Pentecostal movement (and there are good reasons for doing so), I will treat those movements stemming from the 1960s and after that are not a part of classical Pentecostal denominations as "Charismatic."

will overcome their lack of social activism."[8] Kilian McDonnell notes that when denominations formally responded to the Charismatic Renewal, they almost unanimously faulted it for failing to address the social implications of the gospel.[9] Like the criticism of Pentecostal social action, however, much of the condemnation of the Charismatic movement has been due to overgeneralization and a lack of knowledge concerning the global nature of the movement. Veli-Matti Kärkkäinen, speaking of the roots most Charismatics have in mainline denominational churches, holds that Charismatics compared to classical Pentecostals have been "more open to the challenge of social justice, perhaps because most of their churches have been."[10] While not all Charismatics have actively engaged in social action, a number of Charismatic groups have been.

Recent years have seen an increase in academic works concerning social justice within Renewal. Many of these works have focused on Global Renewalism, however, implying a gap in the United States.[11] Still other works within Renewal Theology that have focused on social justice topics have been on the rise such as *A Liberating Spirit* edited by Wilkinson and Studebaker.[12] These are often first forays into various topics from a Renewal theological perspective.

In this chapter, we will argue that despite these quietistic accusations, Renewal Theology itself has helpful resources to offer a theology of poverty, particularly its emphasis on Pneumatology. We will accomplish this by analyzing the work that Renewal Theology has done on poverty already. First, because Renewal Theology is a relatively new player in the academic world, we will introduce the field of Renewal Studies and its approaches. After this we will outline some of the theological work and practical responses to poverty by the Renewal movement. Because Renewal is still rather nascent, we will have to focus a little more broadly on social action at times and draw applications to urban poverty more specifically. We will also have to draw more widely than just from the United States because Renewal in the United States has been more quietistic and, as we are talking about potential, it can look to its global neighbors for inspiration on what Renewal can truly look like.

---

8. Scotland, *Charismatics and the Next Millennium*, 264.

9. McDonnell, *Presence, Power, Praise*, liii.

10. Kärkkäinen, "Mission, Spirit, and Eschatology," 80.

11. See Miller and Yamamori, *Global Pentecostalism*; Petersen, *Not by Might, Nor by Power*.

12. Wilkinson and Studebaker, *Liberating Spirit*.

WHAT IS RENEWAL THEOLOGY?[13]

Before exploring Renewal Theology's responses to urban poverty in the United States and abroad, it will be helpful to introduce Renewal Theology as an approach to the discipline of theology. Many may not be familiar with its advent, its theological content, or why it would be beneficial to explore for the purposes of a Pneumatology of urban poverty. The field of Renewal Studies is an emerging field in the landscape of academic inquiry. It seeks to provide a certain hermeneutic through which to view the world, the history of the people of God (church history), its sacred texts (biblical studies), and its theology. As with all approaches, there is a period of emergence and formation that takes place in which ideas and approaches are more fluid than firm. The same is true in Renewal Studies. In this brief section, I will first give an overview of the emergence of Renewal Studies as an academic field, specifically theology as an approach within that field. Second, I will ask whether Renewal Theology has a method and, if so, what that method is and its promise for a theology of urban poverty.

The Emergence of Renewal Theology as an Academic Approach

Renewal Studies, particularly in the United States, finds its history in the Pentecostal/Charismatic movements of the twentieth century.[14] While Renewal Studies did not develop as an academic field until the late twentieth century, the early years of the movement helped plant the seeds for the worldview that would form the questions later scholars would ask.[15]

---

13. The language of "Renewal" itself comes out of the Charismatic Renewal of the 1960s and 1970s. Over time, there has been a blurring between traditional three wave categorizations of classical Pentecostalism, mainline Charismatics and independent Charismatics. This blurring is furthered by the immense growth of the movement around the world so that it often takes different forms and relationships in different countries and regions globally. When the Pew Forum began studying the movement's beliefs and practices they landed on the term "Renewal" to describe its diversity of movements. See Cartledge, "Can Theology Be 'Practical'?," 18–34.

14. As with any movement, its origins are complex and multifaceted. Most of the early academic approaches to Renewal have been from Western perspectives born out of the United States and Europe. As such, the story of the rise of Renewal Theology largely goes through the Western narratives of the rise of Renewal. For diverse accounts on the movement itself see Hollenweger, *Pentecostals*; Synan, *Holiness-Pentecostal Tradition*; Robeck Jr. and Yong, *Cambridge Companion to Pentecostalism*.

15. Hollenweger specifically identifies the first decade as the formative early years for Pentecostal Theology. Pentecostal scholars like Steven J. Land follow his lead. See Hollenweger, "Pentecostals and the Charismatic Movement," 549–53; Land, *Pentecostal Spirituality*, 47.

The beginning of the movement was focused on mission and eschatology with little concern for academic or theological development. As generations passed and Pentecostal/Charismatics began to attend schools for church history or biblical studies in an attempt to interpret their movement, these early formative questions came to bear on their work before Renewal scholars began to foray into other areas of theology.[16]

The first set of figures in Renewal predated the entrance of Renewal Studies into the academy. I include them because it was not that these early figures did not do theology, they simply did not do it in an academic sense. The movement's first pastors and writers were focused on identifying and defending the experiences they had in various revival and renewal settings. There was little forward movement or attempt to dialogue with the "liberal" academy except to use these other movements' methods and language for Renewal's own purposes. There was very little outside scholarly inquiry into the early Pentecostal/Charismatic movement.

While many examples are available, one person we could draw on is Alexander A. Boddy, often ascribed as one of the founders of Pentecostalism in Europe, particularly in Great Britain. Much of Boddy's work took the form of tracts, some compiled into small books, and his periodical entitled "Confidence." Mark J. Cartledge in his article on Boddy's "Confidence" magazine notes that commentators label Boddy's form of theology "oral theology" and "non-academic theology."[17] Boddy's major dialogue partners consisted of other Pentecostals, largely European, rather than the larger Christian world. Boddy was one of the most educated leaders of the early Pentecostal movement and, having been a vicar in the Anglican church, would have had a broad knowledge of other Christian movements in Europe, but he rarely engaged them. The most that can be said was that the silence was an engagement of indictment.

The one possible exception to this isolationist trend in early Renewal scholarship is Donald Gee who was an early member of the World Council of Churches and encouraged some of the first Pentecostals, including Walter Hollenweger, to engage in academic study.[18] Gee's work represents the greatest example of early Pentecostal engagement on a somewhat scholarly level with those outside Pentecostalism. This trend does not mean Pentecostals were not theological, did not do sound exegesis or were not intelligent.

---

16. Telling the story of the rise of Renewal Theology into the academy is a messy task. There are several possible ways in which the story could be told as it is largely open to interpretation. This is one narrative that certainly has bearing.

17. Cartledge, "Early Pentecostal Theology," 117.

18. Hollenweger, "Two Extraordinary Pentecostal Ecumenists," 391.

It means that they did not engage in the larger academic disciplines of their day.

As early Renewalists did begin to reflect more intentionally on their theology, it often consisted of what might be called a "Bible doctrines" method which restated, organized and synthesized passages of Scripture to affirm various doctrines. Examples of these biblical scholars include Myer Pearlman and French Arrington. They used Scripture to prove every point and to create a theological system of what was important. They had a foundational belief in the truth, accuracy and centrality of the Bible. According to Christopher A. Stephenson, while Renewal academics has gone beyond a simplistic view of the Bible or using only the Bible for theology, the Bible is still central to both Renewal practice and theology and should maintain a central, if not primary, role for any Renewal theological approach.[19]

It was not until the 1960s that Renewalists in the United States began to pursue higher education and enter the academy.[20] The first generation of American Renewal scholars were mostly Pentecostal historians who attempted to tell the story of early Pentecostalism. Their historical narrative primarily ran through Charles Parham, William Seymour and Azusa Street.[21] Around the same time, in Europe, Hollenweger took a more global and critical approach in telling the story of early Pentecostalism.[22]

After these historians, the next wave of researchers consisted mostly of Biblical studies scholars like Roger Stronstad, John Christopher Thomas and Rick D. Moore.[23] At first many of them set out to "retrieve their own traditions and use early Pentecostal sources to develop 'critical constructive scholarship.'"[24] They went beyond the Bible doctrines method by engaging with biblical critical methods and the larger academy. Perhaps the greatest inciting incident to draw these biblical scholars into the larger academic discussion came in the early 1970s with James D. G. Dunn's work on Spirit baptism in Luke. Dunn challenged Renewal understandings and hermeneutics

---

19. Stephenson, *Types of Pentecostal Theology*, 11–27.

20. This entrance largely coincided with Pentecostals being able to go to college on the G. I. Bill in the late 1940s and early 1950s. They then worked their way into higher education and began doing academic work by the 1960s. Before WWII many Pentecostals were too poor to get a university education and the G. I. Bill finally afforded them the opportunity. This is also part of what led to the upward mobility of Pentecostals around the same time.

21. For examples of such histories, see Synan, *Holiness-Pentecostal Movement*; Robeck, *Azusa Street Mission and Revival*.

22. Hollenweger, *Pentecostals*.

23. See, for example, Stronstad, *Charismatic Theology of St Luke*; Thomas, *Footwashing in John 13*; Moore, *God Saves*.

24. Cartledge, "Can Theology Be 'Practical'?," 22.

helping to spur the beginnings of what we might call Renewal Studies. He caused Renewal scholars to begin looking outward and dialogue with the larger academic community. Dunn specifically challenges Roman Catholic and Pentecostal interpretations of Luke's Spirit baptism accounts in Acts.[25] His challenge is against what Stronstad later terms the "vocational view" of baptism in the Holy Spirit which focuses on commissioning and empowerment.[26] Dunn instead proposes an "initiation-conversion view" which holds the disciples in Acts are receiving the Holy Spirit at conversion and the empowerment motif is only secondary.[27]

Scholars like Stronstad responded to Dunn with their own works on Luke-Acts from a specifically Renewal perspective. He held to the "antecedent spiritual state motif" in which Luke reported the spiritual state of being righteous or being a believer and then only after this does the believer receive the Holy Spirit. Spirit baptism then, is an act that comes subsequent to salvation for empowerment, not initiation.[28] This controversy helped lead to the larger academic community engaging more with Renewal's histories and biblical interpretations.[29] These Renewal scholars still largely retrieved the Pentecostal tradition in their work. They focused on themes and issues from the first decade of Pentecostalism, but also began to engage the larger academy.

After a period of intense response to other theologians' work, a group of systematic theologians, such as Frank Macchia and Amos Yong, began to do more constructive work and form a Renewal theological approach.[30] They more fully developed their own biblical hermeneutics, theological categories and concerns within a larger academic context dialoguing with a broader range of ecumenical traditions. Renewal scholars began to take up issues beyond the scope of strictly "Pentecostal" issues and apply a Renewal hermeneutic to larger concerns such as soteriology, Christology, creation etc. At the same time, more scholars, such as those from the Hollenweger school and practical theologians like Mark J. Cartledge, begin to do inter-disciplinary work studying and applying social science principles

25. Dunn, *Baptism in the Holy Spirit*, 140.

26. Stronstad, *Charismatic Theology of St Luke*, 26.

27. Dunn, *Baptism in the Holy Spirit*, 54.

28. Stronstad, *Charismatic Theology of St Luke*, 64–80.

29. This should not be seen as the first time Renewalists engaged outside groups, this was done early on in response to other criticisms about glossolalia for instance, but it was largely in a pastoral context contained within early Pentecostal periodicals. This was one of the first times when Renewal scholars began to engage other academic work about Pentecostalism.

30. For example, see Macchia, *Baptized in the Spirit*; Yong, *Spirit-Word-Community*.

and methods to the history and theology of Renewal movements.[31] So as Renewal Scholars began to do their own constructive work what did it look like? It is to this question we now turn.[32]

A Renewal Methodology?

Renewal Studies is an extremely new field. While a field like Liberation Theology has years of refinement in its methodologies, definitions, scopes of inquiry and interactions with other disciplines, Renewal Studies is still defining these elements of an approach for itself. In the beginning, newer fields of inquiry largely adopt the methods and definitions of other fields and apply them to their own concerns. Only after time does a field begin to define these issues for itself and broaden its inquiry into other areas.

We are in a time where the idea of a Renewal method is rather confused. It is still being formulated and there is little consensus on what constitutes it or if there even should, or can be, a Renewal method. This is because what does exist as Renewal method and its brief history poses a number challenges to the historical understanding of method. First, Renewal method is not systematic or comprehensive and this is the very content of method if we are to rely on Lonergan's definition of method as a "normative pattern of recurrent and related operations yielding cumulative and progressive results."[33] Second, there was no formal education so that early Renewalists were not methodologically aware of or reflective on what they were doing. This means a lot of translation between early Renewal method and modern Renewal method if it is to stay true to the movement and its roots. Third, most Renewalists were informed by pre-critical interpretations and did not explicitly show method in their work. Fourth, only recently have Renewal theologians incorporated philosophical training. Before this, Renewal Theology functioned in a very limited scope and was not as well equipped to speak into all of life. Philosophy is interested in all things, and early Renewalists were not. Fifth, until recently, most Renewalists did not include theological developments from the wider Christian tradition. They were much more confessional and so were neither heavily exposed to, nor did they utilize or dialogue with, other methods.

---

31. For example, see Anderson, "Varieties, Taxonomies, and Definitions"; Cartledge, *Charismatic Glossolalia*.

32. Because of my own focus on systematic theology in this dissertation, we will largely focus on Renewal Theology from a systematic approach.

33. Lonergan, *Method in Theology*, 4.

Perhaps the greatest of these challenges for modern Renewal Theology continues to be how it will define itself over against other hermeneutics and methods. According to D. Lyle Dabney in his article "Saul's Armor," the problem of a Renewal Theology is one of Saul's armor. Modern Renewal Theology has done theology from within the constraints of other approaches and methods less conducive to Renewal. Because Renewal has not been forced to come to a place where their theological work and vocabulary needs to be understood by others, they have borrowed the language of other's, primarily Evangelicals. Often this language does not fit Renewal belief and experience and can even be anti-Renewal according to Dabney.[34] This lack of a strong self-identity among Renewal theologians often stems from the false notion that Renewalism is not a theological tradition. Having absorbed this false belief, Renewal theologians do not approach their history theologically, rather they approach it anthropologically, sociologically or historically.[35] For Dabney then, Renewal scholarship needs to shed these borrowed approaches and forge its own approach which he suggests should be built on its strong pneumatological foundation over against other theological approaches which start from the perspective of the Father or the Son.[36] This is not necessarily a retrieval approach which attempts to goes back to the first decade of Renewal. Instead, for Dabney it forges forward creating new categories, methods and approaches from a pneumatological perspective.[37]

Simon Chan formulates this problem differently. For Chan, Renewalists need to see their distinctives *within* the larger global and ecumenical theological tradition. According to Chan, not seeing their place within this larger context has led to a failure in traditioning in which the Pentecostal reality has not been communicated in all its fullness to a subsequent generation. This failure is what has kept the Renewal theological tradition shallow.[38]

Dabney and Chan represent two ends of the spectrum. One can find more of a middle with someone like Martin Mittlestadt who sees the

34. Dabney, "Saul's Armor," 121.

35. Dabney, "Saul's Armor," 126.

36. Dabney, "Saul's Armor," 129–30.

37. Mark J. Cartledge describes three standpoints in Renewal approaches to theology. The first is the retrieval approach which stays within Pentecostal confines seeing the heart of Renewal in the first decade following Hollenweger. Dabney is a retrievalist in the sense that he wants Renewalists to use specifically Renewal categories and approaches, but he does not necessarily see these in the first decade, but in Pneumatology which may or may not be found in that decade. The second standpoint is the Ecumenical into which Chan would fit. Cartledge's final standpoint is the empirical approach which he himself is representative of. See Cartledge, "Renewal Ecclesiology in Empirical Perspective," 5–25.

38. Chan, *Pentecostal Theology*, 19–23.

challenge as Renewal scholars of the past having been largely uncritical, pastoral or defensive and so lacking in constructive contributions.[39] They have stuck to the traditional topics of Renewal rather than interacting with the larger academy or other areas of theology like ethics, social justice or political theology. Mittlestadt wants Pentecostalism to be fully rooted within the tradition and the larger academic discussion, but to do so constructively and broadly. One way Mittlestadt suggests this happen is through Renewalists reclaiming the early Renewal canon within a canon of Luke–Acts and allowing this unique perspective to speak to larger theological issues. Such a canon within a canon can be somewhat problematic if taken to an extreme, but Mittlestadt's approach does not reject the rest of the canon. Rather it sees Luke–Acts as formative for a Renewal approach, much as Lutheran theology has found Paul formative.

According to these views, a Renewal approach needs to be genuinely Renewal, expressing its core distinctives, but doing so from within the larger Christian tradition. If we follow Chan, we will borrow more fully from other traditions. If we follow Dabney, we will develop our own language and topics of inquiry. I would propose there is room for multiple methods within Renewal Theology. What makes one's theology "Renewal" is not so much the methodological tools one employs, though these cannot be anti-Renewal, but the hermeneutic through which one approaches God, the world and the theological task. I would propose four primary emphases that define parameters for what we might call a Renewal hermeneutic drawn from Christopher A. Stephenson's *Types of Pentecostal Theology*: Scripture, spirituality, experience, and Pneumatology.[40] This list is of course incomplete, but these can be considered central and important for a possible Renewal hermeneutic and have been so for past Renewal theologians.[41]

The first area of a Renewal hermeneutic is the biblical dimension. Renewalists utilized a "Bible doctrines" method which restated, organized and synthesized passages of Scripture to affirm various doctrines. Examples of these biblical scholars include Myer Pearlman and French Arrington. They used Scripture to prove every point and create a theological system of what was important. These scholars had a foundational belief in the truth, accuracy and centrality of the Bible. While Renewal Studies has gone beyond a simplistic view of the Bible or only using the Bible for theology, the Bible

---

39. Mittlestadt, *Reading Luke-Acts*, 11–16.

40. Stephenson, *Types of Pentecostal Theology*, 8–9.

41. These four areas also overlap. Renewalists read Scripture through their experience, spiritual tradition and the Holy Spirit. Likewise, Scripture informs the other three, but they are also distinct enough that each should be treated here, and one could make the case each should be present in some way in a Renewal Theology.

is still central to both Renewal practice and theology. For instance, Amos Yong, a leading Renewal scholar, includes Scripture as central in his hermeneutic outlined in *Spirit-Word-Community*.[42] He also includes a section on Scripture in every chapter of his many forays into applying Pneumatology to other fields of study.[43] The biblical witness should be a, if not the, starting point for a Renewal theological approach. How one approaches Scripture may differ. One may attempt to utilize methods from the first decade of Renewal, read the Scriptures pneumatologically, or through a higher critical method. Usually however, it will in some way interact with these next three dimensions of spirituality, experience and Pneumatology.

A second dimension of a Renewal hermeneutic is spirituality. The seminal work on Pentecostal spirituality is Stephen Land's *Pentecostal Spirituality: A Passion for the Kingdom*. Land argues that theology and spirituality are inseparable. Spirituality is also holistic in that it includes orthodoxy, orthopraxy, and orthopathy.[44] Renewal method therefore needs to include Pentecostal practices, beliefs and affections as primary sources for theology. Land follows Hollenweger in seeing the heart of Pentecostalism as found in the spiritual practices and expressions of its first ten years.[45] These experiences lead to testimony, which lead to the formulation of doctrine, which leads to theologizing. This creates a cycle as our theologizing affects the experiences we have in the future, which then affects our testimonies, doctrines, and affections. It ends up being a kind of Renewal hermeneutical circle. Since this process starts historically, it starts in the experiences of people, though the process can really be entered from any point. Unfortunately, the Renewal spiritual tradition, as we will see, did not address poverty through a social action approach during its early years. Poverty, however was a reality of early Pentecostalism and the spiritual resources that helped these early, poor Pentecostals, such as focusing on healing and even *glossolalia*, have resources we will mine for a theology of poverty.

This idea of experience is the third dimension of a Renewal hermeneutic. Experience is similar to spirituality, but spirituality within Renewal is most often seen ecclesially in specific spiritual practices while the larger

---

42. Yong, *Spirit-Word-Community*, 245–73.

43. See, for instance, Yong, *In the Days of Caesar*. In this volume, Yong includes a section on Scripture in his methodology and addresses at least one passage of Scripture as a way into each of the political topics he explores.

44. Land, *Pentecostal Spirituality*, 37–42. We will look at more global approaches to Renewal Spirituality and poverty from Eldin Villafañe and Samuel Solivan in our next chapter on Pneumatology.

45. Land, *Pentecostal Spirituality*, 13. This spirituality can be found in its songs, prayers, sermons and writings of this first decade.

category of experience is broader and describes one's experience of the world as a whole. Peter Neumann in his work *Pentecostal Experience* holds that, for Renewalists, experience is an authoritative means by which God is known, therefore it holds epistemological value.[46] However, there is a challenge in reconciling experience in Renewalism with theological articulation. This is because once one has an experience they automatically interpret it, meaning that interpretation immediately affects the experience itself. One therefore has a Pentecostal experience most often with a Pentecostal interpretation already in mind.

Historically within Pentecostalism, according to Newman, there are two poles of possible interpretation concerning experience. The first pole says that this experience starts with the human agent. In this view, we immediately experience God as we have been enabled by the pouring out of the Holy Spirit. Methodologically, this means that experience is factual and reveals something true about God. It is primarily interpreted through testimonies of those experiences often using mystical language to denote that it is an experience of the divine.[47] The second pole says that experience starts with divine agency. Since all experience originates with God, it must be interpreted for humans because God is wholly other. Therefore, from the human perspective, experience is always mediated because it is always interpreted. Discernment then is key in this view and methodologically this discernment should come through interdisciplinary activity.[48]

Frank Macchia presents a middle approach in which experience is both immediate and mediated. To demonstrate this, Macchia uses the formative doctrine of Spirit baptism to show how it is punctiliar, but also comes through process.[49] For Macchia, you have the experience of Spirit baptism, but it also comes to encompass the entire salvation process. This aspect of experience is important because it demonstrates the need for a broader tradition to help one discern the meaning of one's experience. Here ecumenical and even interreligious dialogue, while Renewalists have been slow to participate in it, are necessary. This is why we have attempted to address such a broad range of approaches to poverty to help us discern what the Holy Spirit is doing among the poor. Spirituality and experience also put story, specifically of what God has done, at the center of theology. Many also suggest story should be at the center of responding to poverty. Therefore, we

---

46. Neumann, *Pentecostal Experience*, 117.

47. For a historical example of this pole, see Parham, "Everlasting Gospel," 31–44.

48. For a historical example of this second pole, see Seymour, "Doctrines and Discipline," 45–56.

49. Macchia, *Baptized in the Spirit*, 61–88.

have tried to keep stories of the poor at the fore of every chapter. If a theology of poverty does not arise from and affect the experience of the poor it is not a Renewal approach, nor is it a pneumatological approach.[50]

The pneumatological element is the fourth dimension of a Renewal hermeneutic. Amos Yong has been a forerunner in this area, particularly in his development of the pneumatological imagination in *Spirit-Word-Community*. Yong's argument is that a robustly theological hermeneutic is one that aims at interpreting the totality of human experience informed by faith.[51] Procedurally, he starts with pneumatic experience and therefore with Pneumatology, but, for Yong, Pneumatology means that everything is open for theological discussion. This is because the Holy Spirit is the foundational symbol of God's presence and agency in the world. The Holy Spirit therefore stands for everything—how we relate to one another, how we think and how we are. All dimensions of reality can therefore be understood pneumatologically through the categories of relationality (all reality and being is interrelated by the Spirit), rationality (Spirit is the source and communication of rationality in that it reveals the divine mind and provides intelligence, particularity and order) and dynamism (the Spirit transforms the way we relate to God and creation even in an eschatological way).[52] Yong therefore calls for a pneumatological imagination which observes and discerns reality through the Spirit as described above. Yong shows us why Pneumatology is central to a Renewal theological method. Though he expands the idea of what the Spirit entails beyond what some Pentecostals are comfortable with, he helpfully demonstrates how this dimension can truly be foundational for all theological inquiry. We will explore Pneumatology more fully in the next chapter as we agree with Yong that it can be a lens through which to view the entire world since the Spirit is God's agency in the world, particularly for our purposes, in urban poverty.

As we mentioned earlier, these elements do not compose a Renewal method, but rather a Renewal hermeneutic through which to view and approach the theological task. A number of various methods may be employed within these hermeneutical perspectives as long as they are not anti-Renewal. Elements will receive different emphases based on the work, but each will be present in some way through the lens with which the Renewal scholar approaches the theological task. Renewal hermeneutics necessarily clashes with traditional hermeneutical paradigms. The lenses provided by

---

50. I will deal with Yong and his Pneumatology more fully in our next chapter on Pneumatology.

51. Yong, *Spirit-Word-Community*, 6.

52. Yong, *Spirit-Word-Community*, 77.

more traditional hermeneutics do not provide the necessary tools for Renewalists to interpret their own experiences and values in experiencing the world. Renewal Theology, in contrast, proceeds as a particular hermeneutic along the dimensions of Scripture, spirituality, experience and particular emphases (e.g., eschatology, Spirit baptism) centered on the Holy Spirit and directed toward transformation. I would echo Dabney that Pneumatology, however, is really what drives the Renewal hermeneutic and makes the other three elements specifically Renewal. We will explore this assertion in our next chapter on Pneumatology.

Having looked briefly at the field of Renewal Studies and its lack of a specific method but rather a hermeneutic through which to view all of life, will now turn to Renewal Theology's theological and practical responses to poverty.

RENEWAL THEOLOGICAL RESPONSES TO URBAN POVERTY

While often praised for their evangelistic fervor, Renewalists have received strong critique for their lack of social concern.[53] Others, have rebutted this critique by showing that many Renewalists have been involved in various social welfare causes and some have even become involved in social action. Douglas Petersen helpfully delineates the difference between social welfare, which seeks to alleviate the needs of individuals, and social action, which seeks to remedy such injustice on a systemic level by "addressing the basic conditions, structures, or circumstances that are causing the needs."[54] While more Renewalists are getting involved in social action, few have probed into the theology underlying this social action. Such a theology would be helpful in continuing the growing trend of social action and providing resources for those already engaging social issues like urban poverty.

In this section, we will explore five Renewal figures who have made the greatest contributions to a Renewal Theology of social action and we will draw out the implications from their work for urban poverty. I have chosen Murray Dempster, Frank Macchia, Douglas Petersen, and Veli-Matti Kärkkäinen because they are the most representative of the few Renewal scholars who have proposed substantive themes that can be developed into a Renewal Theology of social action and, in turn, a Pneumatology of urban

---

53. For such critiques from Latin America, see Margolies, "Paradoxical Growth of Pentecostalism," 1–5; from Africa, see Wessels, "Charismatic Christian Congregations," 360–74; and from Asia, see Chan, "Asian Pentecostalism," 29–32.

54. Petersen, *Not by Might, Nor by Power*, 112.

poverty.⁵⁵ We will also look at Donald E. Miller and Tetsunao Yamamori's *Global Pentecostalism* as the most helpful exploration of how Renewal approaches poverty from an outsider's perspective. We will see that while a number of Renewal themes have been proposed as starting points, they are not enough for a fully developed theology of social action and better-developed themes are necessary.⁵⁶

Murray Dempster

One of the most prolific writers on the topic of Pentecostal social action is Murray Dempster, professor of social ethics at Southeastern University in Lakeland, Florida.⁵⁷ For Dempster, the largest obstacles to social action for Pentecostals have been their imminent eschatology and fervent evangelism focused on the salvation of the individual soul.⁵⁸ Both have overshadowed the need for larger social transformation and require response.

First, rather than only eschatological hope in the return of Jesus, Dempster holds that the coming of the Holy Spirit at Pentecost should "inspire and shape the mission of the church."⁵⁹ In making this connection between Pentecost and Parousia, Dempster is attempting to draw out the already-and-not-yet nature of the kingdom.⁶⁰ Connecting the future kingdom of Jesus's reign with that ushered in by the Holy Spirit at Pentecost "validates the eschatological significance of the church's work in social service and social action."⁶¹ Social action involves deeds that signify the

---

55. They are not the only scholars who have dealt with poverty and social action from a Renewal perspective, but they are either the most voluminous or make a unique contribution that we want to explore for our purposes of moving toward a Pneumatology of urban poverty. Hopefully each section will bear the burden of each scholar's inclusion. We are omitting here an important stream in Renewal, Latinos Eldin Villafañe and Samuel Solivan, who give theological resources for a theology of poverty, but we will deal with their pneumatological approach by contrasting it with LALT in the next chapter on Pneumatology.

56. While my goal is to provide a Pneumatology of urban poverty and see Renewal as a helpful lens through which to accomplish this, most of the academic theological work done by Renewal Scholars has been done specifically by Pentecostals. For that reasons, as I dialogue with these figures, I will use their own language of Pentecostal where appropriate rather than the more general term "Renewal."

57. Dempster has written at least five articles on the topic of social welfare and action, which far outweighs the one or two common to other Renewal scholars.

58. Dempster, "Eschatology, Spirit Baptism, and Inclusiveness," 115.

59. Dempster, "Christian Social Concern," 55.

60. Dempster, "Eschatology, Spirit Baptism, and Inclusiveness," 165.

61. Dempster, "Christian Social Concern," 54.

transformational nature of the in-breaking kingdom while also pointing to the future age of God's redemptive reign.[62] Dempster biblically demonstrates the link between Pentecost and Parousia by connecting the Acts 2 account of Pentecost with the kingdom mission and ministry of Jesus in the gospels that foreshadows the present-future kingdom he will establish at the Parousia.[63] This kingdom mission is characterized by a moral ethic that calls people to emulate God's character of love and holiness. Dempster also characterizes the kingdom by a prophetic ethic in which the church is called to live out God's character through addressing social issues of "the alien, gender, the poor, economic exploitation and the dignity of children."[64] This prophetic call is based on the church as the new covenant community sealed by the Holy Spirit. As the new community, the church is a "new social reality brought into existence and empowered for mission by the covenant making God of the Old and New Testaments."[65]

Second, Dempster sees theological resources in terms of Spirit baptism and the charisms. Spirit baptism, often seen as empowerment for global evangelism, is also the method through which the Holy Spirit empowers for social action.[66] Spirit baptism is also a sign of inclusion for all peoples in the in-breaking kingdom, excluding no one from the church's mission.[67] Similarly, the social implications of Jesus's healing miracles, one of the charisms, show us that evangelism and the spiritual gifts are not just spiritual in nature, but should have accompanying social implications.

While Dempster mentions the need to move beyond social concern for the individual into social action, he gives few theological resources for this move or for how it should be accomplished. He himself often leaves it on the level of the individual and does not apply his theories to communities and systems. He has laid out helpful building blocks for such a move, however, particularly in his connection of Pentecost with the future Parousia and the kingdom teachings of Jesus. The social vision portrayed in both Pentecost and Parousia reenvision the social order as one of justice and mutual care for the least of these. Dempster connects the two to overcome Pentecostalism's overemphasis on evangelization because of their strong eschatology. One thing he fails to do is connect the Holy Spirit with the

---

62. Dempster, "Christian Social Concern," 63.
63. Dempster, "Pentecostal Social Concern," 138–43.
64. Dempster, "Pentecostal Social Concern," 138.
65. Dempster, "Pentecostal Social Concern," 139.
66. Dempster, "Eschatology, Spirit Baptism, and Inclusiveness," 182.
67. Dempster, "Eschatology, Spirit Baptism, and Inclusiveness," 183.

eschatological vision. We are also left with the question why and how does one move beyond the individual to address the larger systems of injustice at work in world?

Frank Macchia

Having written one of the first Pentecostal theologies through a pneumatological lens, Frank Macchia has been a prominent voice in Pentecostal theology for the last two decades.[68] A lesser-known book is *Spirituality and Social Liberation* a revision of his doctoral thesis. Macchia uses Johann Blumhardt and his son Christoph, German Lutheran pietists of the nineteenth century, as examples of how groups with a more pietistic, inward focused spirituality can and do move toward social action.[69] Macchia indicates that this pietistic, inward focus is also the heritage of modern Evangelicalism and Pentecostalism, both of which have difficulty integrating the spiritual and the social. If either group is to move beyond a gospel that is insufficiently concerned with social liberation they will need "help from those who have had greater success integrating the spiritual and social dimensions of Christian commitment."[70] Macchia proposes this can be found in two major themes from the Blumhardts's theology.

First, Johann Blumhardt emphasized Pentecost as the event in which the invisible realization of the kingdom of God broke in, meaning there is "liberation of the sick and oppressed" in the present, not just in the future Parousia.[71] Christoph Blumhardt extended this liberative healing to include the healing of social relationships not just physical bodies.[72] For Pentecostals who already see Pentecost as a key event and healing as central to the kingdom of God, Macchia encourages them to receive the critique of the Blumhardts and develop a Spirit-Christology that incorporates the healing of social relationships and not just individuals, particularly in light of Luke 4:18.[73]

A second theological resource for social action is the Blumhardt's focus on the divine-human relationship. For instance, Christoph Blumhardt envisions a much more intimate relationship between God's miraculous deeds and the human efforts God uses as signs and manifestations of the

---

68. See Macchia, *Baptized in the Spirit*.
69. Macchia, *Spirituality and Social Liberation*, 1–21.
70. Macchia, *Spirituality and Social Liberation*, 159.
71. Macchia, *Spirituality and Social Liberation*, 160.
72. Macchia, *Spirituality and Social Liberation*, 162.
73. Macchia, *Spirituality and Social Liberation*, 164. This will be part of our task in chapter 7.

coming kingdom.⁷⁴ Macchia uses this connection to assert that Pentecostals should not see the unexplained or what occurs without human instrumentation as the only avenues for the miraculous. Rather, they should also see the work of social action as the work of God and the resulting transformed lives and social structures as part of the miraculous in which God partners with humanity.⁷⁵

Macchia is helpful in providing an example of two people who have come to this conclusion from within a quietist tradition like Pentecostalism. These two emphases can serve as building blocks for developing a fuller understanding of eschatology and the divine-human relationship that supports Pentecostal social action. In particular, it broadens the idea of miraculous, supernatural involvement in the world to include, not just the traditional Renewal categories of salvation or healing, but the transformation that occurs through social action in the lives and community of the poor. In the end, however, the Blumhardts fall short of providing the theological resources for such a reconstruction. Unfortunately, Macchia himself does not address social action much in his following works. The work must be continued by others.

Douglas Petersen

A professor of world mission and intercultural studies at the classical Pentecostal Vanguard University in Costa Mesa, California, Douglas Petersen is also the one of the co-founders of Latin American Childcare, a Pentecostal organization that advocates for and provides children's education in Latin America among the urban poor. His goal in his book, *Not by Might, Nor by Power,* is to develop a social ethic that supports a holistic mission.⁷⁶ He moves toward this goal by providing a number of examples, first of social welfare programs that help to alleviate the needs of people. Second, he gives examples of community-based social action that seeks to reform the basic conditions, structures or circumstances that are causing these needs.

Petersen begins by denying the common accusation that Pentecostalism generates a "passive, otherworldly attitude."⁷⁷ Rather, Pentecostalism challenges its followers to engage in their "own kind of social struggle" within their own context, often implicitly.⁷⁸ For instance, upon conver-

---

74. Macchia, *Spirituality and Social Liberation*, 112.
75. Macchia, *Spirituality and Social Liberation*, 166.
76. Petersen, *Not by Might, Nor by Power*, 187.
77. Petersen, *Not by Might, Nor by Power*, 3.
78. Petersen, *Not by Might, Nor by Power*, 4.

sion and incorporation into a "new vibrant community," new Pentecostals experience a validation of self-worth that has social implications for both the individual and the community.[79] Petersen gives the example that this self-worth can create a "more egalitarian system" in which women are put into leadership, empowered to have better marriages, and are helped to foil machismo attitudes and create a better economic reality for themselves and their families.[80] Most of the assistance that Pentecostal churches provide in Latin America takes place within the church as an alternative way of life.[81]

These Latin American Pentecostal churches also create programs that provide assistance for families in need. They form homes for mothers and children that provide "food, housing, education and love."[82] Whole denominations have created social programs and educational structures within various countries. Petersen uses the example of Latin America Childcare (LACC), of which he is the director, to show the wide impact such an organization can have. LACC seeks to implement a strategy "designed to bring structural change over the long term" and is therefore a great example of Pentecostal social action addressing urban poverty through education.[83] Petersen holds that educating children is perhaps LACC's greatest possible contribution as it shapes those who will be "recreators of social structures" and will then influence the future of their nations.[84] Still, in typical Pentecostal fashion, LACC involves local congregations through sponsoring schools in their immediate area.[85] They would fit Slessarev-Jamir's definition of prophetic activism. Based on LACC's successful work, Petersen proposes Pentecostals continue with the creation of new institutions that help promote social justice among the poor rather than reform present institutions.[86]

Despite these actions, Petersen holds that "little effort has been devoted to the formulation of Pentecostal social doctrine."[87] Still, he believes that there is an inherent agenda of social action in Pentecostalism waiting to be "identified, made explicit, and activated."[88] Petersen even proposes a

---

79. Petersen, *Not by Might, Nor by Power*, 35–40.
80. Petersen, *Not by Might, Nor by Power*, 144–46.
81. Petersen, *Not by Might, Nor by Power*, 119.
82. Petersen, *Not by Might, Nor by Power*, 137.
83. Petersen, *Not by Might, Nor by Power*, 148.
84. Petersen, *Not by Might, Nor by Power*, 167.
85. Petersen, *Not by Might, Nor by Power*, 159.
86. Petersen, *Not by Might, Nor by Power*, 201.
87. Petersen, *Not by Might, Nor by Power*, 186.
88. Petersen, *Not by Might, Nor by Power*, 9.

methodology for such a development. In dialogue with Liberation theologian Juan Luis Segundo's *Liberation of Theology*, he proposes a hermeneutical circle that starts with reflection on Pentecostal experience and intentions before moving to a social doctrine that finally leads to pastoral action.[89] This hermeneutic is always interacting with the biblical text given Pentecostals' commitment to the Bible while also drawing from the concrete historical reality of Latin America.[90]

Petersen gives numerous examples of Pentecostals engaging in social welfare in Latin America and rightly makes the call for them to expand into more explicit forms of social action like that modeled by LACC. What he adds theologically is a framework through which to develop such social action, his appropriation of the hermeneutical circle in dialogue with LALT. We have already explored how this is a useful resource for a theology of poverty and I believe it can also be applied to organizations and theology in the United States as we have seen in BLT. Petersen also proposes Spirit baptism as an interpretive theological structure through which to support the practice of social action for Pentecostals, but puts it on future scholars to develop.[91] One weakness of the model Petersen puts forth through his case study on LACC is that it has a long end-game and he does not address how to fix the social structures now or once these children become adults and presumably gain power to address these structures. These are gaps we will hopefully fill in our final chapter.

Veli-Matti Kärkkäinen

Our final Pentecostal scholar, Veli-Matti Kärkkäinen, professor of systematic theology at Fuller Theological Seminary in Pasadena, California, addresses the issue of Pentecostalism and social justice and action in two articles, "Are Pentecostals Oblivious to Social Justice?"[92] and "Spirituality as a Resource for Social Justice: Reflections for the Roman Catholic-Pentecostal Dialogue."[93] In these articles, he holds that Pentecostalism's focus on evangelization has never been to the exclusion of social concern. Drawing on

---

89. Petersen, *Not by Might, Nor by Power*, 188–92. Petersen is in dialogue with Segundo, *Liberation of Theology*, 9.

90. Petersen, *Not by Might, Nor by Power*, 200–208.

91. Petersen, *Not by Might, Nor by Power*, 203.

92. Kärkkäinen, "Are Pentecostals Oblivious to Social Justice?," 417–31. While Kärkkäinen talks primarily about social justice, his concepts are broader and can also be applied to social action among the urban poor.

93. Kärkkäinen, "Spirituality as a Resource," 83–96.

Miroslav Volf, Kärkkäinen proposes a theology of embrace and spirituality as resources for social justice and action.

Kärkkäinen begins by pointing out that eschatology has been a mixed bag. For many Pentecostals, a belief in the imminent Parousia has blurred the meaning of social improvement since this world will simply fade away.[94] For other Pentecostals, however, an imminent eschatology has brought optimism about their social work.[95] According to Kärkkäinen, Pentecostals believe that empowerment by the Spirit of God equips them to respond in the midst of human suffering and bring healing.[96] One example of such a response is race. During the beginning of the Pentecostal movement in the early twentieth century, Pentecostals were one of the few groups that practiced racial integration in the church bringing healing along ethnic lines. Drawing on this history and Volf, Kärkkäinen proposes a theology of embrace modeled on the embrace of the Trinity rather than a theology of exclusion.[97] Such a Trinitarian theology would move Pentecostals toward engaging the other in both social justice and action. For Kärkkäinen, living out community in Trinitarian-like *koinonia* as Pentecostals did by welcoming all races, has been a major resource for challenging racial and economic inequalities in the past and present. It functions as a social alternative that protests against oppressive structures in its inclusion of all people.[98] A comprehensive Trinitarian theology also emphasizes a life in the Holy Spirit which energizes Christians to "engage in evangelization and to work for justice in society."[99] People transformed by the Holy Spirit are "compelled to transform the world in light of the in-breaking kingdom of God."[100]

Kärkkäinen also puts Pentecostal spirituality into dialogue with Roman Catholic spirituality. Roman Catholic spirituality is the "power source" for its social action and Kärkkäinen wants Pentecostals to view their spirituality similarly.[101] Drawing on the Lord's Prayer, he suggests the practice of daily prayer for the coming of the kingdom as one of the most "basic ways

---

94. Kärkkäinen, "Are Pentecostals Oblivious to Social Justice?," 419.
95. Kärkkäinen, "Are Pentecostals Oblivious to Social Justice?," 419.
96. Kärkkäinen, "Are Pentecostals Oblivious to Social Justice?," 419–20.
97. Kärkkäinen, "Are Pentecostals Oblivious to Social Justice?," 420. Miroslav Volf grew up as the son of a Pentecostal minister and in the 1980s took part in the Roman Catholic/Pentecostal dialogue from the Pentecostal perspective. He does not currently identify himself as a Renewalist in his present works but does often deal with Renewal oriented topics.
98. Kärkkäinen, "Are Pentecostals Oblivious to Social Justice?," 424.
99. Kärkkäinen, "Are Pentecostals Oblivious to Social Justice?," 423.
100. Kärkkäinen, "Are Pentecostals Oblivious to Social Justice?," 423.
101. Kärkkäinen, "Spirituality as a Resource," 84.

in which Pentecostals can cooperate to better the world."[102] Glossolalia also serves as a prayer function that can equip one for service and witness in social action. In the same way, Kärkkäinen proposes that all the charisms can be employed for the sake of such work because they point toward the new creation and the redemption to come.[103]

Kärkkäinen's work gives strong themes through which Renewal can address poverty. In particular, his connection between Pentecost, Spirit baptism, and the coming of the kingdom needs to be fleshed out more fully. These three themes are also intimately connected with eschatology and the Pentecostal view of evangelism, both of which have been seen as hindrances to social action.[104] In addition, we might connect Kärkkäinen's discussion of the charisms with his discussion of *koinonia* and embrace, drawing out how the charisms might be a resource for a larger embracing of humanity, particularly the marginalized and the poor. Finally, Kärkkäinen shows us the necessity of dialogue with another tradition that has a similar emphasis on the Holy Spirit, in this case Roman Catholicism, to uncover resources toward a Pentecostal social action.[105] Petersen made a similar move bringing in the hermeneutical circle from LALT. We will further this dialogue in a specific dialogue between LALT spirituality and Renewal spirituality in our next chapter on Pneumatology.

Donald E. Miller and Tetsunao Yamamori

Finally, we turn to Miller and Yamamori, professors of religion at the University of Southern California, who have written the most comprehensive and recent volume on Renewal social action. They are not writing as Renewalists, but as Protestants sympathetic to the Renewal movement. Their focus is on a group they term progressive Pentecostals, reminiscent of the moniker "progressive Evangelicals" from our third chapter. They define these progressive churches as ones with "active social ministries."[106] This is a minority that is ever growing within Pentecostalism. For the most part, Miller and Yamamori's study is phenomenological, focusing on the practical

---

102. Kärkkäinen, "Are Pentecostals Oblivious to Social Justice?," 89.

103. Kärkkäinen, "Are Pentecostals Oblivious to Social Justice?," 93–94.

104. Kärkkäinen, "Are Pentecostals Oblivious to Social Justice?," 419.

105. One can find most of Kärkkäinen's dialogue with Roman Catholicism in his two volumes on the Roman Catholic-Pentecostal dialogue. The second volume, which covers evangelization, includes the section on social action and poverty. See Kärkkäinen, *Spiritus Ubi Vult Spirat*; *Ad Ultimum Terrae*.

106. Miller and Yamamori, *Global Pentecostalism*, 2.

responses of Renewalists to poverty, but they also do some theologizing about what drives these progressives toward social action.

According to the authors, there is both implicit and explicit social ministry carried out in Pentecostal circles around the world.[107] These Pentecostals' context of poverty dictates a holistic ministry that deals with physical, social, psychological and spiritual needs.[108]

Implicitly, Pentecostal theology and practice empower individuals by supporting them with a "vibrant community of believers."[109] This community functions as an extended family of support for the upward social mobility of its members. For instance, progressive Pentecostal's theology of empowerment deals with the issue of self-worth.[110] Also, a strong emphasis on the priesthood of all believers, because of the Holy Spirit's empowerment of each individual, results in more egalitarian social structures and confidence to step out of one's normal role.[111] The new progressive Pentecostals also act explicitly for social change. Miller and Yamamori tell story after story of work done in the areas of mercy ministries, emergency services, education, counseling services, medical assistance, and the arts.[112] While most of these ministries focus on the social welfare of the individual, there are an increasing number of churches exploring development-oriented social ministries focused on economic development, policy change, community organizing and partnership with non-governmental organizations.[113]

In the end, the authors find these groups can make a positive impact on the problems facing our world.[114] One important move Miller and Yamamori make is the observation that "the single most important element that empowers progressive Pentecostals is . . . their experience of the Spirit in moments of worship."[115] The way in which worship affects social action has rarely been discussed and is an area of possible development. The authors also charge Pentecostals with a major challenge, questioning whether Pentecostals can creatively incorporate ideas from other Christian traditions without losing the fire that drives their compassion.[116] While Miller and

---

107. Miller and Yamamori, *Global Pentecostalism*, 225–34.
108. Miller and Yamamori, *Global Pentecostalism*, 12, 41–42.
109. Miller and Yamamori, *Global Pentecostalism*, 169.
110. Miller and Yamamori, *Global Pentecostalism*, 169.
111. Miller and Yamamori, *Global Pentecostalism*, 179.
112. Miller and Yamamori, *Global Pentecostalism*, 42.
113. Miller and Yamamori, *Global Pentecostalism*, 48.
114. Miller and Yamamori, *Global Pentecostalism*, 221.
115. Miller and Yamamori, *Global Pentecostalism*, 221.
116. Miller and Yamamori, *Global Pentecostalism*, 67.

Yamamori's work is primarily focused on global Pentecostalism, there are an increasing number of examples of progressive Pentecostals in the United States and their theology is equally applicable to poverty in this context.

Evaluation

We have shown numerous themes proposed by Pentecostals toward a theology of social action and how they should be applied to poverty. At the forefront of these proposals has been a unique perspective on the kingdom of God, which serves as an umbrella for various distinctly Pentecostal views. We saw Dempster and Macchia connect the kingdom not only with the Parousia but also with Pentecost meaning that kingdom activities that seek the betterment of humanity, like social action, are necessary for the here-and-now. The baptism of the Spirit, which continues the pouring out of the Holy Spirit from the day of Pentecost forward, is the impetus for the kingdom in the life of the individual and the church. This pouring out of the Holy Spirit is both the sign and the actualization of the reign of God. The continuing work of the Holy Spirit in the church and the individual is the means by which Pentecostals live out the kingdom for both individualistic and social salvation.

In moving Pentecostals from the individual to the social, the Pentecostal distinctive of healing is central. Macchia pointed to the healing of social relationships in light of Luke 4 as central to God's reign. Miller and Yamamori showed how even physical and spiritual healing in the individual serves to reincorporate the person as a full member and participant of society through removing the stigma of disability and giving the physical ability to work and earn an income. Kärkkäinen demonstrated that the healing of relationships and bodies also points toward the egalitarian nature of the kingdom that has been present throughout much of the Pentecostal movement. So then, every human's worth is validated because of the innate presence of the image of God in each person. The availability for the indwelling of the Holy Spirit in every person, regardless of race, gender, or socioeconomic status, points to the nature of the community of God formed in the kingdom. Both Petersen and Miller and Yamamori showed the function of this vibrant alternative community as a form of social action among the poor. Kärkkäinen spoke of this kingdom community as *koinonia* based on the relationship of the Trinity. This idea of *koinonia* also extends to his proposed theology of embrace, which reaches out to the other in the form of social justice and action.

Finally, we have seen most scholars begin dialogue with another Christian tradition. Macchia dialogues with pietism, Petersen with Liberation Theology and Kärkkäinen with Roman Catholicism. Miller and Yamamori also challenge Pentecostals to begin to incorporate ideas from more institutionally oriented movements. Renewal Theology has some resources, but it will require help from others, those we have already explored, on how to develop these new resources and put them into action. We will now look at the practical responses to poverty in Renewal Theology before offering some final reflections on this chapter.

RENEWAL PRACTICAL RESPONSES TO URBAN POVERTY

Renewal social engagement has been a mixed bag particularly in the United States, but this section attempts to demonstrate that Renewal churches and theology have not been wholly quietistic in the area of social action and urban poverty. The following will outline the responses to social issues, both good and sometimes bad, to social issues of a number of Renewal churches, first in the United States, then in Latin America.[117] These examples weigh heavily toward the charismatic side of Renewal because Charismatics have been the most engaged socially. Charismatic Christianity in the United States involved members (often led by pastors) of mainline denominations having Renewal experiences and continuing to pursue Renewal Christianity and its experiential and pneumatological emphases while staying in their own denominations.[118] They inherited their denominations' heritages of social action. This tradition may be part of the explanation that has led to the heightened involvement of Charismatics over against Pentecostals in

---

117. While there has also been social action among Renewalists in Asia and Africa, we have limited space and the Renewal movement has been most influential in Latin American. For some examples on Asian Renewal and social action, see Miller and Yamamori, *Global Pentecostalism*, 121–28. For African examples, see note 151 on page 128.

118. For instance, the Episcopal Charismatic movement began with Dennis Bennett and his church in Van Nuys, CA, and then his church in Seattle, WA. Pioneering pastors can be identified in numerous other denominations such as Harold Bresden and Larry Christenson in the Lutheran Church, Brick Bradford in the Presbyterian Church or Gerald Derstine in the Mennonite Church. These pastors had Pentecostal experiences through various means, which often included Spirit baptism and glossolalia. Rather than joining classical Pentecostal denominations, they chose to stay within their denominations, and the renewal often spread through them to other pastors and churches. See Bennett, *Nine O'clock in the Morning*, 1–30; Synan, *Century of the Holy Spirit*, 151–53.

social action.[119] On the other hand, this legacy also created a heightened expectation for these Charismatics to engage in social action and greater criticism when they did not. From all accounts, such social action was not present in the early iterations of the movement and the ensuing criticism was particularly biting in North America. In many ways, it created two camps within many denominations; one charismatically minded camp and another socially minded camp. Beyond social action among Renewalists in the United States, we are also including a section on Renewal social action in Latin America because of the global nature of Renewal.[120]

Renewal Social Action in the United States

One response of Renewal movements to criticism of quietism has been to defend their contribution to the present social movement as essential even if different. For instance, Dan Danielson held that Renewalists defensively responded by showing the place that worship and prayer have in social justice.[121] He points out that many in the social justice movement have found the need for worship and prayer in their difficult work. Rather than starting by focusing outward, he holds that Renewalists begin with prayer and community and then grow outward "as the Lord leads them."[122] Clark Pinnock adds to this by calling the "radical Christians" in the social movement to be "radically renewed" so that their movement does not die out for lack of spiritual power.[123] These Renewalists seemed willing to dialogue with more socially minded people in their denominations, but they often appeared unwilling to do it at the cost of the increased prayer, worship and use of

---

119. Some trace the reasons early Pentecostals were not involved in social action to their own poverty, but also assert that once they experience upward social mobility they began to become more socially engaged. See Wolfgang Vondey's chapter on "Social Engagement and Triumphalism" in Vondey, *Pentecostalism*, 89–110.

120. Renewal is certainly a global movement. According to the Pew Research Center, in December 2011 there were approximately 584 million Renewalists in the world (8.5 percent of the global population and 26.7 percent of Christianity). According to Todd M. Johnson's research, there were 76 million Renewalists in the United States in 2010, meaning approximately 87 percent of Renewalists live outside the United States. So, to get a representative picture of Renewal practices, we in many ways need to look globally while not forgetting or applying what we learn to the United States. Most research on Renewal social action has also focused on the global movement. See Pew Forum on Religion and Public Life, "Global Christianity"; Johnson, "Global Demographics," 479–83.

121. Danielson, "Charismatic Renewal and Social Concern," 24.

122. Danielson, "Charismatic Renewal and Social Concern," 25.

123. Pinnock, "Charismatic Renewal for the Radical Church," 19.

the charisms that were a hallmark of the movement. Rather, Cardinal Léon Suenens points out that the Holy Spirit and the Spirit's gifts are needed "not only for (one's) personal spiritual life, but so that he may contribute to the healing of society's ills."[124] Even though most Renewalists did not appear to be participating in social action, many still saw it as important enough to dialogue, and they saw the interior renewal they were bringing to the church as a needed contribution to the social movement.

A second response was to defend the distinctives of Renewal as not just support, but as another, possibly more effective, form of social action. Ralph Martin, one of the leaders of the Roman Catholic Charismatic Renewal gave an interview with the *Post American*, the magazine of Sojourners edited by Jim Wallis discussed in chapter 3.[125] In the interview, Martin asserts that the "basis of anything happening in Christianity needs to be a fully healthy local church. . . . A community lifestyle and the breaking out of the power of God is the basis of Christian mission."[126] For Martin, building up the charismatic community of God, functioning in the fullness of the gifts is the best hope the world has of true social change. Larry Christenson, in his book, *A Charismatic Approach to Social Action*, agrees with Martin. The best way to change the structures of society, according to Christenson, is by changing the individuals who comprise those structures and building new, alternative structures altogether.[127] In the mind of many Renewalists, the battle is not primarily fought through political action or even in the physical realm, but through spiritual realities. Hence, prayer and evangelism become the most effective tools of social action. Most Renewalists do not want to deny the need for further engaging in traditional forms of social justice but want to locate the primacy of activity in these more "traditional" functions of the church.

One modern example of this different approach to social action is the Charismatic prayer movement exemplified by the International House of Prayer (IHOP) in Kansas City, Missouri. IHOP also has many offshoot prayer centers around the country and the globe. Part of the organization's vision is "offering Jesus unremitting adoration and taking a stand in prayer for the manifestation of God's justice in every realm of life."[128] They commonly describe the work they do as 24/7 prayer and 24/7 acts of justice.

---

124. Suenens and Câmara, *Charismatic Renewal and Social Action*, 38.

125. Sojourners is more firmly Evangelical though they were very open to Renewal and had members participate in Renewal movements during its early years.

126. Martin, "Interview with Ralph Martin," 12.

127. Christenson, *Charismatic Approach to Social Action*, 39, 70–74.

128. "About the International House of Prayer."

Stuart Greaves, one of the leaders of the movement, has criticized the social action movement for not being christocentric enough and for overlooking the importance of the charisms, prayer, worship, and evangelism as the most powerful tools of social action.[129] He has some harsh criticisms of what he calls the "false justice movement" which focuses on social sin at the expense of personal sin. He includes a number of stories in which IHOP has seen their prayers for justice answered in other places of the globe—for human trafficking in Cambodia for instance—at the exact time they were praying.[130] Interestingly, however, he does not include any examples of works of justice they themselves carry out. Greaves seems to fail to see that it still takes actual people doing actual work on the ground to bring about justice, even if prayer is an engine behind the event.

IHOP illustrates the emphasis of the Renewal movement in the United States on alternative modes of accomplishing justice. Early on, the emphasis appeared to be on spreading the distinctives of this new movement throughout their respective churches rather than being engaged in social action. Examples are not absent, however. Donald Dayton mentions the Jesus Movement as a group who engaged in countercultural activities and provided a "major critique of the middle-class church life" by providing clothes, housing and food for the poor.[131] He also mentioned the Sojourners movement as an Evangelical group that was already doing social action and then became more charismatic. Dayton and Nan Pagano also separately mention the work done by Graham Pulkingham out of Church of the Redeemer, a Charismatic Episcopal church in Houston, TX. Pulkingham created educational programs, after school activities, and other initiatives that sought the transformation of the poor in the community.[132] While the actual examples are rare, there have been Renewalists doing what might be called "traditional social action" in the United States. Some critics consider these actions to be "micro-charity" focused on individuals rather than "macro-charity" focused on groups and systems and call for more macro-charity, however.[133] Most Charismatics are engaging in alternative methods that see the primary loci of social transformation occurring in the individual and

---

129. Greaves, *False Justice*, 27.
130. Greaves, *False Justice*, 83–84.
131. Dayton, "Pentecostal/Charismatic Renewal," 11.
132. Dayton, "Pentecostal/Charismatic Renewal," 12. See Pagano, "Charismatic Social Action," 27.
133. Danielson, "Charismatic Renewal and Social Concern," 25.

the spiritual realm.[134] As we will see, however, Renewalists on other continents have been much more explicitly involved in social action.

Latin American Renewal Social Action

Much like with the United States, we can be certain that the various Charismatic movements' parenting denominations in Latin America have certainly had an influence on its participation in social action. Two other influences deserve mention before we attempt to paint a brief picture of the fact that, despite criticisms, social action is occurring in Renewal churches throughout Latin America. First, we should mention the socioeconomic setting of Latin America. Due to pervasive poverty, corruption, and ineffective social programs in many of these countries, the need for social justice and systemic action is more readily visible. Churches and their parishioners are faced with these realities daily, so much so that they are almost forced to deal with them. This may help in explaining the heightened social action among Renewalists in Latin America, though they are still criticized for an escapist attitude at times.[135]

These socioeconomic and sociopolitical realities led to a number of responses one of which is our second influence, Ecclesial Base Communities (CEBs). In many ways, these communities had their origins within the Roman Catholic action groups that arose earlier in the century and brought "more than two million laypeople into more intense church life through Bible study, prayer, and community action."[136] CEBs were also strongly influenced by Liberation Theology, which was also strongly active in social action. While we may not be able to draw direct links between CEBs and the Renewal communities and prayer groups that equally pervade Latin America, there are a number of similarities including the small group nature, the empowerment of lay people, and a strong influence on the church as a whole. It would be hard to imagine, given the influence of CEBs, that their social activism did not have some influence, positively or negatively, on the social engagement of Renewalists, particularly within the Catholic Charismatic Renewal.

---

134. The transformation of the individual is so embedded in Renewal discourse that is very hard to dislodge, especially when it is bolstered by conservative political views. This is part of why we have brought in a number of voices from ecumenical perspectives that focus more on the transformation of the community. See our discussion on ecumenical perspectives in chapter 4.

135. Suenens and Câmara, *Charismatic Renewal and Social Action*, 29.

136. Cleary, *Rise of Charismatic Catholicism*, 13–14.

Having briefly mentioned some of the history and influences of the Renewal movement in Latin America, we will now mention some of the most significant Renewal groups engaging in social action among the poor.[137] We will give examples from three of the countries where the Charismatic movement has made the greatest impact: Brazil, Argentina and Chile.

One way that Renewalists have been involved in Brazil is through neighborhood associations, a common method of social action in the country. These associations represent a local form of social action, but do important social work nonetheless. They often help to bring positive change to local communities and the neediest families in them through cooperative action. According to John Burdick, Renewalists are once again criticized for not being involved, though it is not due to the commonly cited escapism or hyper-spirituality.[138] Rather, he considers the social marginalization of Renewal movements by those who tend to dominate the associations as the primary reason. When Renewalists are involved, and when they comprise the leadership, they have been respected and seen as doing as good a job or better than their counterparts.[139]

Brazilian Renewalists are often more politically involved than most of their Renewal counterparts in other countries. Renewalists in Brazil have been avid supporters of various political candidates. Second generation Renewalists have even created their own political parties and run for office themselves.[140] The manner in which Roman Catholic Charismatics like Father Marcelo Rossi and the Universal Church utilize media to spread the message of their movements also helps to mobilize these groups as effective in the political realm. Spiritual warfare has been a principal component of the language used in this political action. Such language pits Charismatic and Evangelical politicians against their opponents who are often seen as tools of the devil.[141] Their social action is often couched in the language of spiritual warfare or exorcism with the goal to "free people from spiritual oppressions such as hunger, unemployment, inflation, corruption, organized

---

137. This treatment is by no means exhaustive. We could also mention groups like AJUSCO, led by Father Navarro in Mexico City, which turned the parish into a renewal and evangelization center, and whose "social participation has made a strong impression all over México." See Saracco, "Charismatic Renewal and Social Change," 17. We could also talk about the social action done among teens in Caracas, Venezuela, mentioned in Miller and Yamamori as two of many more examples. See Miller and Yamamori, *Global Pentecostalism*, 84–87.

138. Burdick, "Struggling Against the Devil," 22.

139. Burdick, "Struggling Against the Devil," 26.

140. Cleary, *Rise of Charismatic Catholicism*, 123–26.

141. Freston, "Charismatic Evangelicals in Latin America," 192.

crime."[142] While it may be said that Renewal social action in Brazil may take different tones and forms, it is nonetheless a present and important part of the movement.[143]

Argentina contains one of the largest Renewal communities in Latin America. The movement there has been so impressive that a number of Argentine evangelists, such as Claudio Freidzon and Carlos Annacondia, have become internationally renowned.[144] Argentina has not only led the way in spiritual revolution, but also in social revolution for Renewalists. The Catholic Charismatic movement, for instance, has effectively collaborated with orphanages and homes for foster children to provide increased care from hygiene to education. They have been active in helping during social emergencies such as floods, providing housing and food for evacuees. Norberto Saracco estimates that 50 percent of the movement's tithes go to help the needy.[145] The activity of Catholic Charismatics is not just through the church, but also through participation in social and neighborhood organizations, an even greater mark of dynamic social action.

Miller and Yamamori tell of a Charismatic Baptist church they researched that was completely rethinking their approach to social outreach. They were bucking the perceived trend of Renewal to focus on social action through the individual, what we have called "micro-charity," and focus more on economic development rather than individual social assistance.[146] Another church, Church of the Open Door in Buenos Aires, may foreshadow the future of the Renewal movement in Latin America and globally. The church has over three hundred fifty youth and young adults that participate weekly in twenty different service activities that include giving soup to the homeless, visiting the elderly, and taking mental patients on outings.[147] One of their most well-known ministries that has garnered attention around Argentina involves a group going into jails and helping mentally ill inmates. This may not exactly be fighting for prison reform on a political level, but it is recognized throughout the prison system as the beginning of a larger societal reform because of the individual lives being changed. This is what much Renewal social action entails.

142. Freston, "Charismatic Evangelicals in Latin America," 193.

143. This spiritual warfare language, while characteristic of Renewal movements, is probably more harmful that it is helpful as it can demonize the other and remove any possibility of common ground or collaboration with the poor or other movements that are demonized.

144. Synan, *Century of the Holy Spirit*, 318–19.

145. Saracco, "Charismatic Renewal and Social Change," 18.

146. Miller and Yamamori, *Global Pentecostalism*, 48.

147. Miller and Yamamori, *Global Pentecostalism*, 51.

Latin American social action has not always been glamorous, however. There have been many that neglected the poor and focused only on spiritual matters and this is where much of the criticism has been garnered. Another example, often considered negative, is the political activity of Renewal churches in Chile. Many of these churches joined in what was called the *Consejo de Pastores* (Council of Churches). They unilaterally supported the Pinochet regime known to have committed horrendous crimes against humanity.[148] This group, while trying to speak on behalf of all Christians, was eventually opposed by a number of Evangelical churches that opposed Pinochet's policies that exploited the poor and weak of Chile.[149] So while, Chilean Renewalists became involved in politics during the Pinochet regime, it was often seen to be involvement on the wrong side of the poor. Kamsteeg does point out that these were primarily pastors that gave this support to Pinochet and many church members never became active Pinochet supporters.[150]

As we said previously, the picture of Renewal Christianity in Latin America and their work among the poor is a complex one. So much so that merely criticizing it as quietist or escapist is too simple. Rather, there is an array of Renewal churches, in different nations and cultures, many of which are highly engaged in social action.

Evaluation

We have demonstrated throughout this section the complex nature of social action among Renewal churches in the Americas.[151] While some of the criticism that has been leveled against Renewalists for escapism and quietism is warranted, this cannot be said of the movement as a whole. Sometimes this social action does not look like "traditional" social action and this may be the source of misunderstanding. Still, other Renewalists have engaged

148. Kamsteeg, "Pentecostalism and Political Awakening," 191.
149. Kamsteeg, "Pentecostalism and Political Awakening," 188.
150. Kamsteeg, "Pentecostalism and Political Awakening," 194.
151. There has also been social action among the poor among Renewalists on other continents such as Africa. Cephas Omenyo, for instance, tells us that even though Ghana's Renewal churches did not emphasize social services early on because of being overly concerned with sacred-spiritual matters, things changed with the formation of The Pentecostal Social Services (PENTOS) in 1980. This organization has mobilized Renewal churches to take ownership of local projects that provide social care such as hospitals and orphanages. As another example, Miller and Yamamori tell of Florence Muindi, a Renewal believer in Ethiopia who after training a group of health evangelists has seen substantial improvement in the healthcare of children in their local community and moved toward a community organizing development program. See Omenyo, "Comparative Analysis," 16–17; Miller and Yamamori, *Global Pentecostalism*, 39.

in forms that are more explicit. I believe that the youth movement in Argentine social action will soon find corollaries throughout the rest of the globe. It shows us that there is clearly something in Renewal Theology that has motivated at least some toward action among the poor. Perhaps there is a middle way that recognizes the place of spiritual practices such as prayer and worship in the work of justice but also see that more must be done for true justice to occur that helps the urban poor on every level.

CONCLUSION

Having briefly looked at the academic field of Renewal Studies, the hermeneutic through which it views all of life, and its theological and practical responses to urban poverty, I hope to reflect briefly on its promise as a dialogue partner for a theology of poverty, specifically a Pneumatology of urban poverty. First, we will reflect more fully on a Renewal approach that incorporates Scripture, experience, spirituality and Pneumatology and its promise for a response to urban poverty in light of the theological and practical responses above.

Scripture and experience are ideas that are already at the core of most of the theologies of poverty we have explored up to this point. Verses from the Mosaic law, to the prophetic tradition and the Jesus tradition are used to give direction for why and how poverty should be addressed. We have seen that these biblical texts have largely centered on theistic and christological arguments. Many of the same arguments are used within the little work that has been done on poverty and social justice from a Renewal perspective, but there is a hermeneutical turn as many of these passages traditionally used for social justice are interpreted through the pneumatic experience of Renewal. For instance, let us consider Luke 4:18–19, a passage already mentioned in numerous sections. Normally it is emphasized that Jesus is establishing his kingdom which includes caring for the poor and several other justice categories. A Renewalist reading through a pneumatic lens should notice, however, that Jesus begins this section by saying, "The Spirit of the Lord is on me because he has anointed me." The mechanism through which Jesus addresses poverty is through the anointing and empowerment of the Holy Spirit. Another common passage cited is Acts 2 and 4 describing the first community of Christians who shared everything in common so that no one had need. Not once was it mentioned in any of the literature above that this new community is only formed once the Holy Spirit fell at Pentecost so that this is not just a Jesus community, but a community formed, empowered and inspired by the Holy Spirit. This pneumatic reading of Scripture has huge implications for a theology of poverty.

Experience is another resource that is commonly used in the literature we have overviewed on poverty. Poverty itself is an experience, one that affects the whole person, physically, mentally, spiritually, emotionally and socioeconomically. Stories are told of these poverty experiences, much as we have done at the beginning of each chapter, to attempt and tell the true story of impoverishment that cannot be grasped by just numbers. Likewise, for poverty to be addressed, it cannot remain in the realm of abstract reasoning, but it must be addressed through experiences that transform the lives of individuals and communities. It must be addressed in the realm of the polis, our shared life together, whether that is in politics or civil society. Much like Scripture, however, Renewal Theology sees the Holy Spirit as at the center of our experience in the world. As Amos Yong explains in his pneumatological imagination, the Spirit is at the center of everything, how we live, how we relate to one another and how we relate to God.[152] The Spirit has been poured out on all flesh, including the poor, baptizing our experience of the world but also transforming us to see the divine as central and at work in everything including urban poverty.

The two areas of Renewal Theology that are even more unique are spirituality and Pneumatology. Rarely is spirituality seen as a resource for justice and poverty in the traditional sense. We will see in the next chapter that Jon Sobrino talks about spirituality and Liberation, but it is a very different understanding of spirituality than Renewal's understanding. It is a more "on the ground," praxis-oriented spirituality that is lived through doing justice in our world, but neglects some of the "traditional" spiritual disciplines of the church as resources for justice. When viewed through a Renewal lens, we will see how an experience of God can and should move one out into the world to do justice and love mercy. I propose that a middle way is possible. That one should be empowered by the Holy Spirit to live out the work of the Spirit in the world, in every sector of the world, including poverty.

Finally, in my estimation, Pneumatology is the engine that drives the entire Renewal hermeneutic. Pneumatology underlies Scripture, experience and spirituality, even the very method of inquiry. It is also the most unique endeavor that has not been explored concerning poverty and holds the most promise for new insights. Even Renewalists are still largely wearing "Saul's armor" when it comes to poverty and approaching it from old paradigms and themes. Renewal theologians do talk about the Holy Spirit some, but largely as empowering the individual to address poverty.

---

152. Yong, *Spirit-Word-Community*, 55, 93.

Perhaps this is why Renewal has been such a mixed bag in its practical responses with very few churches doing much to address poverty, particularly in the United States. These theologians and practitioners fail to see that Renewal brings its own set of unique resources in its pneumatic view of the world that should be put into dialogue with other traditions' theologies of poverty. It is not that Renewal is the answer, but that a strong pneumatological perspective, for which Renewal is a great source, can transform the way we look at poverty. Such a dialogue would hopefully move Renewal toward more meaningful and holistic action toward the urban poor, but also be a resource for more mainstream justice movements to recognize the contribution Renewal social action has made among the and the promise of Pneumatology. Our next chapter will explore further what we mean by Pneumatology and the areas of Pneumatology that hold the most promise for a holistic theology of urban poverty.

5

Pneumatological Resources for a Theology of Urban Poverty

INTRODUCTION

I grew up in San Diego, one of the largest cities in the country. As with all metropolitan areas, the number of those in poverty is larger than average. I also grew up attending a Renewal church with my family. This church was a part of the International Church of the Foursquare Gospel (ICFG) founded by Aimee Semple McPherson, a quite controversial figure. McPherson got her start in the Salvation Army, a movement with a rich social heritage.[1] If any early Renewal movement would have had inclinations toward the poor it would have been the ICFG. It had its foundations in the inner city of Los Angeles just before the great depression and was founded by McPherson. In fact, McPherson did have a strong social program out of her famed Angelus Temple in the 1920–1930s that fed over 1.5 million people during her lifetime.[2] As with many of Renewal's early social inclinations, however, they were soon overshadowed by more Evangelical concerns and influences.[3]

Even though it may not have been representative of every ICFG church during the 1990s, the local church I grew up attending in San Diego was much more focused on evangelism and the use of the spiritual gifts than

---

1. Sutton, *Aimee Semple McPherson*, 9, 186. For more on the life of Aimee Semple McPherson, see Blumhofer, *Aimee Semple McPherson*.

2. Sutton, *Aimee Semple McPherson*, 187–88. Even today, Angelus Temple runs the "Dream Center," which Donald Miller and Richard Flory call one of the most successful Pentecostal social ministries in the country. See Flory and Miller, "Dream Center," 9.

3. Robeck cites these Evangelical concerns as "personal salvation, transformed lifestyles, discipling relationships, and hope for the future" (Robeck, "Social Concern," 98). See Kärkkäinen, "Are Pentecostals Oblivious to Social Justice?," 420.

social issues. As an eighth grader, I was baptized in the Holy Spirit with glossolalia as were countless other people in my childhood church around the same time. It was the beginning of what our church, and others in the media, termed a "revival." By the next year, the church was hosting nightly revival meetings that often went four to five hours every night of the week with over five hundred people in attendance each night at its peak. There were reports of people converted, baptized in the Spirit and healed physically, emotionally, and from addiction. My own personal experience with Spirit baptism included an inner compelling to go and help people around the church, particularly the poor. I made a personal commitment to make sandwiches every day for two weeks during the summer and go hand them out to people at the park near our church. I tried to garner support from other church members to go with me, but ended up going myself every time. Everyone else appeared to be more concerned with those already inside the four walls and with spiritual salvation than helping the poor who may never "get their lives straight," as one pastor told me.

This story, while a true experience of mine, is also clearly anecdotal. But it demonstrates much of the discussion between the mainline and Roman Catholic churches we explored in chapter 4 and the Renewal churches we explored in chapter 5. I myself felt a prompting as I was filled with the Holy Spirit to help the poor, something that felt natural and almost sequential to me, but clearly did not resonate with others filled by the same Spirit. As one looks at the history of Renewal, a movement supposed to have the Holy Spirit at its center, one would question whether the Spirit of Renewal cares about the poor or not. We saw in our exploration of Renewal practices this accusation can be true, but it is not the only narrative. It raises the question, however, should a strong theology and experience of the Holy Spirit motivate one toward action on behalf of the poor and does it provide resources through which to think and act? We have already established a gap in the literature, but can Pneumatology fill it? We will answer this question over the next two chapters. In this chapter, we focus on Pneumatology, its history, its place in theology, and the challenges it presents before turning in our final chapter to how this comes to bear most specifically on a theology of urban poverty.

The argument of this chapter will be that a Pneumatology, properly constructed, does have the resources to contribute to a holistic theology of poverty that addresses the complex problems explored in chapter 2 and fills in the gaps left after chapters 3, 4, and 5. We will make this argument by first exploring what Pneumatology is and what its scope should include. Second, we will explore two major challenges to Pneumatology—the interior/exterior and the Spirit/Christ polarities—and how overcoming these challenges gives insight into a holistic pneumatological method for urban poverty. Finally, we will briefly outline this methodology considering what we discover about Pneumatology before fleshing it out more fully and applying it to urban poverty in our final chapter.

WHAT IS PNEUMATOLOGY?

There are several contemporary studies that overview the field of Pneumatology or propose their own pneumatologies.[4] Our purpose is not to write a new Pneumatology, but to quarry the work already done for a new application of Pneumatology to urban poverty. Because of this we must be selective in how we move forward exploring those figures and themes in Pneumatology that have the most relevance for our goal. First, it will be helpful to explore what Pneumatology is.

We are in a kind of pneumatological renaissance emerging from what Vinson Synan terms "The Century of the Holy Spirit."[5] More books have been published than ever before on pneumatological topics. Still, there appears to be a hiddenness to Pneumatology, a difficulty in speaking about the Holy Spirit compared to the Father and the Son, which has made pneumatological approaches slower to emerge. Joel Elowsky puts this difficulty this way, "Any discussion of the Spirit is fraught with the difficulty of speaking about something or someone who defies definition and who purposely averts attention from himself toward someone else. . . . Rather than drawing attention to himself, the Holy Spirit always points us to Christ and his work, which brings glory to the Father."[6] Even with the proliferation of recent writings, many struggle to speak about Pneumatology. For instance, many are hesitant when Pneumatology is at the fore, calling for it to be balanced with Christology instead, even though there are seldom similar calls when Christology is dominant.

A large contributor to this has been the history of Pneumatology and the fact that it has only come to the fore in the church and academy in recent years. It will be helpful to understand what we mean by Pneumatology as a "study of the Holy Spirit" to first look briefly at the history of the field of Pneumatology.

---

4. For perhaps the most thorough overview of the most central pneumatologies in different traditions, see Kärkkäinen, *Pneumatology*. See also Castelo, *Pneumatology*; Jensen, *Lord and Giver of Life*; Dabney and Hinze, *Advents of the Spirit*; Elowsky, *We Believe in the Holy Spirit*.

5. Synan, *Century of the Holy Spirit*.

6. Elowsky, *We Believe in the Holy Spirit*, xiv.

A Historical Inquiry into the Field of Pneumatology

While our primary focus in this chapter is modern Pneumatology, the doctrine of the Holy Spirit in the early church should not be overlooked, either for its contribution to ancient church doctrine, or the way it sheds light on the current challenges in Pneumatology. Definitive statements about the Holy Spirit were slow developing among the earliest church fathers, particularly in the West and before the Cappadocians. Eventually they found such statements to be necessary in the face of controversy. As this Pneumatology developed, it focused primarily on the Holy Spirit's divinity, on its relation to the other two members of the Trinity, and on the unique work of the Spirit in salvation and empowerment.

There was very little said about the Holy Spirit in the Ante-Nicene period. Most of the attention was focused toward more pertinent issues such as apostolic authority or christological controversies. The Nicene Creed, which devotes several descriptors to both God the Father and God the Son, simply says, "and the Holy Spirit." This is also representative of the many times the Holy Spirit is mentioned pre-Nicaea. Most often the Spirit is simply included in Trinitarian formulae like in Clement of Rome's *1 Clement*, "Have we not one God, one Christ and one Spirit of grace that was poured upon us, and one calling in Christ?"[7] Even though some confessed the Spirit as God, as Elowsky says, "They, for the most part, did not work out the implications of that confession until it became an issue of controversy in the middle to latter half of the fourth century."[8]

Another reason little was said about the Holy Spirit is the enigmatic nature in which even Scripture speaks of the Holy Spirit. For instance, believing that the Holy Spirit cannot be fully known, Gregory of Nazianzus comments that, "To be only slightly in error regarding the doctrine of the Holy Spirit is to be orthodox."[9] Because of this, many early fathers, like Cyril of Jerusalem, tried to stick closely to how Scripture spoke of the Holy Spirit: "Let us say about the Spirit exactly what Scripture says and nothing else, and do not let us pry where Scripture does not answer. The Scriptures were spoken by the Holy Spirit himself, and what he said about himself is exactly what he pleased."[10] In staying close to Scripture, there was only so much the church fathers could say. Many, like Didymus in his *Treatise on the Holy*

---

7. Clement of Rome, *1 Clement* 46.5 (*ANF* 1:18).
8. Elowsky, *We Believe in the Holy Spirit*, xxii.
9. Gregory of Nazianzus, *Oration on the Great Athanasius* 21.33 (*NPNF2* 7:279).
10. Cyril of Jerusalem quoted in Ettlinger, "Holy Spirit," 435.

Spirit, were afraid that straying too far from Scripture would result in blaspheming the Holy Spirit.[11]

Eventually, a few controversies came up within the early church that forced it to develop a stronger understanding of Pneumatology. The major dissenting group that caused controversy was the Macedonians, sometimes called the *Pneumatomachoi,* or the spirit-fighters. Several works were written against the Macedonians and demonstrated they taught the Holy Spirit was neither to be called Lord, nor to be glorified with the Father. The Macedonians also did not consider the Holy Spirit a fellow worker with the Father and Son, since it was not capable of creating and giving life.[12] Finally, the Holy Spirit was considered only a minister or instrument of God like the angels, yet not to be considered an angel or creature.[13] It was not just heretical groups that had pneumatological qualms, numerous orthodox scholars had trouble calling the Holy Spirit "God" and some saw the Spirit as God, but to a lesser degree. Origen, influenced by Platonic thought, saw the Father and Son working in all creation, but the Holy Spirit only working in the saints.[14] Athanasius, while fighting the belief that the Holy Spirit was merely a creature, never used the term God for the Spirit, though he does speak twice of the Spirit being of the same *homoousios* as the Father.[15]

Eventually, the church fathers had to make more clear and forceful statements about the Holy Spirit. The primary work on the Holy Spirit was done by the Cappadocian fathers who also did significant work on clarifying the church's Christology and adding significantly to the article on the Holy Spirit at Constantinople. Gregory of Nazianzus, in his fifth oration, contains one of the earliest clear affirmations of the Holy Spirit's divinity saying, "Is the Spirit God? Most certainly. Well then is he consubstantial? Yes, if he is God."[16] This and work by Gregory of Nyssa and Basil of Caesarea

---

11. Didymus quoted in Elowsky, *We Believe in the Holy Spirit,* xxvii.
12. Pseudo-Athanasius quoted in Elowsky, *We Believe in the Holy Spirit,* xxv.
13. Pseudo-Athanasius quoted in Elowsky, *We Believe in the Holy Spirit,* xxv.
14. Origen, *On First Principles* 1.3.5 (*ANF* 4:253).
15. Elowsky, *We Believe in the Holy Spirit,* xxvi.
16. Gregory of Nazianzus, *Oration* 31.10 (*NPNF2* 7:321). For a fuller statement, see Gregory of Nyssa, *On the Holy Spirit* 14 (*NPNF2* 5:320). He says, "We believe and confess that in every deed and thought . . . the Holy Spirit is to be understood as joined with the Father and the Son. Nor is he lacking in any form of will, or energy, or anything else that can be implied in a devout conception of the Supreme Goodness. And so, we believe that, except for the distinction of order (taxis) and person (hypostasis) no variation in any point can be understood. We maintain that while the Spirit's place is counted third in mere sequence after Father and the Son, third in the order of the transmission, in all other respects we acknowledge his inseparable union with them; that is one in nature, in honor, in Godhead, in glory and majesty, in almighty power, and in all devout belief."

led to the Nicene-Constantinopitan creed, which affirmed the Holy Spirit as "the Lord and Giver-of-Life, who proceedeth from the Father, who with the Father and the Son together is worshipped and glorified, who spake by the prophets."[17] Calling the Holy Spirit "Lord" is a clear indication of belief in the Spirit's divinity. This is not just a doctrinal statement, it was reality for the early church. The Holy Spirit was worshipped within their liturgy in conjunction with the Father and the Son as well as individually. Baptism was a major liturgy in which the Holy Spirit was invoked as well as in ordination. Beyond the sacraments, we also see the Holy Spirit in prayers and in worship such as this statement of worship by Gregory of Nyssa, "But with regard to service and worship, we reply that the Holy Spirit is exalted above all that we can do for him with our merely human purpose our worship is far beneath the honor due."[18] The early church fathers focused on three further areas, all present in the creed itself: the Holy Spirit in relation to the Father and the Son in terms of source, the Holy Spirit as the giver of life through salvation, and the Holy Spirit as the one who empowers.

According to Ettlinger, in the earliest period of the church, the precise nature of each of the three persons and their interrelationship were not fully developed.[19] This was especially true of the Holy Spirit and, as a result, he was referred at times to the Father and other times to the Son. The issue of who the Holy Spirit properly belonged to, or who the source of the Spirit's procession was, eventually boiled over with the addition of the *filioque* clause to the Nicene-Constantinopolitan creed causing it to read, "Who proceeds from the Father *and the Son*," at the third council of Toledo in 589.[20] This was soon rejected by the Eastern Church and was a major source of contention in the eventual split between East and West. It also continues to be controversial among modern scholars in Pneumatology. Some, like Pannenberg, reject the clause because it represents a subordination of the Holy Spirit. Others want to maintain the clause but also the unity and equality of all three persons of the Trinity.[21] Potential subordination of the Holy Spirit is a major issue in Pneumatology, but most do not intend subordination. Rather, they follow the Cappadocians in affirming the full personhood of the Holy Spirit. It usually becomes in how people view the

---

17. "Holy Creed Which the 150 Fathers Set Forth" (*NPNF2* 14:163).
18. Gregory of Nyssa, *On the Holy Spirit* 16–17 (*NPNF2* 5:320–21).
19. Ettlinger, "Holy Spirit," 435–436.
20. Elowsky, *We Believe in the Holy Spirit*, 217–218.
21. See, for instance, World Council of Churches, *Baptism, Eucharist, and Ministry*.

activity of the Holy Spirit, or lack thereof, rather than a doctrinal statement like the *filioque*, which would cause subordination.[22]

While little was said about the personhood of the Holy Spirit apart from the Father and the Son, there were more definitive roles ascribed to the Spirit within the working of the Trinity, the body of Christ and the world. The two primary functions discussed come out of the creed itself, the Holy Spirit as the giver of life and the empowerer.

The Holy Spirit as the giver of life is intricately connected with the Spirit's work in creation and its ongoing work of new creation in the salvation in individuals and the church. While many see the Son as the primary source of salvation, it is truly a work of the Trinity in which the Holy Spirit is essential. Within salvation, the early fathers spoke of the Holy Spirit's role in both justification and sanctification. Basil of Caesarea makes the distinction, for instance, that one cannot say that Jesus is Lord, a requisite for justification, except by the Holy Spirit. He asks, "When and what did they confess? For he who does not believe the Spirit does not believe the Son, for none can say that Jesus is the Lord, but by the Holy Spirit."[23]

Even more so, the Holy Spirit was involved in sanctification which Elowsky holds the early church fathers believed to be "the entire process of indwelling by the Holy Spirit by which one is conformed to the image of God, a process that begins in baptism when sin is drowned, and left behind so that new life can begin."[24] Eric Nestler cites Tertullian's view on this when Tertullian declares, "The Lord has sent the *Paraclete*, because human weakness was not capable of receiving the truth all at once; it was necessary that the discipline should be regulated and progressively ordered, until it was carried to perfection by the Holy Spirit."[25] The Holy Spirit's role in sanctification ranged from writing the law upon hearts (Augustine), acting as a conscience counseling us toward good habits (Ambrosiaster), and the idea of *theosis* in the East in which one increasingly participates in the very divine nature (Cyril of Alexandria and Irenaeus).[26]

---

22. The *filioque* has other implications as well such as in debates concerning ontology and function or the equality yet differentiation of the members of the Trinity. For our purposes here, it is simply important to note that while many of the details are debated thoroughly, most try to avoid subordinationism in theory, but fail as their theology plays itself out. For more on the *filioque* debate, see Siecienski, *Filioque*; Habets, *Ecumenical Perspectives on the Filioque*.

23. Basil of Caesarea quoted in Yamamura, "Development of the Doctrine," 15. See also Hilary of Poitiers, *On the Trinity* 2.32 (NPNF2 9:61); Augustine, *Epistle of John* 8.12–14 (NPNF1 7:511–12), cited in Elowsky, *We Believe in the Holy Spirit*, 136.

24. Elowsky, *We Believe in the Holy Spirit*, 171.

25. Tertullian quoted in Nestler, "Was Montanism a Heresy?," 74.

26. See Augustine, *On the Spirit and the Letter* 36 (NPNF1 5:98); Ambrosiaster

The Holy Spirit also empowers the believer to live out God's kingdom in the world. In many ways, the gifts and empowerment that are given to believers through the Holy Spirit make them an extension of the Spirit and his work in creation. One of the ways in which the Holy Spirit empowers believers is by empowering them to speak. According to Alexander of Alexandria, the Holy Spirit did this through the Old Testament prophets and the New Testament Apostles in forming Scripture. He says, "The Spirit has inaugurated both the holy people of the Old Testament and the divine teachers of that which is called the new."[27] The Holy Spirit also inspires modern day prophets to continue to speak the word of God. It was not just the gift of prophecy, but according to Basil it was the "one and only Spirit, the Paraclete who divideth and worketh the charismata that come from God."[28]

These three areas, the divinity of the Holy Spirit, the work of the Spirit in salvation, and in revelation, occupied much of global theology into the modern era.[29] At various times, a figure would come along who would talk more specifically about the Holy Spirit, perhaps even identifying a new metaphor, but it was usually still in these areas reserved for Pneumatology. One example was the Medieval mystics who reemphasized the ability of humanity to experience the Holy Spirit. Elizabeth Dryer says of the mystics that they corrected "the common perception that the doctrines of the Holy Spirit were divorced from the original, polyvalent and enlivening experiences that were its source."[30] Still, much of this experience lived itself out in the traditional ways. For instance, Bernard of Clairvaux, who had a very strong experiential emphasis, spoke uniquely of the Holy Spirit as the "kiss of God." This characterization had two primary functions, the Holy Spirit making knowledge and revelation possible and the intimacy of love between the Trinity and between God and the believer experienced at

---

quoted in Elowsky, *We Believe in the Holy Spirit*, 179; Cyril of Alexandria quoted in Elowsky, *We Believe in the Holy Spirit*, 160; Irenaeus, *Against Heresies* 4.38.3 (*ANF* 1:521–22). The idea of *theosis* finds its roots in Eastern theology as one of the primary modes of speaking about salvation. One increasingly participates in the divine nature eventually becoming "in-godded" through deification. Theosis has even been picked up by Renewal scholars, like Clark Pinnock, as a way of talking about pneumatological salvation. See Pinnock, *Flame of Love*, 149–84.

27. Alexander of Alexandria, *Epistles on the Arian Heresy* 1.12 (*ANF* 6:296).

28. Basil quoted in Stephanou, "Charismata in the Early Church Fathers," 138.

29. You do of course have hints at applying the Spirit to other theological loci, such as ecclesiology, but it by no means makes up the bulk of the pneumatological emphasis prior to the contemporary era.

30. Dreyer quoted in Kärkkäinen, *Pneumatology*, 49.

salvation and increasingly through sanctification.[31] Recently there have been more Renewal scholars attempting to uncover Pneumatology in historical scholars. Some of these such as Joachim of Fiore do add other emphases such as eschatology, though even this is heavily focused on revelation about the eschaton.[32]

This trend in Pneumatology continued until the twentieth century and the rise of modern Pneumatology. Like the first major shift in Pneumatology during the patristic period, the rise of Pneumatology came through historic events that were controversial including the entrance of Eastern Orthodox churches into the World Council of Churches and the spread of Renewal movements globally.[33] Both movements have maintained a more central place for the Holy Spirit in their theology and practice. The presence of both in ecumenical dialogues, and the astounding growth of Renewal in such a short time, has forced scholars to ask more pneumatological questions. This is true both with the rise of Pentecostalism and eventual scholastic debates in Renewal Theology such as with James Dunn over Spirit baptism. It was also true of the Charismatic movement which arose from within mainline denominations like Presbyterians, Lutheranism, Episcopalianism and Roman Catholicism. Each of these movements had their own antecedents of the flourishing of the Holy Spirit in both theology and practice.[34]

In this historical inquiry, we have seen the limited scope of Pneumatology and the subordinate place it has taken to other theological disciplines. This has begun to change in the twentieth century with the rise of Renewal movements and their incorporation into the whole of Christianity through the charismatic movement. Still, the broadening of the scope of Pneumatology has been limited. We will explore in this next section what the scope of Pneumatology should be in light of this historical inquiry and the goals of this thesis.

---

31. See Kärkkäinen, *Pneumatology*, 52.

32. McGinn, *Apocalyptic Spirituality*, 97–148.

33. Kärkkäinen, *Pneumatology*, 11–13.

34. These are by no means the only reasons for the rise of Pneumatology, but they are primary. One could also trace the beginnings of Renewal itself and the way in which the Spirit came more to the fore in Wesleyan and Roman Catholic traditions as precursors to this pneumatological renaissance. Still, if it were not for the immense growth of the Renewal movements, these "roots" may not have come to full fruition. See Kärkkäinen, *Pneumatology*, 73–74; Hocken, "Catholic Charismatic Renewal," 211–14.

The Scope of Pneumatology

In this section, we will explore the question—what is the scope of Pneumatology? Does Pneumatology necessarily need to be limited because of the enigmatic character of the Holy Spirit? Does Pneumatology need to be connected with Christology and if so how? The thesis of this section is that there is a need to move beyond the past limitation of topics in a way that recognizes the unique person and role of the Holy Spirit that permeates every area of creation and theology. One should be able to speak uniquely about the Holy Spirit without Pneumatology being eclipsed by traditional Christology. At the same time, Pneumatology cannot be divorced from, or contradict, Christology because of the nature of the Trinity. We will demonstrate this by analyzing a few methodological approaches to theology within modern Pneumatology—including biblical approaches, integrative approaches, contextual approaches, and what I call holistic approaches—and critiquing them to come to a scope and method appropriate for doing theology through a pneumatological lens.

The simplest pneumatological method would be a kind of biblical Pneumatology. This might be best characterized by Cyril of Jerusalem's earlier quote about not saying anything about the Spirit beyond what Scripture says.[35] The Bible Doctrines Method we explored as an early Renewal methodology would also be an example. For instance, Myer Pearlman, in his book *Knowing the Doctrines of the Bible,* includes a chapter on the Holy Spirit with sections entitled, "The nature of the Holy Spirit," "The Spirit in the Old Testament," "The Spirit of Christ," "The Spirit in Human Experience," "The Gifts of the Sprit," and "The Spirit of the Church." These sections largely consist of systematized biblical quotations with commentary. One also notices that the topics fit exactly into what we have described as the "go to" topics for Pneumatology and do not go beyond them.[36] The Bible Doctrines method was very limited in this regard, largely restating much of what had already been said concerning the Spirit and failing to engage the larger Christian tradition.

---

35. Cyril of Jerusalem quoted in Ettlinger, "Holy Spirit," 435. See this quote on page 135.

36. For a fuller discussion of Pearlman and other early Pentecostals who employed what Stephenson calls the "Bible Doctrines Method," see Stephenson, *Types of Pentecostal Theology*, 11–28. It is important to note that Pearlman and his contemporaries did not employ a strictly *sola scriptura* method, but that they did use tradition, experience and reason to support their interpretations of these biblical texts. The Biblical text, however, determined the topics of discussion and took prime importance in the theological discussion.

Michael Welker, professor of systematic theology at Heidelberg, in his book *God the Spirit*, presents another type of biblically centered Pneumatology. He calls it a "realistic theology" that goes beyond the abstract idealisms and personalistic individualisms common today in Pneumatology to explore how the Holy Spirit is experienced in everyday life. Welker's thesis is that, while God's action as Spirit in the conflicts of human life is not always easy to recognize, God's Spirit is working in the world to overcome debilitating differences in favor of life-enhancing, righteous, constructive differences that contribute to energizing richer patterns of creation.[37] Welker attempted to bridge the charismatic view of the Holy Spirit as ever-present and interactive through ecstatic experience and modern views of the Spirit as largely other and distant.

To relate these experiences of the Holy Spirit, Welker turns to the biblical tradition: the Spirit in the Old Testament, in the Lukan Jesus and in Pauline literature. Welker paints a view of the Spirit that attempts to counter disintegration through debilitating differences and to form a community of justice and freedom. He interprets these Scriptures in a much more theological and historical method than the Bible Doctrines Method by incorporating a wealth of other scholarship from progressive and diverse theological backgrounds. For instance, Welker adopts Pannenberg's view of the Holy Spirit as a "field of force" generative of concern for and love of others that works for the good of all.[38] Even condemnation and judgment enacted by the Spirit is ultimately for the sake of redemption. To establish this new idea of the Holy Spirit's personhood, Welker draws on Pentecost as an ongoing event of overcoming disintegration and bringing redemption. He also draws heavily on Liberation Theology for his themes of redemption, oppression, and overcoming disintegration.[39] In dealing with such a wide range of Biblical passages, Welker does not attempt to synthesize them into a clean systematic statement or doctrine of the Spirit, but seeks to allow a plurality of witness to the Spirit and the Spirit's work in the world.

These biblical approaches to the Holy Spirit are helpful and necessary to construct a Pneumatology, but are limiting. Welker expands what a biblical theology of Pneumatology can look like by incorporating more Scripture, more dialogue partners and not trying to synthesize everything too cleanly so that varying views of the Holy Spirit are not lost. He falls short in incorporating experiences of the Spirit, however, particularly from

---

37. Welker, *God the Spirit*, 25–27.
38. Welker, *God the Spirit*, 227–46.
39. Welker, *God the Spirit*, 16–17. Welker engages figures like Boff and Boff, *Introducing Liberation Theology*; Gutiérrez, *Theology of Liberation*; Sobrino, *True Church and the Poor*; Cone, *God of the Oppressed*.

Renewal traditions, in his attempt at what he calls "realism." His goal in his realism seems to be to stay away from the supernatural and escapist forms of Pneumatology and so neglects what many see as "real" experiences of the Holy Spirit.

A second approach to the scope of Pneumatology involves more integrative approaches within systematic theology. One examples would be Wolfhart Pannenberg in his *Systematic Theology*. In these three volumes, Pannenberg does not provide a dedicated section to the Holy Spirit, but rather takes what Killian McDonnell calls an "integral pneumatological approach."[40] Pannenberg sees the Holy Spirit as the life principle of all creation.[41] As such, he connects the Holy Spirit with each of the main theological loci, allowing pneumatological foundations to imbue them instead of treating the Holy Spirit as a "gap-filler," according to Kärkkäinen.[42] Still, in my estimation, Pannenberg's pneumatological applications fall short in various places as he strays away from the Holy Spirit in key areas of his theology that would have been helpful to apply Pneumatology.[43]

Another example of an integrative approach, though very different from Pannenberg's, is Clark Pinnock in his *Flame of Love*. While Pinnock also attempts to bring Pneumatology into various loci of theology, he does so more explicitly. He asks what the Sprit has to do with the Trinity, creation, Christology, ecclesiology, soteriology, and a theology of religions. Even in this approach, however, Pinnock at times reverts into christological categories that restrict him from new potentialities. For instance, in his criteria for evaluating religions, he uses primarily christological criteria which leads to closing the evaluator off to other religions in a way that a pneumatological approach would leave more open and dynamic.[44] Finally, Pinnock does not continue his work beyond the limited number of loci in this one work. He picks some of the major areas of theology to tackle, but it is often the way

40. McDonnell, *Other Hand of God*, 114. See also Varkey, *Role of the Holy Spirit*, 383.

41. Pannenberg, *Systematic Theology*, 2:20–34.

42. Kärkkäinen, *Pneumatology*, 20.

43. For instance, in volume 3, Pannenberg starts out strong in speaking of the Spirit in soteriology but gets away from the Spirit in speaking of the kingdom, the Church and the law just after. The Spirit is not wholly absent but does seem to take a back seat. This is fine because Pannenberg's goal is not a pneumatological systematic theology, but his ending application in his section of the gospel and the law might be different if he had been more pneumatologically driven bringing salvation and completion of the law more clearly into the present.

44. For instance, Pinnock says, "The question to ask is christological. . . . The truth of it is precisely the point about Christ's being the criterion of Spirit activity" (Pinnock, *Flame of Love*, 208–211).

these topics are worked out in the details that provide the real meat of theology and its application to our lives in the world. Discernment of religions or interreligious dialogue are equally important as salvation in religions, but Pinnock only deals with the latter.[45]

Another approach to Pneumatology includes contextual theologies that attempt to ask the question of how Pneumatology fits within and enhances a theological system one already find themselves in based on personal context. José Comblin's *The Holy Spirit and Liberation* is a prime example as he asks what the Spirit has to do with LALT and its major themes of liberation, freedom and local community development.[46] Elizabeth Johnson takes a similar approach for Feminist theology in *She Who Is: The Mystery of God in Feminist Theological Discourse*.[47] Blair Reynolds does the same for process theology, particularly drawing on the wells of mysticism for his view of the Holy Spirit.[48]

A final approach to the scope of Pneumatology is what I call the holistic approach. Holistic approaches attempt to allow pneumatological concerns to set the very agenda of the theological project. This does not mean that one will eschew christological concerns but that one will, at every turn, allow the pneumatological to speak and critique former modes of theology. Two attempts to move this direction include Frank Macchia's *Baptized in the Spirit* and Amos Yong's *Spirit-Word-Community*.

Macchia, like Pinnock, attempts to apply pneumatological themes to various traditional theological loci. He goes a step further in that his approach to this Pneumatology employs a specifically pneumatological structure through the metaphor of Spirit baptism. Macchia uses Spirit baptism as his organizing principle and gateway into each theological locus.[49] He covers topics like anthropology, soteriology, eschatology, ecclesiology and the sacraments. Unfortunately, sticking specifically to the metaphor of Spirit baptism throughout his whole work creates problems. First, he stretches the metaphor beyond what it can handle in certain areas. In these areas,

---

45. Moltmann provides a kind of hybrid view between the two. For instance, he has a monograph that is pneumatologically focused in *The Spirit of Life* that includes some originality in several topics and insights, but still follows more traditional patterns in how that agenda is set. He also has a strong Pneumatology in other works as well in search of what he calls a "holistic" Pneumatology that also deals with more concrete realities like the human body and the earth. See Moltmann, *Spirit of Life*, xiii. For an example of him applying Pneumatology to one specific loci like Pinnock, see Moltmann, *Church in the Power of the Spirit*.

46. Comblin, *Holy Spirit and Liberation*, 19.

47. Johnson, *She Who Is*.

48. See Reynolds, *Toward a Process Pneumatology*.

49. Macchia, *Baptized in the Spirit*, 17.

other metaphors of the Spirit may be more appropriate. Second, there are times when he does bring in other metaphors and moves into other areas of the Spirit, but continues to call it Spirit baptism for the sake of his project. Finally, it is interesting that he ends up staying with many of the same theological loci as Pinnock does in his *Flame of Love* and that neither moves into other areas of theology. Both of their ideas of what constitutes the center of theology still seems to be tied up in previous versions for better or worse.[50]

Amos Yong in his book, *Spirit-Word-Community*, may take the scope of Pneumatology to the furthest reach to date.[51] His is truly a pneumatologically centered methodology with what he calls foundational Pneumatology and the pneumatological imagination at the center of it. These two ideas are the basis of his metaphysics and his epistemology, respectively. The Holy Spirit is the foundation of a metaphysics because the Spirit is the foundational symbol for God's presence and agency in the world. This symbol points to the third person of the Trinity, but it also stands for everything—how we relate to one another, how we think, and how we are. All dimensions of reality can be understood pneumatologically in that the Holy Spirit imbues relationality, rationality and social dynamism.[52] Since, for Yong, all reality is built on the Spirit, all reality can be studied and known through the Spirit. Because Pneumatology and pneumatic experience extends to every level of reality it means that everything is open for theological discussion. This blows the proverbial theological doors wide open and allows Yong to move into areas of theology and life in a pneumatic way.

While this idea of Pneumatology as everything means it does not have to be the Holy Spirit one is talking about for it be pneumatological, Yong, as a Renewalist is still very Spirit-centered which leads to his idea of the pneumatological imagination as a way to know and discern reality. This pneumatological imagination is built on biblical discernment, the reality of the person of the Holy Spirit (not just as a metaphysical concept) and on community which often takes the form of ecumenical and interdisciplinary engagement. So, for instance, when Yong seeks to engage theology and science, he begins with Scripture and sees that the idea of creation is very

50. There have been other scholars who have taken Pneumatology into other areas of theology, for instance political theology, but they often stay in these specific loci rather allowing these concerns to arise out of a more systematic Pneumatology. Those that attempt to be systematic have still centered on similar concerns by and large. For an example of a politically oriented Pneumatology, see Müller-Fahrenholz, *God's Spirit*.

51. Yong's complete hermeneutic includes Word and Community as his title describes, but even his use of Scripture and theological tradition flow out of his use of the Spirit in his pneumatological imagination. He goes on to employ this methodology to various theological loci in future works.

52. Yong, *Spirit-Word-Community*, 4.

present in Scripture. Yong then looks for a root metaphor through which to engage the topic of creation which for him is the Holy Spirit because of the Spirit's presence at and role in sustaining creation.[53] Yong then speaks about how the Holy Spirit works in creation in as many ways as possible, including even the parapsychological.[54] He engages a wide variety of disciplines and voices because spirit is not just symbolic for the third person of the Trinity, but for all creation, all knowledge and all disciplines.

This is a rather limited understanding of Yong's complete hermeneutic, but it shows the scope with which he desires to employ Pneumatology even expanding beyond what one may find in the "Spirit-proper" in Scripture or in traditional Spirit-themes. Such an understanding of the Spirit opens Yong up for criticism of stretching things too far in the name of Pneumatology and at the cost of Christology. Still, his willingness to explore various metaphors within a pneumatological imagination that still has the Holy Spirit at its center allows him to go wide in a responsible and reasonable manner. His pneumatological preference is more chronological than substantive. At times his "Spirit" connection may seem a bit contrived or forced, but the work he does around that metaphor remains more pneumatological than most.[55]

Perhaps my order of approach reveals my own biases towards Yong's approach. This preference does not negate the pneumatological approaches mentioned before, rather it takes them to their natural, or at least possible, conclusion. Any Christian Pneumatology, especially from an Evangelical or Renewal perspective, should have a strong biblical component and Yong himself starts with Scripture in every major section of his work. Pneumatology will also naturally deal with the largest areas of theology but should approach their subsets in more systematic ways. This of course in not the purpose of this thesis. We ourselves will probably be open to similar criticisms as I have leveled at points here, but hopefully I will also move toward establishing a helpful paradigm for a holistic Pneumatology through the singular example of applying it to urban poverty while not over stretching the metaphor so the outcome becomes unhelpful in actually addressing poverty. I suspect I may be open to some of these criticisms because there

---

53. Yong, *Spirit of Creation*, 29.

54. Yong, *Spirit of Creation*, 184–95.

55. For instance, Yong uses the category of Christ as Sanctifier but sees this applying pneumatically to a theology of culture. The Spirit is certainly involved in culture, and he does demonstrate how Pentecostal views of holiness do affect their view of culture, but the connections seems forced. Of course, the work he does on a theology of culture is helpful. Perhaps when one is trying to work from a thoroughly pneumatological paradigm when the categories have not been previously established such forced jumps are at times necessary. Perhaps similar criticisms will be made of our pneumatological attempts in the next chapter. See Yong, *In the Days of Caesar*, 166–67.

are some natural challenges that arise in doing theology from a pneumatological perspective. It is to these challenges we now turn.

CHALLENGES TO PNEUMATOLOGY

While we cannot move forward the entire field of Pneumatology in this limited work, our hope is to overcome, or at the very least address some of the challenges that have limited Pneumatology in the past. Doing so will allow us to make a unique pneumatological contribution to urban poverty and theology as a whole. Our response to these challenges will underlie our holistic pneumatological method in the next chapter and help to structure our approach to urban poverty. These are by no means the only challenges in Pneumatology, but they come to the fore in each attempt described above and below in this chapter and will be present in our final chapter. The two greatest challenges facing Pneumatology are balancing the exterior and the interior and balancing the place of Christology and Pneumatology. Both of these stem from the limited nature of past pneumatologies and the newness of the endeavor. They also both directly affect our attempt to apply this Pneumatology to urban poverty.

Challenge One: Exterior and Interior

The first challenge to Pneumatology involves balancing the exterior and the interior. This balance can take many forms including exterior/interior, social/individual, or praxis/theory. Many who have been most concerned with the Holy Spirit from the Monastics, to the Medieval mystics and early Renewalists have been accused of having impractical theology. They are seen as only focused on spiritual experience in a very individualistic and escapist manner that has little application for life lived in this world. At the same time, these spiritual experiences have been extremely transformative for those experiencing them so that there is a hesitancy to eschew them in favor of what we saw Welker call "realistic Pneumatology."

Those proposing more socially driven pneumatologies, like Welker, can be accused by those of a more spiritualist persuasion as not caring about individual transformation or the interior of a person in their desire to help a person physically or address social, exterior structures through their praxis. Instead, our desire is to recognize the supernatural or inner spiritual life as realistic, but also that the political, economic, etc., is equally spiritual even though it takes what appears to be more concrete, exterior forms.

Another way to term the impasse is in the way one defines "spirituality." All theological movements purport a spirituality, but their definition of this spirituality is different. I attempt to overcome this challenge through a dialogue between two of these traditions, LALT and Renewal Theology. Looking at their views of Pneumatology and spirituality will help us argue that the impasse between the interior and exterior may never be completely solved, but should be an ever-present tension that directs us to pay attention to both and put them in dialogue with one another as two perspectives on the same issue.

Latin American Liberation Pneumatology[56]

The Spirit in the Historical

LALT is centered on the idea of a theology that has practical and historical implications for the world in which we live. Theology is always a second step because praxis, historical being in the world, is the first step. One of the founders and strongest proponents of Liberation Theology, the Brazilian priest Leonardo Boff, states that the Father is seen as one who forms his people and who "frees his people from oppression. The Father hears the cry of his downtrodden children; intervening in history to redeem them from their slavery and lead them back to their freedom."[57] This historical presence is seen even more in the person and praxis of Jesus. Jon Sobrino emphasizes Jesus as the mediator of the reign and ultimate will of God for the poor, a mediator that has a "concrete, specific history."[58] He makes this even more implicit in saying that Christology must come into confrontation with the reality of the poor as its object because, "the Son of Man is present in the poor of the world."[59]

Theology not only looks toward history, it arises out of the history of a people; it is historical and contextual. For Juan Luis Segundo, no theology is absent of a "prior political commitment."[60] This is made explicit by LAL theologians, who reread theology from the reality of the poor of Latin America. It is because of this historicity and contextuality that these scholars emphasize the historical Jesus more than the Christ of faith. As Sobrino

---

56. One can find this next section published in its entirety in Kertson, "Pneumatology in Latin American Liberation Theology," 85–99.
57. Boff, *Trinity and Society*, 176.
58. Sobrino, "Systematic Christology," 445.
59. Sobrino, "Systematic Christology," 458.
60. Segundo, *Liberation of Theology*, 94.

says, "The Christ discovered in Latin America is also a 'lived' Christ: a Christ of living experience."[61]

The Holy Spirit is conceived as part of the same historical and contextual praxis. José Comblin's method in *The Holy Spirit and Liberation* is "to bring out what is really fundamental in these experiences, leaving aside manifestations that St. Paul and the other New Testament authors judged to be secondary. The basic manifestations are historical which mean they fit into a context of action in history."[62] It is for this reason that Comblin begins with discussions of the experience and action of the Holy Spirit in the world before the Spirit in the church or in relation to the Trinity. Humanity does not experience the Holy Spirit apart from history. According to Comblin, "There is no separation between what the Spirit does and what human beings do, despite the fact that far from everything that they do proceeds from the Spirit."[63] Divine revelation of the Trinitarian persons, including the Holy Spirit, is not through ecstatic experience; it is through the concrete and historical.[64] Not everything we experience is God, but we do experience God in acts of freedom, prophetic speech, action, community and life.[65] Surely, the Holy Spirit is other than this world, but Liberation theologians question what point there is in talking of the Holy Spirit in supernatural terms. If the Holy Spirit has not been revealed through historical manifestations, supernatural revelation has little for theology. For these reasons, LAL theologians find the Spirit not in what Comblin called secondary manifestations, which include spiritual gifts or devotional practices, but in a historically and politically based spirituality lived among the poor of the world.

The Spirit in Spirituality

Traditional Christian spirituality usually includes practices centered on Scripture, prayer, contemplation, and the sacraments.[66] For LALT, theology and liberation are lived spirituality. José Maria Vigil explains this in saying, "The option for the poor is the adoption of a spiritual practice (wholly human and therefore also social and political) in favor of the poor in their

---

61. Sobrino, *Spirituality of Liberation*, 176.
62. Comblin, *Holy Spirit and Liberation*, 19.
63. Comblin, *Holy Spirit and Liberation*, 61.
64. Comblin, *Holy Spirit and Liberation*, 4.
65. Comblin, *Holy Spirit and Liberation*, 61–75.
66. See, for instance, the topics covered in Cunningham and Egan, *Christian Spirituality*, iii; Bacik, *Catholic Spirituality*, v–vi.

concrete social, historical, and conflictive situation."[67] Like theology, spirituality is not esoteric, supernatural, or otherworldly, nor does it have to be conjured through specialized practices or persons. Rather, according to Gustavo Gutiérrez, spirituality is "learning to live a new way; led by the Spirit. This is a lifestyle and not just an inner living."[68] While spirituality is seen primarily as following Jesus, we do this according to the Spirit, as this "is the area of the Spirit's action."[69]

What does this concrete and historical spirituality look like? For Gutiérrez, spirituality includes solidarity, gratuitousness, joy and community. This is a similar list to Comblin's description of how we experience God. Notice Gutiérrez includes joy, which can be understood in more emotional or abstract terms. For Gutiérrez, however, it is still rooted in experiences of solidarity and community lived with one another and through the Holy Spirit. Comblin at one point even communicates the idea that spirituality is expressed in the language of prayer.[70] He therefore connects his spirituality to "traditional" spirituality, but even here, prayer is an expression of lived spirituality that finds its root in life with, among and on behalf of the poor.

In his work on spirituality and liberation, Jon Sobrino makes spirituality even more connected with praxis and concrete lived experience. The spirit "actually becomes present in human beings and animates their thoughts, feelings, and actions."[71] This concrete spirit is the spirit of an individual or group "in relationship with the whole reality."[72] Spirituality is always present within the historical life and can be seen in any group or religion in how they interact with ultimate reality.[73] A Christian spirituality would likewise be life lived in a particular spirit, the spirit of Jesus.[74] Rather than contemplative practice, Sobrino's spirituality is centered on the political. That is, "Action directed toward structurally transforming society in the direction of the reign of God, by doing justice to the poor and oppressed majorities, so that they obtain life and historical salvation."[75] This action includes proclamation, evangelization, discipleship (though

---

67. Vigil, "Option for the Poor," 12.
68. Gutiérrez, *We Drink From Our Own Wells*, 79.
69. Gutiérrez, *We Drink From Our Own Wells*, 91.
70. Comblin, "Holy Spirit," 481.
71. Sobrino, "Spirituality and the Following of Jesus," 680.
72. Sobrino, *Spirituality of Liberation*, 13.
73. Sobrino, *Spirituality of Liberation*, 30.
74. Sobrino, *Spirituality of Liberation*, 2.
75. Sobrino, *Spirituality of Liberation*, 80.

all significantly revised), and conflict that all result in changes leading to liberation. He also sees the "spirit of the beatitudes" as a formative spirit for liberation.[76]

Liberation is the goal of spirituality and therefore the Holy Spirit. Because the Holy Spirit is constitutive of praxis for LALT, the unique person of the Holy Spirit is at times downplayed or conflated with a broader spirituality. This ambiguity concerning the Spirit is particularly found in the work of Sobrino who does not delineate a specific role for the Holy Spirit in spirituality. This becomes a tension within LALT's Pneumatology and spirituality. In response, some like Comblin write more about the traditional roles and work of the Holy Spirit, but without divorcing spirituality from praxis or the poor. For both Sobrino and Comblin, however, the Holy Spirit is always the engine that drives spirituality. Spirituality is about living a life of the Spirit to further the liberating work of Jesus in the world.

The Spirit of Liberation

Who then is the Holy Spirit in LALT? Few statements are made explicitly to describe the Holy Spirit because we learn about the Spirit through its actions. When these scholars speak of the Holy Spirit, it is done in ways that buttress the idea of liberation.

One way that Leonardo Boff chooses to interpret the Holy Spirit is through the lens of the Trinity and society. For Boff, this triune communion is a source of inspiration for Christians committed to social change. He writes: "A society that takes its inspiration from Trinitarian communion cannot tolerate class differences and domination based on power. . . . The sort of society that would emerge from inspiration by the Trinitarian model would be one of fellowship, equality of opportunity, and generosity."[77] For Boff, if we learn about the divine character from divine action within society, then we know that the Holy Spirit is the liberating Spirit, for where the Spirit of the Lord is there is freedom. Likewise, a theology of the Holy Spirit can only emerge from the "praxis of a free Christian people."[78]

The Holy Spirit is also seen as liberation in its role in new creation. The idea of life is central to the understanding of liberation. God is life and the Spirit is the giver of life, the one through whom we access God. Boff explains it this way, "The Holy Spirit is first and foremost life and communication of

76. Sobrino, "Spirituality and the Following of Jesus," 692.

77. Boff, *Trinity and Society*, 151. Boff is largely dependent upon Moltmann for his discussion of the social Trinity, esp. Moltmann, *Trinity and the Kingdom*.

78. Comblin, "Holy Spirit," 466.

life through communion and union."⁷⁹ The experience of life is also central to the liberating message of Jesus as he stated: "I have come that they may have life, and have it to the full" (John 10:10). This life is realized in the experience of the Holy Spirit, Lord and Giver of Life.

This life is also seen in the resurrection where the Spirit is the giver of new life. José Comblin tells us that the Holy Spirit is "sent to the whole world to bring about a new creation. The Spirit's action in the church is subordinate to this goal of new creation."[80] The Holy Spirit's work goes beyond political, economic or social change to complete transformation of these systems. Theologically, this aspect of the Holy Spirit can be traced to the work of the Spirit in the resurrection of the body. This resurrection is not just Jesus's resurrection or our eternal resurrection, but since the Holy Spirit is already present, resurrection is also obtainable in this world. As Comblin points out, "The Spirit actually generates a new human being. The Holy Spirit is the presence, in our own time, of the reign of God."[81]

The Holy Spirit brings life to the individual and communities, empowering them to bring life and liberation to the poor of the world. Comblin describes this empowerment as an experience of the Holy Spirit that "launches men and women out into the world as though imbibed with superhuman energy to tackle superhuman tasks."[82] He later describes these tasks as furthering the kingdom of God and mission of Jesus. Boff also describes this experience corporately noting that, "The Holy Spirit does not act only in the multiplicity of men and women, especially the poor. Its favored manifestation—sacrament—is in the community of those who follow Jesus. The church is the sacrament of Christ and also that of the Holy Spirit."[83] The Spirit gives life and empowers the people of God to give life through embodying the kingdom in our present-day contexts.

Finally, the Holy Spirit in LALT points us to Jesus's life and example of liberation. Comblin tells us "the Holy Spirit enables us to understand Jesus's life, his actions.... We understand his work by taking part in the actions to which they refer."[84] He says this even more explicitly in the statement, "the Spirit cannot separate itself from Jesus."[85] Likewise, in summarizing the work of the Holy Spirit, Boff says it "consists basically in revealing the Son to

---

79. Boff, *Trinity and Society*, 216.
80. Comblin, *Holy Spirit and Liberation*, 43.
81. Comblin, "Holy Spirit," 472.
82. Comblin, *Holy Spirit and Liberation*, 6.
83. Boff, *Trinity and Society*, 209. See also Gutiérrez, *Theology of Liberation*, 143–61.
84. Comblin, *Holy Spirit and Liberation*, 155.
85. Comblin, *Holy Spirit and Liberation*, 156.

all and in working out the liberation action of the Son."[86] Finally, we also saw in Sobrino's work on spirituality that Liberation spirituality focuses on the works and life of Jesus. This gives further evidence that the work of the Holy Spirit in Liberation Pneumatology is to further the work of Jesus.

This is not altogether different from traditional pneumatologies, which have been hesitant to speak of the Holy Spirit beyond Scripture or a Christocentric paradigm.[87] It is significant for Liberation Pneumatology, however, because the Spirit's pointing to Jesus is the central reason one knows that the Holy Spirit is the Spirit of liberation. It is also important that, while the Spirit's role is reimagined in light of Liberation's rereading of Jesus as liberator, the function of the Holy Spirit within the Trinity remains unchanged. This is a move made more recently in Renewal Theology, which attempts to construct a theological framework in which the Holy Spirit and the experience of the Spirit in the world by the people of God is a central feature.

Renewal Pneumatology

Three Pentecostal authors present themselves as good candidates to help begin a dialogue with LAL Pneumatology. I will begin with Steven Land's *Pentecostal Spirituality: A Passion for the Kingdom* whose proposal is the broadest. I will then overview Eldin Villafañe's *The Liberating Spirit: An Hispanic American Pentecostal Social Ethic*, which narrows in on a specifically Latino context before turning to Samuel Solivan's *The Spirit, Pathos and Liberation: Toward an Hispanic Pentecostal Theology*. These three scholars represent a limited sampling of the Renewal landscape and are not necessarily representative of the movement as a whole. Nevertheless, though each very different, they are illustrative of the resources available within the movement that can be used to dialogue with LALT.

Like LAL theologians, Land sees spirituality and theology as intricately connected. Theology is not just discursive reasoning, "but also engagement of the whole person within the communion of charisms."[88] Theology is in the service of spirituality and emerges out of spirituality. Orthopraxy is just as important as orthodoxy. This moves the center of theology and Pneumatology away from the abstract and towards the historical. Similar to LALT, Land sees the center of spirituality and the Holy Spirit's work, as focused on the kingdom. The Holy Spirit is the agent of the kingdom, so for Land, Pentecostal spirituality centers on a passion for the kingdom through a life

---

86. Boff, *Trinity and Society*, 34.
87. See Wiles and Santer, *Documents in Early Christian Thought*, 81.
88. Land, *Pentecostal Spirituality*, 23.

that honors God and seeing the kingdom advance in this world, primarily through evangelism.[89] This praxis is quite different and more abstract than what we have seen in LALT. With the concept of kingdom, Land connects the idea of orthopathy, or right affections. By orthopathy, Land means a "religious experience as an event of knowing between the Divine source and human participation" that in turn develops "affections which motivate the heart and characterize the believer."[90] One develops this affection through prayer and mission done in light of eschatological fervency. Orthopathy serves as the third leg of the theological stool along with orthodoxy and orthopraxy: being, believing and doing. It orients one's beliefs and praxes through engagement with the Holy Spirit and makes for a lasting change in the individual and the world. These are affections "which dispose the person toward God and the neighbor."[91] All three "orthos" are necessary and central to the theological task, living by the Holy Spirit and in relating to God and others.

In his book *The Liberating Spirit*, Eldin Villafañe also sees spirituality as central to Renewal. He calls spirituality "a style of living the life of the Holy Spirit" but calls for Pentecostals to have a more holistic spirituality relevant for all of life.[92] Different from Land, such spirituality would include both personal transformation and social transformation through justice, advocacy, and social action. Distancing himself from LALT, he insists that the primary motivator for spirituality is an encounter with the Holy Spirit, who pours the love of God into our hearts making love the dominant relationship of the believer to God and others. Therefore, Spirit empowered love becomes the source, motive and power of living ethically. The Holy Spirit's work goes beyond the church as Spirit-empowered people are called to discern the Spirit's work in the world and join with the Spirit in bringing about the reign of God.[93] This comes through sharing love and justice via fellowship, worship, proclamation and service in the power of the Spirit.[94]

Samuel Solivan also develops the idea of orthopathy, though independently and differently than Land.[95] While his central claim is still based

---

89. Land, *Pentecostal Spirituality*, 44.

90. Land, *Pentecostal Spirituality*, 33.

91. Land, *Pentecostal Spirituality*, 136. Land does not talk specifically about the poor in his vision of mission. He takes a more traditional Renewal approach focused on the interior. At the same time, he provides the language of "orthopathy" and right affections which are an important component for poverty.

92. Villafañe, *Liberating Spirit*, 164.

93. Villafañe, *Liberating Spirit*, 191.

94. Villafañe, *Liberating Spirit*, 216–21.

95. Solivan, *Spirit, Pathos, and Liberation*, 12.

on right affections, he has a very different vision of what these affections entail. In my view, his theological move provides more of a middle ground between Land and LALT. Pathos, rather than passion for the kingdom, is the situation of suffering and self-alienation many Hispanics experience in the United States. Orthopathos, or right pathos, then is the manner in which suffering can be a source for liberation and social transformation through the Holy Spirit.[96] Orthopathy is pneumatologically driven and focuses on the whole person. The person, the community, and even social structures can be transformed physically, psychologically, socially and spiritually through the Holy Spirit.[97] This occurs as the people of God experience the power and presence of the Holy Spirit among them and then provide hope in the Spirit as a living witness to the presence of God among the suffering poor.[98] Here is where he connects with LALT. He insists that this pathos-suffering is the point of connection between the divine and the suffering poor. The God who suffered takes sides with those who suffer because of injustice. The role of the Holy Spirit is in "linking us with Christ's own source of power.... [The Spirit] is that gift of God to us that equips us to do battle and win over the forces of evil and injustice. It is the same Holy Spirit who gives us wisdom for engaging the principalities and powers that daily seek to overwhelm us."[99] Solivan agrees with LALT that orthodoxy is not enough to overcome the systemic evil of this world. He goes a step further in saying that orthopraxis is also not enough if the people's suffering is not transformed into hope by the power of the Holy Spirit, thereby changing the very constitution of the person, the community and the society not just socioeconomically, but holistically.

Making the Connection

So, what does this mean for Pneumatology? First, there are similarities in these two views of the Holy Spirit. Both Renewal Theology and LALT envision the Holy Spirit as an historical reality experienced in the day-to-day life of people. This historical experience expands beyond the church to include the larger kingdom of God and the experience of the Spirit in the world. The Holy Spirit both points back towards Jesus's work in the kingdom of God, but also inspires innovation among others in advancing this work. For both Renewal and LALT the Holy Spirit is also the liberating Spirit. These

96. Solivan, *Spirit, Pathos, and Liberation*, 61–62.
97. Solivan, *Spirit, Pathos, and Liberation*, 100.
98. Solivan, *Spirit, Pathos, and Liberation*, 111.
99. Solivan, *Spirit, Pathos, and Liberation*, 131.

similarities continually have to be nuanced, however, because while they use similar language, which opens up possible dialogue, what each movement means is very different. Here, for instance, while both see the Holy Spirit as the liberator, these two movement's views of liberation have traditionally been different: Liberation theologians focused on the social-economic aspects while Renewal scholars focused more on spiritual liberation. Theologians like Villafañe and Solivan help us bridge this gap making Liberation not just spiritual but holistic.

This discussion begins to point to some of the pneumatological differences between the two movements and what they can learn from one another. There are many differences, but I will briefly discuss two possible avenues that can serve as dialogue points for mutual enrichment: one, the scope of the Holy Spirit's work, and two, the nature of the Holy Spirit's work in spirituality.

Concerning the scope of the Holy Spirit's work, Renewal Theology envisions the Spirit as being poured out on all flesh while LALT sees the Holy Spirit particularly at work in the poor and marginalized majorities of the world. That said, the work of Solivan provides a middle ground perspective expanding the idea of poor to include all suffering peoples. This does not result in an either-or dialogue but both-and dialogue. While the Holy Spirit is poured out on all flesh, it is for the sake of the poor and the suffering to bring transformation and it is in this relationship that all parties can be changed. While Liberation Pneumatology has taken this a step further in seeing the work of the kingdom as related to historical salvation, Renewalists have often limited this work to spiritual concerns. Certainly, in a Renewal vision the Holy Spirit is experienced through the historical, the bodily and the concrete, but the primary implications are traditionally seen as spiritual and geared toward eternal, otherworldly salvation.[100] This is an area that Renewal Theology can continue to learn from LALT. The Holy Spirit is also at work in political, economic and social liberation, not only spiritual liberation.

On the other hand, Renewal Theology provides a paradigm that is more inclusive of spiritual realities in its view of liberation. For instance, it is common among Renewalists to view the Holy Spirit as enacting healing for the body, emotions, and psyche. There is a need, however, to move beyond seeing this healing as symbolic for an ultimate spiritual healing and broaden our understanding of healing as applying to every area of life (the social, economic and political) and communities and systems, not only

---

100. This is what we saw in Land, for instance, though this has begun to change with works like Althouse, *Spirit of the Last Days*.

individuals. Another example would be evangelism. Renewalists see the Holy Spirit as empowering for witness. Does this witness need to be only for individual spiritual salvation? Renewalists should be challenged to expand their vision of the kingdom of God and the scope of the Spirit's work by allowing a Spirit-driven orthopathy to motivate a holistic and historically rooted orthopraxy that includes spiritual practices, as well as political and social action. In view of this discussion, it becomes obvious that there is need to develop a Renewal Pneumatology that is more intentionally holistic; a Pneumatology that while it celebrates the importance of individual spiritual health, it can also emphasize the need for social and political justice in the larger society

A second area of mutual dialogue is the nature of the Holy Spirit's work in spirituality. For LALT, the very act of being involved in liberation is a spiritual act in which one follows the way of Jesus empowered by the Holy Spirit. For Renewal Pneumatology, however, seeing the Holy Spirit involved in history gives greater importance to the unique person and role of the Spirit. Renewal Pneumatology challenges LALT by insisting that it is important to encounter the Holy Spirit for the sake of the Spirit and not just for liberation, although for Solivan these encounters of the Spirit are the very engine that drives liberation through the idea of orthopathos. Renewal Theology can learn from LALT that liberation is indeed a spiritual practice; one can encounter the Holy Spirit and be used by the Holy Spirit in liberation. Liberation can also learn from Renewalist thought. As Land discusses, it is important to develop orthopathy as much as orthopraxy. This is developed in passion for the kingdom, through passionate prayer, worship, service and encounter with the Holy Spirit. Solivan and Villafañe echo these concepts as important for orthopathic liberation and right living by the Spirit. Orthopathos can also be developed through right practice through participation in liberation as posited by Liberation spirituality. Renewal spirituality also affirms the importance of an encounter with the person of the Holy Spirit through various traditional spiritual practices. While these practices may include liberation, they ultimately help develop one's orthopathy toward a greater passion for the kingdom and for liberation.

Conclusion

Looking back, the conversation between Liberation and Renewal is certainly not new. As early as 1979, Cardinal Léon Joseph Suenens, Charismatic liaison to the Pope John Paul I, and Liberation theologian, Hélder Câmara, coauthored a book entitled *Charismatic Renewal and Social Action*.[101] This book brought together these two Renewal movements, one that has been traditionally seen as focused on spiritual renewal and one that has been seen as focused on political renewal. Cardinal Suenens contention was that the practices of prayer and worship in which Charismatic Roman Catholics have encountered the Holy Spirit can be motivation and empowerment for liberation practices. Câmara responded that experiences of the Holy Spirit are of little good if they do not lead to such liberation.

In a more contemporary vein, I have tried to show in this section that a dialogue concerning Pneumatology between LALT and Renewal Theology can show that the two are not mutually exclusive. Rather they are crossing the same bridge of renewal from different vantage points and have theological ideas and resources that can contribute toward a shared goal of the liberation of creation and the urban poor. A spirituality for the urban poor should address both the exterior and interior of the person. It should address both the spiritual and physical, both the individual and the social. As we saw in our second chapter, both are affected by poverty.

Challenge Two: Pneumatology and Christology

A second challenge is the interaction between Christology and Pneumatology. Historically, Christology has taken precedence in this relationship as described in our historical inquiry above. Many are hesitant to leave Christology behind in their attempt to be pneumatological. It is questionable whether it is even possible to leave Christology behind because one of the central roles of the Holy Spirit is to point to the Son. It boils down to a Trinitarian problem of the relation, in similarity and differentiation, between the persons of the Godhead. In speaking of one member, Trinitarian theology dictates that any statement must be true of the others. At the same time, if there is no differentiation between the members, one moves into either a oneness position or a heavy kind of subordinationism often with Jesus as the head practically, but the Father theologically. In purporting a strong Pneumatology, I desire to give a unique role to the Holy Spirit, while recognizing it can never be wholly unique from Christology. Still, my belief is that the wells of Pneumatology have barely been explored and this exploration has been held back by fears of abandoning Christology. One movement that has attempted to address this quandary is Spirit-Christology. In this section, we will explore modern approaches to Spirit-Christology and assert that the

---

101. Suenens and Câmara, *Charismatic Renewal and Social Action*.

complimentary model is the best approach through which to put forward a holistic Pneumatology of urban poverty.

Samuel Alfaro in his book *Divino Compañero* gives one of the more recent overviews of modern Spirit-Christologies from Roman Catholic, Protestant and Pentecostal perspectives.[102] He categorizes these Christologies into three approaches: replacement, revisionist and complementary.[103] The first category includes the replacement models of Geoffrey Lampe, Paul Newman and James D. G. Dunn.[104] Replacement Christologies attempt to supplant the traditional Chalcedonian view of the two natures of Christ. They reject traditional views of the incarnation and see the Holy Spirit as the divine influence over the human Jesus.[105] It is the Holy Spirit who accounts for the divine element in the life of Jesus. This perspective leads to a strong Pneumatology. For instance, Lampe sees the Holy Spirit as the primary actor in salvation saying it was the Spirit who resurrected Jesus and that same Spirit who resurrects or recreates us today.[106] This strong Pneumatology is at the cost of Christology, however.

The revisionist approach, is represented by Roger Haight and Piet Schoonenberg.[107] Alfaro identifies these approaches as revisionist rather than Ralph Del Colle's identification of them as replacement theologies because of Haight's and Schoonenberg's own insistence that their Spirit-Christologies are meant to run parallel to Logos-Christology, that both Christologies are important, and that both insist on maintaining the divinity of Jesus.[108] Still, these views reinterpret orthodoxy and Christology. For instance, Schoonenberg sees the biggest difference being that in Logos-Christology Jesus descends from God, in a Spirit-Christology Jesus ascends to God. This is a theology of becoming in which Jesus becomes the son of God through the Holy Spirit rather than Jesus being fully God at birth.[109]

---

102. Alfaro, *Divino Compañero*, 62–86.

103. This is over against Ralph Del Colle's two classifications of replacement and complementary. Alfaro adds the third category of "revisionist" for reasons described below. See Del Colle, *Christ and the Spirit*.

104. See Lampe, *God as Spirit*; Newman, *Spirit Christology*; Dunn, *Jesus and the Spirit*.

105. Alfaro, *Divino Compañero*, 64. Some, like Lampe, more clearly reject the incarnation while others like Dunn are heavily revisionist, especially when looking from a Pauline perspective.

106. Lampe, *God as Spirit*, 144.

107. Haight, *Jesus, Symbol of God*. Schoonenberg, *Der Geist*.

108. Alfaro, *Divino Compañero*, 77.

109. Schoonenberg, *Der Geist*, 125.

The final approach to Spirit-Christology outlined by Alfaro is the complementary view.[110] Such approaches include the work of Charismatic scholars like Clark Pinnock, Jean Jacques Suurmond and Ralph Del Colle.[111] The complementary view wants to establish the role of the Holy Spirit in Jesus's life without rejecting or revising incarnational Christology. It seeks to maintain the divinity of the Holy Spirit and Jesus as well as the hypostatic union. For instance, Suurmond wants to assert the necessary nature of both a Logos- and Spirit-Christology in that they balance one another in a "yin-yang manner," one being from above, the other from below; one providing order, the other dynamism.[112]

Other Renewal approaches to the Spirit-Christ problem have taken a complementary approach.[113] Myk Habets, in his book *The Anointed Son*, believes Spirit-Christology should seek to maintain both the *filioque* and the pneumatological aspects of Christology, it must be fully Trinitarian, and finally it should be scriptural.[114] Amos Yong draws on both Irenaean Trinitarianism, seeing the Son and the Holy Spirit as the two hands of the Father, and *perichoresis* as the mutual interpenetration of the Son and the Holy Spirit. These concepts maintain both the sameness and the uniqueness of the Holy Spirit and the Son.[115]

These Spirit-Christologies give some perspectives on possible interplays between Pneumatology and Christology, though all of them focus more on how Pneumatology interacts with Christology than the opposite. It shows the central place that Christology continually takes over Pneumatology. In terms of our approach, complementarian is the most helpful because it still gives a prominent role to the Holy Spirit while not denying the equally important place that an incarnational, fully human and fully God, Christ takes in the Trinity. At the same time, this author does see a need to ask questions from a more pneumatically centered perspective than is done in Spirit-Christology. For instance, how does Christology affect Pneumatology? If we were doing strong pneumatological theology this would be a more pressing question.

Amos Yong in his Spirit-Word-Community gives a number of reasons why it is reasonable and even advantageous to start with the Holy Spirit in

110. Alfaro, *Divino Compañero*, 82.

111. See Pinnock, *Flame of Love*; Suurmond, "Ethical Influence"; Del Colle, *Christ and the Spirit*.

112. Suurmond, "Ethical Influence," 41–45.

113. All of Alfaro's examples of the complementary view—Pinnock, Suurmond, and Del Colle—are Renewalists.

114. Habets, *Anointed Son*, 229–31.

115. Yong, *Spirit-Word-Community*, 49–59.

theology. He mentions the pedagogical reasons that because Christ has come first so often, starting with the Holy Spirit equalizes this trend.[116] Second is his Spirit-Christology which says that the Holy Spirit is what makes Jesus the Christ. Jesus's "teaching, preaching, healing, exorcism, liberating, delivering, and saving words and deeds are the result of the Spirit's anointing."[117] The Holy Spirit unites the divinity and humanity of Jesus. The Holy Spirit is also integral to the cross, resurrection, ascension and return of Jesus, and the time in between. Still, Yong holds his pneumatological imagination has a christomorphic structure one cannot get around because of his, and our, conviction to remain wholly Trinitarian and biblical.[118] Still, for Yong, the pneumatological imagination must remain distinctly charismatic and pneumatic.

For our purposes, this means our Pneumatology will provide critique and complement to the christological and theistic views of urban poverty we have explored so far in this thesis. It will necessarily be connected to christological and theistic views of urban poverty while striving to maintain a pneumatological center.

CONCLUSION: A METHODOLOGY FOR A PNEUMATOLOGY OF URBAN POVERTY

In this chapter, we have explored Pneumatology as a step toward putting forth a holistic Pneumatology of urban poverty in our final chapter. We have explored the history of Pneumatology and the scope of Pneumatology because we have perceived a pneumatological gap in the previous Evangelical, ecumenical and Renewal literature on urban poverty. While Pneumatology has been quiet throughout the ages, there has been a renaissance of the Holy Spirit in the last century both ecclesially and academically. However, we are still in the very early phases of exploring and applying this Pneumatology to the whole of theology. Increasingly, scholars are calling for theology to move beyond basic scriptural inquiries or speaking about the Holy Spirit as a gap-filler in a number of theological loci. Instead, some theologians are putting forth a pneumatologically driven theological method, what we are calling a holistic Pneumatology, which seeks to see all of life and reality from a pneumatological perspective.

Still, we have seen some challenges that come with a pneumatological theology. The first of these challenges is overcoming a series of polarities, such as the interior and exterior, or the natural and supernatural polarities.

---

116. Yong, *Spirit-Word-Community*, 28.
117. Yong, *Spirit-Word-Community*, 28–29.
118. Yong, *Spirit-Word-Community*, 36–37.

A Pneumatology, especially if it is Trinitarian, must be holistic and address both extremes. The second challenge was that of how Pneumatology applies to Christology. We have seen that it must have a complementary christological element that helps keep it grounded and stay true to Scripture. If our theology is to be truly Trinitarian, however, the Spirit must also be able to speak uniquely and holistically to a situation like urban poverty and not be subsumed by Christology.

We have not, in this chapter, explored various pneumatological themes because every theological theme should be able to be spoken about pneumatologically. What is more important is the pneumatic method through which we think and approach any given topic of theology. To do this concerning urban poverty, we will follow Amos Yong's idea of the pneumatological imagination described above.

I will propose a methodology centered on a holistic pneumatological reworking of the four-fold gospel of Jesus as savior, baptizer, healer and soon coming king, as at the heart of a Renewal response to urban poverty. Donald Dayton has proposed that such a four-fold gospel is at the heart of Renewal Theology and some have picked up on this theme for their own modern constructions.[119] To develop this method, I utilize Amos Yong's pneumatological imagination to identify a possible pneumatic metaphor to provide a bridge between Pneumatology and poverty. Yong himself does not develop a theology of poverty but does deal with poverty in different segments of his book *In the Days of Caesar*, particularly chapter 7, in which he talks about economics and explores the health and wealth gospel as a Pentecostal response to poverty.[120] Yong uses his pneumatological imagination to identify salvation as a primary pneumatic metaphor for political theology, but then proceeds to interpret this metaphor of salvation through the christological five-fold gospel rather than interpret salvation in a pneumatological manner.

I also want to propose the pneumatic metaphor of salvation but want to interpret it in a pneumatological manner based on the passage Luke 4:18–19, "The Spirit of the Lord is on me because he has anointed me to proclaim good news to the poor. He has sent me to proclaim freedom for the prisoners and recovery of sight for the blind, to set the oppressed free to proclaim the year of the Lord's favor." Jesus himself says that his mission was to proclaim the gospel to the poor (salvation) which includes restitution to community for the prisoner (Spirit baptism) and healing the sight

---

119. See Dayton, *Theological Roots of Pentecostalism*, 21–23. The four-fold gospel has in fact been applied to social issues, but not within a pneumatological framework. See Clifton, "Preaching the 'Full Gospel'"; Swoboda, *Tongues and Trees*.

120. Yong, *In the Days of Caesar*, 257–74.

of the blind (healing) all seen in an Eschatological framework, the year of the Lord. However, it is often overlooked that this was a pneumatic mission empowered by the Holy Spirit. When most people talk about social action toward the poor, at its core they are talking about salvation. This is not just a spiritual salvation, but a holistic salvation that includes personal, familial, ecclesial, material, social, and cosmic aspects, all of which are affected by poverty and in need of the saving work of the Holy Spirit.

As Yong points out in *The Spirit Poured out on all Flesh*, salvation is not just a function of the Son, but the Holy Spirit is involved at every level of salvation.[121] This Renewal tradition has perhaps the strongest emphasis on the Holy Spirit. Yong is right that Renewal's four-fold gospel serves a holistic soteriological framework that deals with salvation physically (healing), emotionally (healing), personally (savior), communally (Spirit baptism), ecclesially (Spirit baptism), and cosmically (soon coming/eschatology).[122] Luke 4:18–19 also reflects each of these four-fold functions of the pneumatic mission to the poor. Many of these spheres in which salvation works overlap but naming them demonstrates that the four-fold gospel has the capacity to cover a holistic vision of salvation for the urban poor.[123]

To complement the christological focus of the four-fold gospel within the Renewal tradition, I will develop the four-fold gospel in a pneumatological way in which the Spirit functions as savior, baptizer, healer, and entelechy of the eschatological kingdom.[124] This is not to replace Christ in salvation or the four-fold gospel, but to show the important and sometimes unique roles the Holy Spirit also plays in salvation. This methodology will be developed into a holistic Pneumatology of the urban poor in the next chapter.

---

121. Yong, *Spirit Poured Out*, 91–109.

122. Yong uses the five-fold gospel because he wants to include sanctification in his discussion, even though he himself does not come from the holiness-Pentecostal tradition. I, also an assemblies of God minister, will use the four-fold gospel more often used by non-holiness Pentecostals.

123. The four-fold gospel has in fact been applied to social issues, but not within a pneumatological framework. See Clifton, "Preaching the 'Full Gospel,'" 117–19.

124. For another example of someone using a pneumatological version of the four-fold gospel see Swoboda, *Tongues and Trees*. See also Tallman, "Pentecostal Ecology," 136. Tallman, however, only interprets the third tenant of Spirit baptism as "Pneumatology," still speaking of salvation, healing, and eschatology christologically rather than interpreting the whole framework through a pneumatological lens.

6

Pneumatology and Urban Poverty in the United States

INTRODUCTION

I have one last autobiographical story illustrating my hope in creating a holistic Pneumatology of urban poverty in this dissertation. I was a young pastor, just fresh out of university. Having learned everything from higher critical methods, to spiritual disciplines, to how to live with people who were not my family for the first time, I, like most twenty-two-year-olds, felt ready to take on the world. My wife and I were running a performing arts studio in Southern California at the time. This included a children's performance group that would perform Christian songs and dances at churches, retirement homes, or in public spaces. There was a diversity of race, age and socioeconomic status among the young people in our group. Some received scholarships to be in the studio because their parents did not have enough money to pay, but many were rather well off. My wife and I often took this group to perform for the more marginalized in our society—the elderly, mentally ill, and the poor. We did this because we knew these groups could use some extra joy in their lives that can only be brought by children. We also wanted our students to hear stories they probably would not hear otherwise in hopes of creating some form of present and future solidarity.

One Wednesday night we got the opportunity to take the studio's performing group to a large Baptist church that had a weekly feeding program. Each week the church fed dinner to over three hundred people who needed a free meal. Many were homeless, many were families, all were experiencing difficulties during this season. During the meal, the church liked to have entertainment when possible. The church had asked me to share a short devotional thought after our kids performed. Having been a recent college graduate from Azusa Pacific University studying various theological movements around the world, I knew exactly what I should share. These people needed to know about Latin American Liberation Theology. They needed to know that God was for the poor. They needed to know they were special to God even in the midst of their poverty. My heart was in the right place coming from my cosmopolitan setting into these borderlands. In the midst of my short talk, however, in all my young enthusiasm, I said these words, "God loves the poor so much. You are the luckiest people on earth. Sometimes I wish I was poor!" Immediately someone shouted back, "Well, let's trade place then!" I was so embarrassed. To this day I do not even remember how I responded. I think I repressed it somewhere deep in the recesses of the shame I felt. I had clearly misunderstood the theological drive for the option for the poor and had also offered an idea that would not really help.

Sometimes we have the best intentions in trying to help people. Many have good intentions to help the poor in their community, but a number of roadblocks stand in the way. They may not understand the individual and systemic causes of poverty, they may not know the best approach, or they may lack resources. The thesis has been put forth in this dissertation that there has been a gap in the theological approach to urban poverty and that a holistic pneumatological approach can help to fill that gap. While the Pneumatology put forth in this chapter may not keep embarrassing moments like mine from happening, anytime we can come to a fuller understanding of something we are better for it.

Chapter 6 described what Pneumatology is, the scope of Pneumatology, and sought to overcome two major challenges to a Pneumatology of poverty—the imbalance between the interior and exterior and between Pneumatology and Christology. In this, our final chapter, we outline the beginnings of a holistic Pneumatology of urban poverty using the metaphor of salvation as seen in the four-fold gospel: the Holy Spirit as savior, baptizer, healer and entelechy of the eschatological kingdom. Before exploring each of these areas, we will first engage in a brief pneumatic reading of Luke 4 which provides us with our primarily pneumatological metaphor of the Holy Spirit as savior for the urban poor.

PNEUMATIC READING OF LUKE 4

In the end of chapter 6 we described our method, following Amos Yong's pneumatological imagination, as identifying a key pneumatic metaphor through which to address the problem of poverty. We identified this metaphor as "salvation" drawn from Jesus's own pneumatic mission statement to proclaim the gospel to the poor. Before unpacking what we mean by this salvation theologically, it will behoove us to briefly explore the passage on which we base this reading within its Lukan context and allow it to inform our theology.

The placement of the Luke 4:18–19 pericope is situated in a pivotal location for Luke's narrative as whole.[1] It transitions the reader from Luke's introductory material about Jesus's early life and preparation for ministry to his ministry proper. Before this passage there are no miracles attributed to Jesus. After this proclamation, healing and exorcism become regular.[2] This is not the first mention of the Holy Spirit in Luke. Jesus was conceived by the Holy Spirit (Luke 1:35). The Holy Spirit presided over his dedication as a baby. (Luke 2:25–32). Jesus grew strong in wisdom, a concept often associated with the Holy Spirit (Luke 1:80; 2:52; cf. Isa 11:2). The Holy Spirit descended upon Jesus at his baptism (Luke 3:21–22) and led Jesus into the wilderness (Luke 4:1) helping him to overcome temptation and return filled with the power of the of Holy Spirit for his ministry after this pneumatic inauguration (Luke 4:14).[3]

After this inauguration, Jesus lives out this anointing by the power of the Holy Spirit doing exactly what he said he would do. Immediately, Luke relates Jesus setting an oppressed person free by casting a demon out of him (Luke 4:31–37), healing Simon Peter's mother from a fever (Luke 4:38–39) and then providing a generalized description of the many who were healed of various diseases and freed from different spirits (Luke 4:40–41). Luke continues interspersing such Holy Spirit empowered salvific acts throughout the whole book. Many of Jesus's words are also pneumatic either being empowered by the Holy Spirit or speaking about the Spirit (Luke 10:21; 11:13, 20; 12:10, 12; 24:49).[4] Luke 4:18–19 then stands at the center of these two pneumatic movements. Jesus looks backward, "The Spirit of the Lord is on me, because he has anointed me" and forward, "to proclaim good news to the poor." The Holy Spirit is central as the one who prepares Jesus for his ministry and empowers him to live out his mission.

What do these verses mean concerning the poor, our theme of salvation, and a holistic Pneumatology of the poor? It is at the Holy Spirit's

---

1. Both R. Alan Culpepper and Walter E. Pilgrim, for instance, see Luke 18:19 as part of the larger passage in Luke 4:16–30, and place it at the beginning of a major section of Luke's gospel that encompasses Jesus's ministry in Galilee from Luke 4:14 to Luke 9:50. See Culpepper and O'Day, *Gospel of Luke*; Pilgrim, *Good News to the Poor*.

2. Thomas, "Spirit, Healing, and Mission," 432.

3. For pneumatic readings of Luke-Acts, see Menzies, *Empowered for Witness*. See also Yong, *Spirit Poured Out*, 84–91; Mittelstadt, *Reading Luke-Acts*.

4. Menzies, *Empowered for Witness*, 157–72.

prompting and empowerment that Jesus centers his ministry upon the poor and the marginalized. The Holy Spirit should take a similarly central role in our own theology and action toward the poor, both motivating us and empowering us in our action. Addressing poverty is a pneumatic act as it seeks to further human flourishing in the world.

It is important to note how Walter E. Pilgrim establishes clearly that Luke's portrayal of the poor to which Jesus is ministering clearly involves the economic poor.[5] Luke's use of *ptóchos* for the poor, while it may have spiritual nuances, is an economic category with socio-economic implications. Luke portrays Jesus meeting the concrete needs of people who are poor and oppressed throughout the gospel. In Luke 6, Jesus declares, "Blessed are the poor," and the ensuing woes concerning the rich and the well fed make it clear Jesus is talking about the poor economically and socially, not just spiritually (Luke 6:20, 24–25).[6] Likewise, in Luke 14, Jesus challenges the Pharisee with whom he is eating to invite the poor, the maimed, the lame and the blind to the meal. These groups comprise a class of people that parallels Luke 4. It is a group that cannot repay someone for the hospitality they receive. Even the opening of the book of Luke paints the beginning of a drama in which God puts down the mighty and rich from their positions of power and raises up those who are lowly (Luke 1–2). One cannot limit the afflictions of these groups to economic problems. Rather these afflictions encompass a range including social, spiritual, economic, and even physical marginalization. If there is any spiritual connotation at all in Luke's usage of the poor, it is that whatever one's economic state, they should put their full trust in God for everything.

S. John Roth in his book *The Blind, the Lame and the Poor*, makes similar assertions concerning these groups that are lumped together in Luke 4:18–19. He argues, the "captive, the shattered, the blind, the deaf mute, the lame, the lepers, the maimed, the dead and the poor should be considered together as a set of types."[7] Roth looks toward the Septuagint (LXX), which Luke would have been dependent on for his use and understanding of these words, for elucidation as to what Luke means by these categories. In the LXX, each of these types has no personality. They are not actors but

---

5. Pilgrim, *Good News to the Poor*, 71.

6. Matthew does seem to spiritualize the concept of poverty in his gospel, particularly in his version of the beatitudes where he says, "Blessed are the poor in spirit" (Matt 5:3). This cannot be extrapolated onto Luke's theology, however, and both nuances of poverty should be held in tension with regards their portrayal of Jes

7. Roth, *Blind*, 78. Roth follows Rudolph Bultmann in this argument but refines it by finding understanding of these types through the LXX rather than the world of Luke's time. See Bultmann, *History of the Synoptic Tradition*, 67.

acted upon within the divine story. Even when a person is characterized in a particular story about Jesus, such as his healing a blind person (Luke 18:35–43) or a person with leprosy (Luke 5:12–16), these characters are not given names or very few, if any, defining characteristics. In Roth's reading of the LXX he does not even see much to distinguish these categories from one another, but rather they almost function synonymously as types of the "neglected mass of humanity in the LXX . . . that are acted upon in the course of human events. Correspondingly, they are at the mercy of others. Importantly, however, these types routinely attract the sympathy of the LXX reader."[8] They are an oft clustered group of stereotypical characters that take an even broader shape when mentioned together in a number of specific texts (Job 29:12–17; Ps 145:7–9; Isa 29:8–10; 35:4–6; 42:6–7; 58:6–7; Jer 35–37). The clustering also has a rhetorical effect according to Roth in that it serves to "heighten the magnificence of God's saving action, or in the case of human generosity, to exaggerate the giver's virtuous character or to magnify the evil of the sinner who routinely acts against them."[9]

Taking Pilgrim's and Roth's understandings of these groups, we should not spend too much time exploring the specifics of each individual group. Both authors come up with largely the same results for each group. One question the text does present however, is whether or not the first phrase, "To proclaim good news to the poor," is meant to be an inclusive heading subsuming the prisoners, the blind, and the oppressed. It is hard to be certain of Luke's intention and either reading can be defended. Each one of the individual actions can be seen as a proclamation of good news, for instance. As we have seen, the dynamics and complexity of poverty provide that prisoners, the blind/disabled, and the oppressed can all fit into a matrix of poverty. Each one can be a cause and a result of poverty. At the same time, the fact that Jesus, relying on Isaiah, does not just give us a laundry list, but a specific action attached to each group is significant. Even though there are different groups that can be included within poverty, a holistic pneumatological approach based on Luke 4 should not provide one "catch-all" solution for all of poverty but reach into each unique situation and provide a tailored response. This is what the Holy Spirit does in our own lives and how we should seek to respond to our world though it requires being Holy Spirit-led and locally focused.

The next phrase of Luke 4:18–19 is that the Holy Spirit has sent Jesus to "proclaim freedom for the prisoners. The word Luke uses for "freedom" here is a technical term in the LXX specifically connected with the year of

---

8. Roth, *Blind*, 140.
9. Roth, *Blind*, 141.

Jubilee in Leviticus 25–27 and the Sabbath year described in Deuteronomy 15:1 and Exodus 23:11. Apart from this instance, the word *aphesis* is usually translated as forgiveness. Connected with the adjective *aichmalōtos* which means "captive" or "prisoner" however, freedom makes sense. Still, it carries with it the sense of being forgiven from debts in the Jubilee paradigm. The biblical story that connects the most directly with this statement of Jesus's is the Gerasene demoniac in Luke 8. He was bound not just by demons, but literally kept under guard and bound in chains. Jesus, empowered by the Holy Spirit, addresses his whole situation, addressing the spiritual, the causes of why he was imprisoned, and helping him reintegrate into society by telling him, "Return home and tell how much God has done for you" (Luke 4:39). Such healing would have had economic consequences by making him fit to work.[10] Prisoners and ex-convicts who have also been kept under guard and bound in chains in the United States, are often some of the poorest in our society. There are also direct connections to one's poverty level and one's chances of being incarcerated.[11] Perhaps the greatest issue for prisoners is the social stigmatization. Often ex-convicts remain in poverty and oppression because of an inability to find good paying work post-incarceration or even to reintegrate into society. Their criminal records follow them throughout their whole lives. Freedom for a prisoner that truly addresses poverty would include not just being set free from prison but reintegration into society and a forgiveness of economic and social debts. We will address such debts, social separation, and the need for reintegration in our section on the Holy Spirit's salvific work in Spirit baptism which focuses on the Spirit's creation of a new community among the poor.

The next phrase in Luke 4 is Jesus's pneumatic proclamation of recovery of sight for the blind. Pilgrim notes that Luke only uses the term blind as a metaphor once (Luke 6:39). Every other time the word has a literal meaning.[12] The blind is a type especially representative of the extraordinarily vulnerable and as such are also the recipients of both divine and human magnanimity. This is illustrated in the one account Luke has of Jesus healing a specific blind person as opposed to mentioning the blind in a laundry list of miracles Jesus performed. In this account, the blind person is a beggar and clearly looked down upon by onlookers (Luke 18:35–43). Being able to heal someone who is blind is also proof not just of one's generosity, but of

10. In Acts 16:16–19, Paul's exorcism of a spirit from a young slave girl who prophesied for money also had direct economic consequences, though there were negative consequences for the girl's master.

11. See Hall et al., "Postincarceration Policies and Prisoner Reentry," 56–72; Heller, "Poverty," 219–47.

12. Pilgrim, *Good News to the Poor*, 67.

the power of God and of God's agent Jesus. Perhaps the greatest commonality between various mentions of the blind in the LXX, according to Roth, is their connection with the "day of the Lord."[13] Jesus's own messianic mission as well as the Holy Spirit's salvific work through Jesus should be seen in an eschatological framework in which there will be no more pain or tears (Rev 21:4). The way that Jesus addresses blindness is through bringing healing. Only after the most acute problem is addressed do spiritual problems also get addressed.[14]

Again, we see that a pneumatic response will not be general but specific to the causes of poverty. It will also be holistic by addressing physical, spiritual, social and economic elements. We noted in chapter 2 the effects poverty has on the physically and mentally disabled and how these groups are particularly prone to poverty. They often cannot contribute economically except through begging. We will specifically address this type of poverty and the physical nature of poverty in our exposition of the Holy Spirit's saving work in healing, though we will not limit this to physical healing, because healing for the poor, like salvation, must be holistic.

The last specific group Jesus mentions is the most general group along with the poor, and that is his proclamation that he will set the oppressed free by the power of the Holy Spirit. The word *thrauō* which is translated "oppressed" in the NIV literally means those broken to pieces or crushed under a weight (see Exod 15:6; Num 24:17 in the LXX). According to Pilgrim, this phrase would suggest a series of social injustices in line with Isaiah 58:6 where the phrase is paralleled with loosing the chains of injustice.[15] Again, these shattered are not presented as characters. They are a nameless faceless type. Roth notes the warfare imagery often connected with this particular character.[16] They are the lowly that Mary says the Lord will lift up and reverse their situations with the powerful who helped cause their oppression (Luke 1:46–56). This is nothing less than salvation, a concept which we will deal with more fully in our first section on the Holy Spirit as savior below.

The whole passage is put into a jubilee framework by the final phrase "to proclaim the year of the Lord's favor." This phrase, along with the opening phrase, "to preach good news to the poor" bookend the more specific groups of poor and set the framework for how we should understand them and

---

13. Roth, *Blind*, 106.

14. In Luke, this can be seen in the blind person following Jesus and praising God. In the expanded Johannine account, the man actually makes a faith profession in Jesus and also evangelizes the religious leaders on Jesus's behalf asking if they want to become his disciples too.

15. Pilgrim, *Good News to the Poor*, 68–69.

16. Roth, *Blind*, 103–4.

Jesus's pneumatic mission toward them. In the same way, our first and last section below will set the framework for how we look at salvation. The first section on the Holy Spirit as savior will define what we mean by salvation, its scope and its applications. Our final section will put all of our work in an eschatological framework as the Holy Spirit is the entelechy of the eschatological kingdom and holistic pneumatological salvation must be seen in an eschatological light. Also, like Luke 4, the middle sections on Spirit baptism and healing will provide the meat that is fleshed out into specific examples and applied to specific groups. All of it is good news for the urban poor.

THE PNEUMATOLOGICAL SALVATION OF THE URBAN POOR

Are the poor in need of saving? We have seen that according to Luke 4:18–19 they are. Every one of the actions the Holy Spirit anoints Jesus to perform involves some form of salvation for a marginalized group of people. So, the question arises, what does "salvation" look like for the urban poor in our context? In many ways, most theologies of poverty are trying to provide a theological response that answers this question. It is Jesus's proclamation in the beatitudes, "Blessed are the poor" (Luke 6:20). Unfortunately, as we have seen, salvation is usually considered the realm of Christology. This, at its best, has been a bifurcation with justification centered on Jesus and ongoing salvation through sanctification centered on the Holy Spirit. Rather, we should see the whole of salvation as the complementary work of Christ and the Holy Spirit. In the *ordo salutis*, the Holy Spirit enables the proclamation, hearing, and understanding of the gospel. The Holy Spirit justifies through the resurrection of Christ, provides for the adoption of believers, accomplishes rebirth and renewal, sanctifies hearts and lives, and provides the down payment for eschatological transformation.

We have adopted the Renewal four-fold model of salvation because it covers a holistic vision of salvation with each area specifically affecting the poor and is also clearly seen as the work of both the Holy Spirit and the Son according to Luke. It is also a contained way through which we can show the pneumatological potential for a theology of poverty that was missing in those theologies previously surveyed. Each element has clear pneumatological themes even though they have traditionally been understood christologically. We are not simply appropriating this christological doctrine, to another member of the Trinity, the Holy Spirit. Rather we are holding that the theological locus of salvation is an area that is equally the realm of the Spirit, not just because of the doctrines of *perichoresis* and appropriation, but because biblically, salvation is just as much the realm of the Holy Spirit as it is the Son. We can in fact apply the doctrine of appropriation and say that the Holy Spirit, also uniquely at work in salvation, has as much to say about the topic as any other member of the Trinity. What is true of one is true of all three.[17]

This is equally true of the other areas of the four-fold gospel. While traditionally envisioned christologically, such an envisioning disregarded Trinitarian theology. Each of these four areas, including salvation proper, are the realm of both the Son and the Holy Spirit. This is evident biblically that the Holy Spirit is active in the economy of salvation, Spirit baptism, healing and eschatology in an equal and a unique way to the Son that demands we speak uniquely of the Spirit yet still within this Trinitarian framework. Because these areas have been spoken of christologically, and because of the pneumatological focus of our work, we will focus only on the Spirit here and allow our work in chapters 3 and 4, as well as in other Soteriologies that are more christologically focused, to stand for themselves.

There is not just overlap and uniqueness in the persons of the Trinity, but in each of the four elements of the four-fold gospel. For instance, the salvation motif encompasses all four elements, while also constituting the first. We will therefore treat the topic of the Spirit as savior as a kind of comprehensive introduction to the topic of the salvation of the urban poor as a whole while the other three sections will flesh this out in greater detail. In the same way, Spirit baptism and healing are both salvific and eschatological acts. Healing can and does occur within Spirit baptism and the community that ensues. The ancients for instance, understood salvation as healing from disease followed by the restoration of the individual to community.[18] Healing can both precede and occur through such restoration to the community. Still, while there is much overlap, there are also nuances that require looking at each separately to gain a more complete picture of the potential for a holistic Pneumatology of poverty.

The Holy Spirit as Savior

Tom Greggs in his article "Communio Ecclesiology" gives us a helpful starting point by asserting that, in order to have a pneumatological view of

---

17. For Barth's doctrines of *perichoresis* and appropriation, see Barth, *Church Dogmatics*, 1/1:368–96. See also our discussion on our Trinitarian approach in the introduction on pages 2, 8.

18. See Witherington III, "Salvation and Health," 821–43.

salvation, one must also have a pneumatological view of the fall.[19] Such a view sees the fall as not just vertical but horizontal, rupturing relations with God, between humans, and with creation. Gregg defines sin as the heart turned upon itself, human individualism and self-centeredness in relation to the rest of the created world.[20] Such a view of the fall demonstrates that it is not just the poor who are in need of salvation, but the rich as well. Because of the divine connection between humans created by the same Spirit who breathed into all of humanity at creation, both the aggressor and the victim experience the effects of sin in different ways that require salvation. In terms of poverty, both the rich and the poor are affected by the sinful systems and actions that create poverty. The poor are hurt economically, socially and emotionally through their experience of poverty. The rich are also affected through their participation in these systems, explicitly or neglectfully, which keep the poor impoverished. Both the rich and the poor experience a lesser version of what it means to be fully human that causes their need for salvation.

While our definition of poverty is primarily economic, we have seen clearly the social, emotional, spiritual and physical effects of poverty and the need for holistic solutions. Still, as we saw in our pneumatic reading of Luke 4, Jesus often started with the most pressing matter at hand, the primary cause of the poverty be it blindness, demon possession, or some other illness. Still, Jesus did not leave it at this level. It is easy to fall into a trap in which we lean too far on one side. We have seen this in our survey of previous theologies of poverty. Many on the ecumenical side focus on the economics of poverty without dealing with the other facets. Many on the Evangelical side focus too much on spiritual causes and trust that these will fix the economic problems. They do not see the economic as a real problem or ignore the relationship between poverty and healing. Being economically poor does not make one less human, live less of a life, or have less happiness. Rather, it is the other dimensions, the underside of poverty, that really take the toll on the humanity of a person. These cannot be separated from the economic realities and the fact that poverty becomes a cyclical vortex difficult to climb out of. This is important because in speaking of the salvation of the poor we want to address the whole person, recognizing economics is a part of the need, but not the whole need. We also must recognize the poor are not in any more need of saving than the rich. Rather, economic poverty is one facet of a complex reality that affects people from all socioeconomic backgrounds. In this light, we will describe what we mean by a

19. Greggs, "Communio Ecclesiology," 347.
20. Greggs, "Communio Ecclesiology," 348.

pneumatological salvation that can be applied to poverty and brings hope to all humanity for a new way forward in every dimension of life.

Any salvation proposed must be multidimensional. Poverty is multidimensional. The work of the Holy Spirit in salvation is also multidimensional. A holistic pneumatological approach moves beyond the exclusivity of one approach. It holds together the individual and the communal. It reaches into each individual situation locally and addresses its needs while also recognizing the person is part of a community that must also be addressed. We see the Holy Spirit in Scripture addressing both the individual and the societal. The Holy Spirit empowers Jesus to address every level of poverty.

There are two ways we can approach describing the multidimensionality of salvation we hope to put forth to holistically address poverty. One is the various forms of salvation that affect the person and community including, personal salvation, familial salvation, material salvation, social salvation, and cosmic salvation.[21] Each of these have scriptural precedence and are important in a pneumatological vision of salvation addressing the complexities of poverty. The second way we can approach the multidimensionality of salvation is to outline the various types of personal conversion an individual can have beyond spiritual salvation. These types of personal conversion make salvation holistic for the person by moving them into more responsible living as a global citizen, in our case in respect to poverty. These aspects include intellectual, affective, moral, sociopolitical and religious conversion.[22] Both of these approaches to salvation are important because together they recognize the complex multidimensionality of the salvation of both the poor and the rich, both the individual and the community, both the interior and the exterior.

First, we will explore the dynamic nature of soteriology in a pneumatological paradigm. The first aspect is personal salvation in which individuals encounter and are transformed into the image of Christ by the Holy Spirit. It includes elements such as deliverance from oppressive situations, release from spiritual captivity and the exorcism of demonic forces.[23] Steps the individual takes in this salvation include repentance, baptism, the

---

21. These aspects of salvation are primarily drawn from Amos Yong's discussion on the multidimensionality of salvation in Yong, *Spirit Poured Out*, 91–98.

22. These types of personal conversion are outlined by the late Donald L. Gelpi, a Charismatic Roman Catholic theologian, in Gelpi, *Conversion Experience*. See also Gelpi, *Charism and Sacrament*. Another source of discussion on this topic is Rambo, *Understanding Religious Conversion*.

23. The Gerasene demoniac is of course a great example of such personal salvation, though as we mentioned, his personal salvation also had social implications.

forgiveness of sins, and the reception of the gift of the Holy Spirit.[24] Often these elements are individualized, but each of these occur within and to communities as well. We already discussed how the Holy Spirit is at work in each part of this *ordo salutis* commonly cited in personal salvation.[25] Evangelicals are often seen as the strongest proponents of such a personal salvation and critics often worry that it is to the neglect of other dimensions, but this is not necessarily so. One cannot neglect the individual either.[26] There is a sense in which, even if a person has not personally assented to a mode of being or a paradigm of living, nothing a community does will sway this person toward their own conversion. In terms of poverty, this is seen in the oft quoted phrase, "some people simply want to be poor." At its worst, this idea is applied to all the poor asserting it is always one's individual choice to be poor. On the other side, one can abnegate the personal dimension completely. Each person and situation must be addressed individually. Each circumstance must be discerned to see if there are personal elements that have led to poverty that need help without this becoming a scapegoat for dealing with larger systemic issues.

Personal salvation also cannot be simply seen as spiritual. Rather as Gelpi outlines, there are various areas of life in which a person needs conversion including the intellectual, the affective, the moral, the sociopolitical and the religious. Religious conversion is just one aspect. Gelpi defines conversion much in the same way we have been here as a turning from something and turning to something new.[27] For instance, one turns from irresponsible to responsible living in some realm of experience. Conversion is a personal experience; hence we have included it within personal salvation, but as we have described, Gelpi also believes it occurs within a matrix of social processes unique to each person, situation and location. Similarly, each domain affects the other domains while also being separate. One can be religiously converted but not have experienced conversion in any other area. Still one's religious conversion will affect every other realm of one's living.

Intellectual conversion takes responsibility for the truth or falsity of our beliefs and for the explanatory frameworks within which our beliefs

---

24. Yong, *Spirit Poured Out*, 93.

25. This list is of course not exhaustive and there is no singularly agreed upon *ordo salutis* between traditions. These elements are common to most descriptions of personal salvation, however. For such a classical vie, see Gause, *Living in the Spirit*.

26. There may even be a case for arguing that personal salvation is primary for Luke as there is no evidence of Jesus directly challenging the social structures. If social structures were challenged, it was largely through the work done in individual lives.

27. Gelpi, *Conversion Experience*, 24. See also Rambo, *Understanding Religious Conversion*.

sit.²⁸ Intellectual conversion is necessary for both the rich and the poor. It includes false mindsets and beliefs that have helped lead one into poverty as well as false beliefs about the poor that have caused the neglect of poverty as a societal problem. Educational programs that teach people about the realities of poverty are central to addressing the need for intellectual conversion in the area of poverty. These should address people's views of wealth, of how to handle finances, the true causes of poverty and its complexity. Many people simply do not know why they continue to find themselves in poverty or why poverty continues to exist in our world.

Another facet of intellectual conversion that should be mentioned is the fact that mental disability is so common among the poor. For many it is not just knowing the right information but a matter of how one's mind works. Such mental issues are not a simple matter and cannot be addressed in the scope of a thesis such as this.²⁹ Help should be created and given to those with mental disabilities, whether affected by poverty or not, through programs that help with mental development as well as with financial assistance for those who need it.

Intellectual conversion is not enough. One can know everything there is to know about poverty, but not be moved to help. Affective conversion takes responsibility for our emotional health and maturation.³⁰ We saw in our chapter on Pneumatology a discussion about the importance of orthopathy, or right affections. Samuel Solivan is the most helpful in this regard as he talks about the solidarity that God has with the pathos or suffering of the poor. He describes orthopathos as the proper relationship between correct belief (orthodoxy) and proper ethics or action (orthopraxy).³¹ Affections are a necessary step between intellectual conversion and moral conversion. If we shelter our emotions and stay in an infantile state in which we are not confronted with and moved by the plight of the suffering poor, we have not been converted in our affections.

The greatest thing to move one's affections is personal experience. Experiencing poverty for oneself has a way of driving its reality home.³² This can occur through intercultural or inner-city trips where one can meet and hear stories of those most affected by poverty. It would be easy to see such

---

28. Gelpi, *Conversion Experience*, 33.

29. For more on the topic, see Eide and Ingstad, *Disability and Poverty*. For more theologically, see Yong, *Bible, Disability, and the Church*.

30. Gelpi, *Conversion Experience*, 34.

31. Solivan, *Spirit, Pathos, and Liberation*, 13.

32. Even reading of journalist Barbara Ehrenrich's experience of trying to live on minimum wage in America moved my affections for the working poor when I first read it in university back in 2002. See Ehrenreich, *Nickel and Dimed*.

a response to poverty as trite and minimizing the poverty experience to an intellectual exercise. But for many of the rich who have the power to make systemic changes in our culture, they are so removed from poverty that only such experiences can change their affections toward the poor. Solivan says that for the rich in society to help affect hope it takes an existential link to the poor, not just an intellectual link.[33]

A conversion of affections is not just important for cosmopolitans. It is equally important for those living in the borderlands of poverty. For Solivan, right affections among the poor looks like the "power of the Holy Spirit in one's life that transforms pathos, suffering and despair into hope and wholeness. Orthopathos is a holistic, liberating process that engenders hope in their suffering."[34] For the poor it looks like a holistic approach to poverty that results in a distinction between suffering which results in self-alienation, and suffering that can somehow be a source for liberation and social transformation. It becomes the transformation of one's affections and suffering into hope and change. A major part of Solivan's picture of how this works practically among the Hispanic poor in the United States involves the creation of a new community by the power of the Holy Spirit that the communal nature of Hispanic culture already has the resources to provide.[35] We will explore what this new community can look like in our second section on Spirit baptism.

The conversion of one's intellect and of one's affections mean little for the plight of the poor if it does not result in moral conversion. Such a moral conversion takes responsibility for our practical deliberations and our choice of actions within interpersonal relations.[36] A moral conversion recognizes that one's actions have a butterfly effect that impacts the poor. These actions have a broad range, from political actions in how one votes, to how and where one spends their money or the hiring practices of corporations. Such actions are important on both a communal and individual level for both the rich and the poor. The Old Testament prophets often called out whole societies for their lack of morality specifically citing their neglect of the poor.

The idea of moral conversion also recognizes that while the actions of one's society may affect one's economic situation, your own personal actions and morals are also part of the cause. How one has handled money is the simplest example. Other moral choices we have seen can be contributing

---

33. Solivan, *Spirit, Pathos, and Liberation*, 36.

34. Solivan, *Spirit, Pathos, and Liberation*, 27–28.

35. Solivan, *Spirit, Pathos, and Liberation*, 140. Unfortunately, Solivan does not fully grapple with Luke 4 in terms of poverty. In this way, we are improving on his already helpful work.

36. Gelpi, *Conversion Experience*, 28.

factors to poverty, however. We have seen that single mothers make up a major percentage of the poor.[37] This can occur for non-moral reasons such as the death of a spouse. But individual choices regarding sex before marriage, divorce, and our society's proclivities toward these realities are also contributing factors. Changing one's actions is a difficult task, but it is done primarily through changing the mindsets and affections already mentioned above.

It is also important to recognize that our moral choices naturally have sociopolitical consequences. Gelpi mentions sociopolitical conversion as a subset of moral conversion and both are equally important.[38] A pneumatological framework, as we have discussed, addresses both realities. Jesus in Luke 4 was anointed by the Holy Spirit individually, but for the sake of community. In Acts 2, the Holy Spirit fell on each individual, but within a communal setting that formed a new community of solidarity that had economic, personal and sociopolitical ramifications. We will unpack this more fully in our section on Spirit baptism below.

A final area of conversion Gelpi discusses is religious conversion. Remember that each of these conversions can be separate from one another, but also are integrated in the way they affect one another. In fact, Gelpi has two separate sections, one of which includes "secular conversion" to show how these various types of conversion can look outside of a religious setting, while also recognizing that they can look different alongside religious conversion.[39] Religious conversion should affect one's posture and actions toward the poor. This is more likely to be the case if one goes through a holistic conversion. Only a religious conversion does not appear to be enough. Still many religious organizations, for instance those explored by Helene Slessarev-Jamir in *Prophetic Activism,* have been central to modern responses to poverty in the United States.[40] We also saw in Miller and Yamamori how religious conversion can result in a kind of social uplift that affects the poor as they also have certain moral and intellectual conversions that accompany their religious conversion.[41] Still the best approach is a holistic approach. This approach has not been fully connected with Luke 4, but we will see as we continue that these categories of poverty and the way in which we should seek the salvation of the poor certainly includes all of these dimensions of salvation.

Due to the intricacies of the personal level of poverty in that every person may have a different combination of issues and conversions in different

---

37. DeNavas-Walt and Proctor, *Income and Poverty,* 12.
38. Gelpi, *Conversion Experience,* 31.
39. Gelpi, *Conversion Experience,* 42–57.
40. Slessarev-Jamir, *Prophetic Activism.* See our discussion in chapter 4.
41. Miller and Yamamori, *Global Pentecostalism,* 33.

areas, a personalized approach to poverty is necessary. We will discuss more systemic modes as we progress, but we have continued to hold that the personal and individual are just as important pneumatologically. I propose a kind of life-coaching that coaches the whole person. In my own sphere of life, I have found that this specificity and individualization, done within community and including an emphasis on how to live within community, is the best way to affect transformation in someone's life. In my own sphere of college campus ministry, we call it discipleship, though in practice it looks more like whole life coaching from a particular religious perspective. Such an approach is built on relationship in which one gets to know the person, their predicament and how best to help that person. It allows the solution to be tailor made and holistic focusing on every area of life contributing to and affected by poverty.

Just as in discipleship, a one-size fits all mcdonaldization model cannot truly address poverty.[42] This is not a program the government alone can institute, it would cost a fortune. The best approach is one that comes from partnership between the main sectors of society: government, religion, civic society, and business. Certain individuals distrust one or more of these institutions, but there is one that fits each person as well. It ensures there are religious approaches for every religion and secular approaches run by government or business. This is best accomplished locally, particularly through local social work agencies, both governmental and non-profit. For instance, when dealing with unemployment, one should deal with the whole person and the particularities of that person by looking into their work, financial and family history and by coaching them in all of these areas, referring them to specialized help when necessary. For example, if emotional outbursts or mental health are major reasons for a person not holding a job, working out salvation in that person's life in a pneumatological fashion involves connecting them with a mental health professional.

Churches should also be equipped to offer holistic life coaching or discipleship for people that includes financial and emotional well-being tailored to the individual. The church and business sectors are particularly poised to address the rich concerning their own need for conversion in regard to poverty. Even instituting such programs in a holistic manner would

---

42. While there are many books on the McDonaldization of society, one I found particularly helpful in that it wrestles with the topic on the borders of economics and theology is James, *McDonaldisation*. In particular, he talks about the Indian appropriation of mass televangelism that occurs in what he calls a "glocal" way in that it appropriates a global phenomenon with local flavor and implications. Televangelism is just one example of an attempt at mass-driven discipleship and traditioning rather than a localized, personal approach fitting the person's community and situation. For a treatment more focused on the United States, see Lyon, *Jesus in Disneyland*.

bring about change for those participating from a cosmopolitan perspective. This will result in the creation of a new community as people's suffering would turn into hope and the very source of transformation as these programs take place within communities of poverty helping one another.

We have seen that even within what we have called personal salvation, there are other dynamics that work besides the personal as we live in an intricate and interconnected web called humanity accentuated by the pneumatological reality of each human having the Spirit-breath of God breathed into them. These are expounded more fully in the other forms of salvation outlined by Amos Yong, familial, material, social and cosmic salvation. Each one also has important pneumatological implications for poverty.

Salvation occurs not just for individuals but for families. We see this biblically in the accounts of Cornelius (Acts 11:14), Lydia (Acts 16:14–15), the Philippian jailer (Acts 16:31–33) and Crispus (Acts 18:8). Amos Yong mentions that, while many see salvation of whole families or clans as an ancient practice and salvation shifting toward an individual phenomenon in modernity, salvation of the individual is still the exception throughout history.[43] Certainly, family is still an integral part of salvation spiritually, but also on every other level we have discussed. When one person finds conversion in an area of life it can easily have ripples throughout the whole family. This is especially true within more communally oriented cultures that are continuing to grow within the United States and are also the most affected by poverty including Hispanic and many Black cultures. Family is particularly important when it comes to poverty. We saw in chapter 2 that one's family heritage as well as the current make up of one's family has important implications for how one is affected by poverty. In particular, the sins of a father can have lasting negative effects on the rest of a family.

As such, when we speak about salvation and poverty, it should not just focus on the individual or political, but on civil society, particularly the family. We saw such approaches particularly present in progressive Evangelicals like David Gushee.[44] The salvation of families includes an emphasis on healthy families no matter their shape. Intentional and intact families clearly make the biggest difference for poverty, however. As we saw statistically, families where a member is ripped away through divorce, death, or imprisonment suffer economically and in a myriad of other ways.

The personalized life-coaching solution we proposed above for personal salvation will help to address families as it addresses the family situation

---

43. Yong, *Spirit Poured Out*, 92.

44. See our discussion of Gushee in chapter 3. See also Gushee, *New Evangelical Manifesto*; *Toward a Just and Caring Society*; "Rebuilding Marriage and the Family"; Monsma, "Poverty, Civil Society," 46–71.

no matter what it looks like. As one individual is helped in a family, the whole family situation can be changed. This would especially be so if families are involved in the process which is more likely if change were affected on the local and civil levels through churches, community organizations, or even families themselves that are helping other families in their community. Amos Yong also draws out the eschatological and pneumatological dimensions of familial salvation seeing the family as an eschatological sign of the reign of God.[45] This is particularly seen in Acts 2 as the Holy Spirit creates a new, inclusive family of God as an eschatological act, something we will more fully explore in our section on Spirit baptism below.

A third form of salvation beyond the personal and familial is material salvation. This salvation addresses the embodied nature of human beings. When Jesus administered salvation through healing by the power of the Holy Spirit it involved the healing of the mind, soul and body. Often the body was first. Amos Yong says, "Material salvation is primarily directed to the poor, the marginalized and the oppressed, perhaps because they experience their diseased and deprived conditions in palpable ways."[46] Jesus did not just address material salvation by divine healing, but also through feeding the hungry himself and blessing the poor and those who hunger or thirst. Jesus called the rich young ruler to a material salvation asking him to sell his possessions and give them to the poor in Luke 18:18–23.

This carried forward into the ethos of the early church. Once they also experienced the Holy Spirit fully, they insisted on ministering to the sick, the impoverished, the naked, the stranger and those in prison. In Acts 2 they gave up their own material wealth to help those in need, particularly to care for widows and children.[47] We also see the importance of materiality in the bodily resurrection of Christ, the church and the renewal of the physical earth by the power of the Holy Spirit. Materiality involves not just our bodies, but the material possessions we have including our wealth. It includes the way that we treat possessions, recognizing that things do not belong to us, but everything belongs to God. Material possessions are important but only in how they help us to live in relationship with one another and with God. We will address the materiality of salvation more fully as we explore the Holy Spirit as healer below.

The fourth area of salvation is social salvation. It is very similar to sociopolitical salvation described above. On the one hand, it refers to reconciliation in interpersonal relationships. On the other hand, it refers to

---

45. Yong, "Sons and Daughters," 148–49.
46. Yong, *Spirit Poured Out*, 93. See also Volf, "Materiality of Salvation," 447–67.
47. Yong, *Spirit Poured Out*, 93.

the redemption of socioeconomic and political structures.[48] Galatians 3:28 describes reconciliation among three groups through the outpouring of the Holy Spirit at Pentecost: Jew and Greek (racial reconciliation), slave and free (class reconciliation) and male and female (gender reconciliation). Even though class reconciliation appears as if it would have the most direct bearing on a Pneumatology of poverty, racial and gender reconciliation are equally important. Poverty looks very different along racial and gender lines. One cannot fully address poverty without addressing all three of these issues. Indeed, all were addressed in the early church. At Pentecost, speaking in glossolalia signified the gospel overcoming racial and cultural divisions while still keeping the uniqueness of each culture in that those hearing the gospel still heard it in their own native tongue (Acts 2). The Holy Spirit, through a vision, also led Peter to reach out to the Gentile Cornelius overcoming sacred cultural taboos and boundaries (Acts 10:9ff). Even in early Pentecostalism, Frank Bartleman talked about racial barriers being washed away by the blood at Azusa Street, a revival led by a Black man, William Seymour.[49] Paul's interpretation of the Pentecost event through the lens of the prophet Joel included him saying that the Holy Spirit was poured out on servants and men and women, young and old (Acts 2:18). The church then went on to share everything they had with those of lower classes (Acts 2:45). We will address social salvation more fully in our section on Spirit baptism and the creation of a new community by the power of the Holy Spirit.[50]

The final area of salvation is cosmic salvation which involves the interconnectedness of human beings and their environment. Even creation is involved in Pentecost (Acts 2:19–20) and salvation is not just for humanity but is leading to the redemption of all creation (Eph 6:12; Rev 21:5). In Luke 4, we saw the Holy Spirit pointing toward the day of the Lord through Jesus, the same day of the Lord that is mentioned by Peter in Acts 2 in connection with creation. As Amos Yong points out, pneumatologically, Paul connects the cosmic salvation of all creation and the human redemption of the body

---

48. Yong primarily draws on Walter Wink in this section to talk about fallen and destructive power structures as public and social manifestations of the demonic. See Walter Wink's *Power* trilogy: *Unmasking the Powers*; *Engaging the Powers*; *When the Powers Fall*. Wink sees the powers as emergent powers and not necessarily embodied powers; I think there is room for both possibilities.

49. Bartleman, *Azusa Street*, 59.

50. We should note that slaves in Luke were healed but not freed. While social issues were addressed, social stratification was not necessarily removed. Jesus, according to Luke, also did not appear to challenge the existing political structures explicitly. These political structures also allowed less room for them to be challenged than the democratic society of the United States today.

with the work and groaning of the Spirit of God (Rom 8:19–23).[51] In terms of poverty, it is not just humanity that is affected by poverty, but all of creation.[52] Countries where poverty is the worst also have some of the greatest environmental problems. When we think of creation, we often think of the mountains, forests or oceans, but one of the places where environmental issues are equally felt is the inner city where the environment has been all but stripped away and the air quality is the worst. Eschatologically, in the vision of a new creation, there is also a special emphasis on the new city (Rev 21:2). The idea of cosmic salvation is often connected with an eschatological focus which is what we shall focus upon in our final section on the Holy Spirit as entelechy of the eschatological kingdom.[53]

To give a brief summary of this section, we have explored salvation as personal in all its multidimensionality, as familial, as material, as social and as cosmic. The Holy Spirit is involved in each of these areas of salvation and has a bearing on urban poverty. The Luke 4 passage we began this chapter by exploring has room for each of these dimensions in the broad and holistic categories through which it defines poverty. We will demonstrate this as we continue to draw in Luke and Acts in each section below. We spent the most time unpacking personal salvation in this section because we will explore social and familial, material, and cosmic salvation more fully in the next three sections respectively. In our unpacking of personal salvation, we saw the need to focus on the individual but within a local community setting of civil society, particularly the family. Both the rich and the poor need salvation. Our approach should be personalized to each person which is best accomplished through face to face interaction that happens through whole-life coaching. Finally, this coaching can and should be done through all three major sectors of our society in the United States: the government (though on a local level), religion and business.

---

51. Yong, *Spirit Poured Out*, 95.

52. For more on the environment and the Spirit, see Swoboda, *Tongues and Trees*. And, "Creation Care as 'Keeping in Step with the Spirit,'" 248–64. For more on the connection between the environment and poverty see Bass, *Reducing Poverty*.

53. This should not necessarily be the case that the salvation of creation should have the closest connection with eschatology, though it often does. Like other ideas in eschatological salvation we will explore, the salvation of creation should also be sought as a realized eschatological reality that is addressed in the here and now even if it is not fully realized until another era.

The Holy Spirit as Baptizer

We have discussed in previous chapters the need to address not just the individual but communities of poverty. We also saw that a holistic view of salvation includes the familial and the social. This idea of community is what I believe is really at the core of Spirit baptism in which a new community of God is created which supersedes race, gender and socioeconomic status. While a major focus of Spirit baptism is on community, it transforms both the individual and the community. It does this by the individual helping to transform the community and the community the individual so that neither is of first importance. We see this in Jesus's Luke 4 proclamation that he was "sent to proclaim freedom for the prisoners." As we explored in our pneumatic reading of Luke 4, the freeing of a prisoner is an individual act, but it includes a restoration to community and an inclusion in society. This section will demonstrate that the theme of Spirit baptism gives the pneumatological resources through which to address the social dynamics of poverty. The social dynamics of poverty come to the fore in the generational and familial nature of poverty and in the ostracization and the poor's stigmatization from the rest of society. We will show how Spirit baptism addresses these social dynamics through the creation of a new community, an impetus for hospitality, and also the empowerment through which to create this new community and overcome poverty.

Theologically, Spirit baptism has historically been understood as occurring at salvation when the Holy Spirit came upon the believer as a seal of salvation.[54] Classical Pentecostals have seen Spirit baptism as a second, or even third, experience after salvation that empowered the believer for witness.[55] Each group has attempted to define Spirit baptism in a particular way through doctrinal statements. These statements try to identify it as an experience in a certain order within the *ordo salutis*, as having glossolalia as

---

54. Kilian McDonnell and George T. Montague argue that the dominant view of the early church was of the reception of the Spirit through the rites of initiation such as water baptism and Eucharist. They do not deny that early church Fathers saw the possibility of numerous impartations of the Spirit but that this was an actualization of the Spirit originally imparted at initiation. See McDonnell and Montague, *Christian Initiation*.

55. This view of a third experience of the Holy Spirit its roots in John Fletcher and found its popularity with B. H. Irwin, both of Wesleyan-holiness traditions. Those who hold Spirit baptism as a second experience are of the finished work Pentecostals. Even this paradigm is somewhat simplistic. Oneness Pentecostals believe Spirit baptism occurs at salvation which only comes with water baptism. Later in his life, Irwin himself taught that there were six further baptisms of fire. See Synan, *Holiness-Pentecostal Movement*, 51–57; Hunter, *Spirit-Baptism*, 187.

the initial physical evidence of Spirit baptism or having certain outcomes.[56] Ultimately these statements function as a lowest common denominator upon which everyone can agree. The actual testimonies of early Pentecostal believers described Spirit baptism in much more dynamic terms than such static doctrinal statements.[57]

In this section, we will give a broader vision of Spirit baptism as the ongoing and dynamic work of the Holy Spirit in the individual the community. This can include a specific experience of the Spirit accompanied by glossolalia as prescribed by many classical Pentecostals but is much more. One can argue that this "classical" experience is the root experience, but it is hard to argue it is a first or necessary experience to experience the Holy Spirit at all. The testimonies of many Pentecostals override such an inclination. Classical Pentecostal scholar Frank Macchia uses Spirit baptism in a similar manner, as a larger metaphor for the work of the Holy Spirit in the Christian life and even outside of the church. He connects the metaphor primarily with the eschatological kingdom of God rather than the church. In this way, Spirit baptism is a multidimensional and ongoing experience.[58] In connecting it with the eschatological kingdom, it also moves Spirit baptism beyond the church into the world at large. This move is supported scripturally in the Luke 4 language in which part of Jesus's pneumatic mission is to proclaim the year of the Lord's favor and in the similar eschatological language found in the Pentecost account of Acts 2. This broadening is an important aspect of Spirit baptism but will also be important for healing in our next section. Though the church has a central role to play in bringing salvation to the poor, the Holy Spirit's work is much broader and holistic as the Spirit who has been poured out on all flesh is moving all creation toward being made new.

We will now turn to what Scripture has to say about Spirit baptism to help us unpack the primary pneumatological themes we will draw out to concerning urban poverty. Our primary text for this chapter has been Luke 4 and the line we are focusing on in this section is Jesus proclamation "he has sent me to proclaim freedom for the prisoners." Such a statement is by no means out of the realm of even traditional understandings of Spirit baptism. Two common themes in the testimonies and teachings of early

---

56. Take for instance the doctrinal statement of the assemblies of God in their 1916 Statement of Fundamental Truths, which reads: "All believers are entitled to, and should ardently expect, and earnestly seek the promise of the Father, the baptism in the Holy Ghost and fire. . . . The full consummation of the baptism of believers in the Holy Ghost and fire, is indicated by the initial sign of speaking in tongues, as the Spirit of God gives utterance" (General Council of the Assemblies of God, *Minutes*, 10).

57. See my own work on this topic in Kertson, "Spirit Baptism," 244–61.

58. Macchia, *Baptized in the Spirit*, 16, 85.

Pentecostals concerning the results of Sprit baptism include freedom from sin and habits that have held one bound and also healing from all types of afflictions including physical and emotional, even the healing of relationships. For instance, Stanley Frodsham testifies that there is "nothing compared to the fellowship we had together since we were baptized in the Holy Spirit."[59] E. N. Bell tells readers, "Ever since the Lord baptized me with the Holy Spirit . . . God has put a longing in my heart to see all schismatic, narrow, sectarian lines wiped out, and all God's people truly made one. I believe this desire is in the heart of every baptized Saint."[60] Finally, A. P. Collins makes a "plea for unity" drawing on 1 Corinthians which says that we are all baptized into one Spirit.[61] Biblically, whenever a person was freed from the prison of sin, demon possession or physical or mental disease, they were also restored to community. There was a simultaneous victory over the social ostracization that had kept the person imprisoned from the mainstream of society, the same kind of ostracization we have described the urban poor as experiencing in the United States today.

We already mentioned the story of the lepers as a prime example of such restoration to community. In Acts 2, after the outpouring of the Holy Spirit at Pentecost, the passage that follows Peter's explanation of the event is a description of a new community.

> They devoted themselves to the apostles' teaching and to fellowship, to the breaking of bread and to prayer. Everyone was filled with awe at the many wonders and signs performed by the apostles. All the believers were together and had everything in common. They sold property and possessions to give to anyone who had need. Every day they continued to meet together in the temple courts. They broke bread in their homes and ate together with glad and sincere hearts, praising God and enjoying the favor of all the people. And the Lord added to their number daily those who were being saved. (Acts 2:42–47)

This new community is focused on learning, praying and eating together. But a hallmark of the community is actually economic in nature. These believers had everything in common. They were even willing to sacrifice their own riches to make sure that no one went wanting. This was a community people wanted to be a part of demonstrated by people joining the movement daily. A similar description is given of the early church in Acts

---

59. Frodsham, "Sunday School Lesson," 12.
60. Bell, "Baptized Body of Christ," 4.
61. Collins, "Plea for Unity," 3. All three of these quotes from the *Christian Evangel* are also found in my article Kertson, "Spirit Baptism," 256–58.

4:32–35. Even on the heels of persecution they continued to be of one heart and mind. How were they of one heart and mind? No one claimed any of their possessions were their own, but they shared everything they had. Some even sold their homes and brought the money of the sale to the apostles to distribute to the needy.

This is a picture of how the church was meant to address poverty and it was connected with the quintessential pneumatological event in Scripture. Among Renewalists, much is discussed about speaking in glossolalia in relation to Spirit baptism. Spirt baptism's purpose is most commonly framed as the power to witness. It is often overlooked, however, that the direct result of Spirit baptism in Luke's account of Pentecost in Acts 2 is the creation of a new salvific community of God. Yes, the community is empowered to witness, and people are added to their number daily, but the Holy Spirit also empowered them to function as an inclusive community that overcame social barriers including socioeconomic, gender and race.

Glossolalia, which is featured in this Acts 2 narrative, is usually seen by many Renewalists as an evidence, or the evidence, of Spirit baptism. Others see it as a way to speak to God through your spirit or in the Acts 2 narrative as simply a prophecy, that by being in tongues, demonstrates the prophecy is truly of the Holy Spirit.[62] These glossolalia, however, also served the purpose of a sign of the community of God that is supernaturally being established by the power of the Holy Spirit in the Spirit's being poured out on all flesh. While the speakers spoke in different languages, each person in the crowd heard the message in their own language. This demonstrates a unity in diversity that is a hallmark of Spirit-established community. There is diversity in that each believer spoke a different tongue verbally and those in the crowd were from a diversity of backgrounds hearing the message in their own diverse tongue. This diversity crossed social lines no person would usually cross except by the Holy Spirit. Included in the list of those there were Arabs and Egyptians, both of whom were responsible for keeping Israel captive during their history. Even Cretans are included of whom it was said they are liars, brutes and gluttons (Titus 1:12). All of these heard the message in their mother tongue and were invited to belong to the new community of God by the Holy Spirit being poured out that day.

Still, in the midst of this diversity, there is one message and one purpose. As Paul says, there is one Holy Spirit and this Spirit transcends these

---

62. R. Hollis Gause purports these traditional views of speaking in tongue. He says, "The Holy Spirit's presence is signaled by His speech." Gause seems only concerned about proving people spoke in glossolalia every time they were Spirit baptized and not in describing the purpose of these tongues beyond their use for witness. See Gause, *Living in the Spirit*, 133.

ethnic and language barriers, "For in the one Spirit we were all baptized into one body—Jews or Greeks, slaves of free—and we were all made to drink of one Spirit" (1 Cor 12:13). Much as in the bringing of possessions to lay at the apostle's feet, each person brings their own race, language and culture and puts them at the disposal of the new community, the hallmark of which is a communion, a *koinonia*, that results in the needs of everyone being met. For instance, slavery was not overturned in the New Testament, but it was subverted as slaves received the same inclusion in the new family of God.

This leads us to discuss the way in which Pneumatology, particularly Spirit baptism, helps us to address urban poverty. First, Spirit baptism creates a new community. This occurs through the breaking down of social barriers. Primarily our focus is economic barriers here, the gap that exists in the United States between the rich and the poor. It is also a spatial gap as the poor often live in metropolitan urban settings or isolated rural settings while the rich live in the suburbs or metropolitan high rises above the rest of society. There has been little to narrow this gap over the past decades, in fact it has grown. Only a move of the Spirit of God who creates new community can overcome these barriers.

There are also racial barriers. Certain minorities, particularly of African and Hispanic descent, are the greatest victims of poverty. Even these races are often secluded from one another in their own ghettos. Gender barriers were also significant as women, who have significantly less earning power than men, are especially susceptible to falling into poverty. In Spirit baptism, each of these issues are overcome by the creation of a new community where there is neither Jew nor Gentile (racial), neither slave nor free (socioeconomic) neither male nor female (gender) (Gal 3:28).[63] These barriers are brought down as people are released from the captivity of their isolation, their discrimination, and the powers that oppress and separate humanity.

The Holy Spirit causes and empowers people to reach out beyond themselves to those they would never otherwise reach. Two metaphors commonly applied to the church that is empowered by the Holy Spirit are hospitality and *koinonia*. These two concepts work hand in hand with one another. Amos Yong says, "Salvation now needs to be understood in terms of hospitality: being reconstituted into the divine community, the new people of God. The needy are best able to appreciate the divine hospitality given through Jesus and the Holy Spirit, and the saved then become instruments of

---

63. Again, these distinctions are not removed, but all of them are included in a new family where they once would not have associated with one another. There is still diversity, but unity is found in the midst of that diversity. Such a vision did not change the cultural views of these categories immediately but subtly and progressively subverts it.

divine hospitality heralding the eschatological kingdom."[64] Such hospitality reaches beyond itself welcoming the other in. It creates room within itself for the other much as the Trinity made room for humanity within its own communion. Hospitality also gives of itself for the other as we saw in Acts 2.

Such a hospitality does not work, however, if there is not an attractive community to which one can belong. This is where *koinonia* comes in. Frank Macchia says, "The Spirit is the Spirit of communion. Spirit baptism implies communion. This is why it leads to a shared love, a shared meal, a shared mission, and the proliferation and enhancement of an interactive charismatic life. Spirit baptism thus implies a relationship of unity between the Lord and the church that is not fundamentally one of identity but rather communion."[65] Even if a community reaches out to the other, if it is not an attractive community, one with unity within diversity, one that continues to seek healing even within itself, the other will not want to belong. The power of *koinonia* and communion within the context of Spirit baptism is that it has the power to not just appropriate people into a singular community but to replicate itself into numerous communities much as the early church did. Much as the CEB's of Liberation Theology sought to do among the poor of Latin America. In this way, a poor urban community on the south side of Chicago can hear the proclamation of Jesus for good news, receive healing and Spirit baptism that forms it into a new community of health and restoration. The divisive social structures within that own community will be overcome as well as those which separate it from those outside. It may then even replicate itself into other Chicago communities and beyond.

How does Spirit baptism affect such a community? There is a realization of the power of the Holy Spirit that has already been poured out on all flesh that is beyond human control. A miraculous work of which it might be said, "'Not by might, not by power, but my Spirit,' says the Lord Almighty" (Zech 4:6). We also cannot forsake one of the most common themes of Spirit baptism, that of empowerment for witness. Those open to and filled with this Holy Spirit are empowered by that Spirit to partner with the Holy Spirit's work in the world for a holistic salvation. This is what it means to be empowered for witness. One powerful image of how this empowerment by the Spirit works is the image of the Holy Spirit's work on the cross with Jesus. Lyle Dabney highlights that the Holy Spirit not only enables Jesus's offering of himself on the cross for the sake of the world (Heb 9:14) but also remains present with Jesus through the passion. Jesus's cry, "Abba, Father" (Mark 14:36a) is enabled, as Paul notes elsewhere, by the Spirit (Rom 8:15,

---

64. Yong, *Spirit Poured Out*, 90.
65. Macchia, *Baptized in the Spirit*, 156.

Gal 4:6).[66] In the same way, the Holy Spirit sits with the poor in their suffering and empowers us to do likewise.

A major part of the holistic pneumatological response to poverty that Spirit baptism provides is the same gift of presence promised in the pouring out of the Holy Spirit. This presence is built into the communion of the new community. It is the same gift promised through sacraments like the Eucharist. This presence is also for the poor. Our primary solution we have been outlining of one-on-one life coaching that seeks healing and salvation for the whole person is infused with this presence. Having someone to talk to and to be with, whether they are from a cosmopolitan or a borderland setting, is an empowering reality. The Eucharistic practices, we will outline in our section on healing is a communion building setting that also calls for reaching beyond the community in hospitality. We have already talked about the need for most of this work to be done at the local civic level which also helps to build a more close-knit community through already present communities like churches, social agencies and non-profits. Another level of this would be to create small groups, similar to the CEBs of Liberation Theology, in which communion and hospitality was occurring. They would be Acts 2 communities where needs—financial, social, physical, spiritual, intellectual and emotional—are presented and met. Together these communities can help move one another toward health and life, peace and wellness, in other words the shalom of God. Together these communities can identify systems in their communities and in the laws that have helped to create these social stratifications, that have helped to put people in the bondages from which the Holy Spirit is working to free us. This is what the Holy Spirit is moving us toward. This is the kingdom vision in which we participate. But it is still a process. We live in the already and not yet tension of the eschatological kingdom which we will explore in our final section on the Holy Spirit as entelechy of the eschatological kingdom. Before this we will first explore the Holy Spirit as healer.

The Holy Spirit as Healer

Our third area of holistic pneumatological inquiry into a theology of poverty comes in the area of healing. Healing was central to the pneumatic declaration of Jesus in Luke 4 where he proclaimed recovery of sight for the blind. Similarly, when John the Baptist's disciples wanted to know whether Jesus was the Messiah, Jesus's answer was not a theological treatise, but calling John's attention to what was happening, "Go back and report to John what

---

66. Dabney, "Naming the Spirit," 58.

you have seen and heard: The blind receive sight, the lame walk, those who have leprosy are cured, the deaf hear, the dead are raised, and the good news is preached to the poor" (Luke 7:21–22). This statement from Jesus and his larger healing ministry demonstrate that healing does not just confirm the proclamation of the gospel but is itself gospel proclamation.[67]

Similarly, directly after Pentecost, the very first descriptive story of this new community in action involves Peter and John healing a lame person at the temple gate (Acts 3:1–10). This act of healing serves to show that Peter and John walked in the same power of the Holy Spirit Jesus did partaking in the same salvific healing ministry. This healing also preceded Peter's second sermon in the book of Acts. Peter's first two sermons follow miracles of the Holy Spirit again lending credence to our statement of healing, and other gifts of the Spirit, being gospel proclamation. Healing is central to the work of salvation affected by the Holy Spirit and to a pneumatological response to poverty. In this section, we will unpack what healing is in connection with salvation, then apply it to poverty in three holistic ways by discussing the healing of individuals, the healing of communities and the eschatological dimension of healing.

Healing is intricately connected with salvation and as such is a key metaphor for thinking about how to address urban poverty holistically in the United States. While it is a key component of salvation, it is not synonymous. As a component of salvation, healing is that part of salvation which helps move it from the ethereal to the concrete. Salvation is not just an intellectual assent, a set of beliefs, or even a forensic transaction. It makes a tangible difference in the life of an individual and the life of a community. The same should be true for any proposal concerning poverty. Laws can be changed, money can be raised, education can be given, but until the miracle of a healed and changed life occurs, salvation has not been fully experienced. This is in fact the whole goal. We cannot just talk about poverty, we must do something. Norberto Saracco calls illness a "manifestation of 'anti-life' that is more than a physical and individual phenomenon. It has also to do with the mind, emotions, interpersonal relations, i.e., human beings as whole persons."[68] This statement could easily be transferred onto everything we have learned about poverty. Healing within salvation also reminds us of the ongoing nature of salvation, or sanctification, because our complete healing will not be in this life, but it incrementally moves us toward who we will fully be one day.

---

67. John Christopher Thomas comes to a similar conclusion based on more thorough evidence in Thomas, "Spirit, Healing, and Mission," 421.

68. Saracco, "Holy Spirit," 414.

Healing is also clearly connected with the Holy Spirit in Scripture, both in what we saw in Luke 4 and Acts 3 above, but also in the earliest days of Christianity. In Paul's letter to the Corinthians he says, "There are different kinds of gifts, but the same Spirit distributes them . . . to another gifts of healing by that one Spirit" (1 Cor 12:4, 9b).[69] There is also a clear christological component of healing in that the apostles were healing in the name of Jesus (Acts 3:6). The Holy Spirit who empowered Jesus to heal also empowered the early Christians to minister healing to the sick.

With this statement of the Spirit's centrality in healing, we come up against the problem of healing done outside of a Christian context. In the United States this includes medical treatments, alternative medical treatments, as well as psychological and psychiatric treatments for mental and emotional illness. If we are to look at healing in a global context, Christopher H. Grundmann tells us healers can include shamans, diviners, medicine men, prophets or physicians.[70] Even biblically, it was recognized that while healing was central to the church, it was not exclusive to the church. In Luke 9:49–50, the disciple John tells Jesus "Master, we saw someone driving out demons in your name and we tried to stop him, because he is not one of us." Jesus responded, "Do not stop him for whoever is not against you is for you." In Matthew 12:27, Jesus indicates the Pharisees drove out demons. According to Grundmann, healing is a privilege, not a prerogative of the church.[71]

The church as a charismatic body should be at the center of healing because it is clearly a manifestation of the kingdom of God and the presence of the Holy Spirit. Still, it must recognize the possibility, and even the need, to partner with those working for the same healing from outside of the church. Healing is an integral part of addressing poverty because of the physical, mental, and emotional causes and repercussions of poverty that are common. We already talked in our last section about material salvation. Healing is normally thought of as bodily, mental or emotional.[72] Even, Amos Yong's description about material salvation focuses on these elements.[73]

I want to take healing even a step further to include the salvation of the material nature of one's exterior life, not just one's interior or spiritual

---

69. Scholars unanimously situate the letter to Corinthians as being written well before either Luke or Acts making it a possibly truer indication of beliefs in the earliest parts of the church.

70. Grundmann, "Inviting the Spirit," 54.

71. Grundmann, "Inviting the Spirit," 57.

72. The latter two are often connected biblically with demon possessions which had the effect of healing outward symptoms caused by some kind of inner turmoil such as demon possession.

73. Yong, *Spirit Poured Out*, 93.

life. By exterior life I mean the material element, the economic element, and even socio-political relationships. The healing of one's economic situation may necessitate conversion morally or socio-politically to make correct choices in one's life or in the political systems of our world. Just like the healing of one's body, it takes faith that one's economic life can find healing and restoration. It may take hard work, even prayer and fasting, to see the economic structures of our country change to provide equal opportunity for every race and gender, but it is possible to find salvific healing in our internal and external material lives. Healing is not just material, however. There is also healing of social divisions through Spirit baptism and the healing of communities. Such broken relationships are perhaps the most catastrophic result of poverty that mars the divine image in humanity, but healing can be an integral part of this social healing as well.[74] So, what does healing for the poor look like? We will explore this by looking at the healing of both individuals and communities.

In speaking of the healing of individuals in poverty, we have already mentioned that we should consider a holistic approach to healing. John Christopher Thomas, in surveying just the four healing events in the book of John, demonstrates that they reveal the "holistic nature of healing and salvation in the fourth gospel."[75] One particular story worth mentioning is the healing of the invalid man by the pool of Bethesda in John 5. This man was among the poor of his day sitting by the pool day after day hoping to find healing for his physical body so that his social relationships and financial situation could also be healed. Here, Jesus does not just ask the man, "Do you want to be healed?" but, "Do you want to be whole?" (John 5:6). We have also mentioned the story in Acts 3 with Peter and John at the temple gate. The lame person desires economic salvation, but Peter and John give him a holistic answer that addresses his physical, social and economic needs. In speaking of healing, Norbert Saracco holds that "We should understand the human condition as one single entity, in which personal, social, cultural, and environmental elements are not watertight compartments, but parts of an inseparably inter-related whole."[76] Individual healing of poverty must strive for this holistic approach.

---

74. I say not always because I have a hard time asserting that someone cannot be happy, live a full life, or have meaningful relationship while in poverty. But statistics do show the toll that poverty takes on individuals and on our society.

75. These four passages include the healing of the noble-man's son (John 4:46–54), the healing of the man at the pool (John 5:1–18), the healing of the man born blind (John 9:1–41), and the resurrection of Lazarus from the dead (John 11:1–57). See Thomas, "Spirit, Healing, and Mission" 435.

76. Saracco, "Holy Spirit," 417.

There are a number of physical ailments that can affect one's ability to earn money. Having a physical disability can hinder one's ability to hold certain jobs. For those able to work, there is often discrimination in hiring practices and pay.[77] The American Disabilities Act has made huge strides to rectify these issues, but statistics show the system is far from fixed resulting in the physically disabled still being disproportionately poor. While physical issues are important as a possible cause of poverty, we must also recognize poverty causes physical problems that need healing. One dangerous result of poverty is malnutrition from improper access to enough food, healthy food, or education about proper eating habits. Malnutrition creates vitamin deficiencies resulting in greater health problems which creates a cycle of poverty through high medical bills or an inability to work and earn a living wage.[78]

Health care is a second dangerous aspect of poverty. The poor have no health coverage often causing them not to seek medical care and remain sick or incur high bills, both of which perpetuate a cycle of poverty. Education and coaching individuals to take care of their whole selves because of the effects health can have economically is an important aspect of helping individuals find healing for physical ailments. Many ailments can be healed through simple medicinal and nutritional changes. From a systemic level, much has been done with food stamps and the American Disability Act to address these needs, but there is a continual need for refinement to help keep people from slipping through the cracks.[79] Even programs like WIC (Woman, Infants, and Children) and food stamps have moved to more healthy foods being available, but even stricter guidelines are necessary. A more decentralized system such as the life coaching model we have suggested would be a big step in helping people to not fall through the cracks.

Mental disorders also have enormous implications for poverty. Due to the complexity of such diseases, it is often hard to tell which precedes the other, mental illness or poverty. The relationship is often cyclical as poverty increases the risk for mental disorders and having a mental disorder increases the likelihood of poverty. Statistics show common mental disorders

---

77. A study by Baldwin and Choe found that 10 percent of wage discrepancies for disabled men could specifically be attributed to disability discrimination. The figure was 20 percent for disabled women. Baldwin and Choe, "Re-Examining the Models," 1393.

78. Heltberg, "Malnutrition, Poverty, and Economic Growth," S77–88.

79. Healthcare is a whole other issue in the United States. Even the working poor in the United States struggle with health care, and it is a very convoluted system which makes it even easier to "slip through the cracks." Other Western countries, such as Canada, provide a much more equitable system. See Weitzman and Berry, "Health Status," 87; Baum et al., "Changes Not for the Fainthearted," 1967–74.

are twice as common among the poor as the rich.[80] There are also connections between mental disorders and hunger, debt, overcrowded housing, low education and unemployment.[81] Most countries, including the United States, commit only a low percentage of their national health budget to mental health and even less of this money makes it to the poor.[82] Likewise, psychiatrists often do not stay in poor areas because they do not earn as much money. People with mental disabilities need to be targeted for poverty reduction and development programs to help break this cycle. A holistic approach that can help provide psychological or psychiatric referrals affordable for the poor as well as job placement and training to fit the person is necessary. Good people who have the love of Christ need to rise up and help take care of those who have fallen through the cracks in the system.

The final area of individual healing includes emotional healing. Psychologically, this is usually included under mental disorders. For instance, depression may often be thought of as emotional issue, but it is considered a mental disorder by the American Psychological Association. This stems from the materialistic belief that everything is controlled by the brain. This is neither right nor wrong. As we have already mentioned, the person is an integrated whole. When I think of emotional problems, I think of them usually being caused by something more than chemicals in the brain, though these are clearly at play, but rather caused by disruptions in one's life such as financial problems, divorce, or natural disasters.[83] If these emotional issues become unremitting, there is probably something mental going on as well. Still, many mental problems like depression are triggered from emotional unhealthiness or outside struggles. The solutions are very similar to mental disorders among the poor, but a strong community to belong to that will walk with the person, i.e.—the church, is also key.

As what I would consider a progressive Renewalist (see our conversations about progressive Evangelicals and Renewalists and combine the two), in talking about healing, the progressive part of me does not want to discount the clinical help available as we seek to holistically address poverty in a pneumatological fashion that addresses the whole person in their own unique situation. There are different ways that people receive healing and even some of Jesus's miraculous healings appear to be incremental (Mark

80. Patel et al., "Women, Poverty," 1461–71.

81. "Mental Health, Poverty, and Development."

82. Only 2 percent of the average country's health budget is dedicated to mental health with 37 percent of countries contributing nothing to mental health. See "Mental Health, Poverty, and Development," 3.

83. For instance, post-traumatic stress after war or child birth is a common cause of depression. See Greenawalt et al., "Posttraumatic Stress Disorder," 386–93.

8:22–25; John 5). Still, the Renewalist in me who believes the same Holy Spirit that anointed Christ to heal the blind in Luke, and, as Paul says, the same Spirit that raised Christ from the dead, is the same one poured out upon his church at Pentecost and in Pentecostal experiences today empowering us for healing in the here and now.[84]

The church should not co-opt healing but include government and business in the process because they will reach individuals the church cannot reach and provide resources the church cannot provide. Still, the church is the hope of the world against which the "gates of hell cannot prevail" (Matt 16:18). Healing is meant to flow through the church if it will allow it. I have also found Jesus's example in Luke 8:30–39 to be enlightening. In this story, Jesus tries to cast a demon out of a man, but it does not come out. In fact, it says the demon tortured the man. Jesus then addresses the demon and asks its name. After learning the identity of the demon, Jesus casts out the demon. There is a need to know the individual situation and the complexities of what is causing poverty in a person's unique story. Once they are identified, preferably through a coaching type relationship as we have described, they can be exorcised. Renewal recognizes many of these issues can be addressed through identifying them and exorcising them through prayer. But some, as Jesus told his disciples, only come out through prayer and fasting (Mark 9:29), that is through a plan and hard work in the midst of community and led by the Holy Spirit. In particular, we see directly below how community can address these emotional wounds that help perpetuate the cycle of poverty.

We have so far been addressing the healing of individuals in their unique situation. Our sociological study of poverty and the ecumenical theological approaches which critiqued the individualistic approaches of Evangelical Christianity, however, demonstrated poverty is not always caused by an individual's choices. Often, an equal cause of poverty is the systems or the powers at work in the United States which suppress and exploit whole communities of people.[85] Again, like the healing of individu-

---

84. I fall into the description Veli-Matti Kärkkäinen gives when he says "Pentecostal spirituality usually involves an emphasis upon dramatic religious experience. Prayer for physical or mental healing of a sick person is a telling example: Pentecostals are exceptionally optimistic about both their present and future existence. Their theological conviction that the God who performed mighty works in the New Testament continues to act in miraculous ways through the empowerment of the Holy Spirit provides the great majority of Pentecostal believers with a sense of hope for the present" (Kärkkäinen, "Mission, Spirit, and Eschatology," 47–48).

85. Again, refer to Walter Wink's trilogy of books in the bibliography, but especially Wink, *Unmasking the Powers*. Wink does not have an ontology of the powers, rather he sees them as emergent forces. While I think it is problematic to take a completely

als, these systemic powers need to be unmasked and named, which figures within Liberation Theology like Cornelius West are at the forefront of doing. Beyond laws, there are generational cycles of poverty that are extremely difficult to identify and overcome. Because of this, the church, if it is truly to fight poverty, needs to be at the fore of policy change that helps and benefits the poor and that creates programs to provide financial help where necessary. The church must also seek funding for civil groups and local social work organizations involved in the lives of individuals and communities to intercede for their healing. Only when we are with a community in solidarity can we name the powers that oppress it and begin to address them.

There is also a biblical paradigm for communal healing. Amos Yong sees communal healing taking place when Jesus gives back to his father the boy freed of the epileptic spirit in Luke 9:42. The boy receives physical healing, but the father and the community emotional healing. Similarly, Peter and John in Acts 3 tell the lame person at the gate of the temple to return to his community and the community is visibly affected and moved toward God.[86] Perhaps the greatest example of healing as a communal experience is the case of the cured lepers in Luke 17. Here a whole community receives healing as they seek it together and then that same community becomes an agent of healing as they are allowed to return to their homes and communities from which they had been ostracized. This becomes a process of social transformation in which the whole community is engaged and social taboos are broken. Even the eschatological vision of the new city of God (notice the urban imagery) in Revelation 22 describes trees of life that are for the healing of the nations. Whole communities and nations can find healing. This happens as we take a two-pronged approach of seeking the healing of individuals within poor communities to transform the community into a healing agent, but also focus on the laws and programs that are currently ineffective for whole communities in poverty. Discriminatory laws that allow adults to earn less than a living wage or to go without healthcare benefits, and that allow the rich to get richer while the urban poor languish separated from the mainstream of society marginalized, even ostracized at times through banishment laws, should be refined or replaced.[87]

This cannot happen overnight. It may never happen completely. Part of the Christian story is the eschatological dimension we will explore fully in our next section on the Holy Spirit as the entelechy of the eschatological

---

non-ontological view of the spiritual realm, it is also possible to talk about these larger societal powers and their influences as greater than what can be contained ontologically or personally while not denying the ontological existence of spiritual beings.

86. Yong, *Spirit Poured Out*, 90.

87. Beckett and Herbert, *Banished*.

kingdom. Eschatological hope cannot be an escapism allowing us to push aside today's problems for tomorrow's solutions. Rather, eschatology reminds us that the healing we see through the work of today is just the beginning. The healing of one person or community is a sign of hope for that day when all will truly be made new. This healing is a genuine foretaste of what God has promised to bring about in the end and is only truly recognizable when we seek healing in the present.[88]

This eschatological imagining of healing as both a community act of giving and receiving brings up one final practical response to poverty within the realm of healing. Renewalists have traditionally believed that healing can be found in the celebration of the Lord's Supper, of the Eucharist meal. To internalize the body and blood of Christ is to release healing for broken bodies. The Eucharist is also a communal act in which, to quote Alexander Schmemann, individuals "come together in one place to bring their lives, their very world with them and to be more than what they were: a new community with new life."[89] Through this communal act, the presence of God through the power of the Holy Spirit is mediated through material means to bring healing and salvation to the whole person.[90] The supper is a political and prophetic act whereby the "enacted and enacting body of Christ provides and mediates an alternative way of life through the gracious activities of the Sprit."[91] This supper can take place as people meet together for life coaching sessions enacting solutions of healing as we do life together, enacting solidarity and healing. This does not need to be ceremonial but can also be in simply getting together for communion and food for the purpose of holistic healing. It also should happen within communities in a more formal setting asking for the healing of poverty through the physical, mental, and emotional healing of the participants, their families and their communities.[92]

---

88. Grundmann has good reflections on this pointing out that healings are always "provisional mendings postponing but not preventing death." So, Christians keep striving for healing. In this way healing can only ever be temporary and always looks forward eschatologically. The same is true for poverty. To paraphrase the wisdom of Job, we die the same way we came into the world, with nothing (Job 1:21–22). Grundmann, "Inviting the Spirits," 71.

89. Schmemann, *For the Life of the World*, 27.

90. Wolfgang Vondey, in his book, *People of Bread*, has a helpful discussion on the communal nature, the healing nature and the eschatological nature of the Lord's Supper from a Pentecostal, if not a pneumatological, perspective. See Vondey, *People of Bread*.

91. Yong, *Spirit Poured Out*, 165.

92. I imagine something here similar to what M. L. Daneel started in Zimbabwe, interreligious Eucharist services that brought together various religions in solidarity for the restoration and healing of the impoverished earth but applied to urban communities that have similarly been stripped bare within the United States. See Daneel, "Earthkeeping in Missiological Perspective," 130–88.

The Holy Spirit as Entelechy of the Eschatological Kingdom

In our final section, we will put a capstone on our exploration of a holistic pneumatological approach to poverty by exploring the Holy Spirit as the entelechy of the eschatological kingdom. I borrow this term "entelechy" from David Coffey who sees the Holy Spirit as the "directive principle."[93] He sees the Holy Spirit directing creation toward Christ as the end goal, but I would broaden this to include the Spirit's direction of the cosmos toward the eschatological kingdom over which Christ reigns. It is also important to recover the essence of the philosophical definition of entelechy. Entelechy, a term rooted first in Aristotelian metaphysics and later Leibniz's physics, usually has the meaning of the vital principle of a living organism or organization, or that which realizes or makes actual what is otherwise merely potential.[94] In this way, the Holy Spirit can be seen as a personal force which is moving the world from the potential of the eschatological kingdom, which the Spirit-anointed Christ inaugurated, to its full actualization at the return of Christ.

This eschatological dimension is important for addressing urban poverty because we must recognize that the salvation of the poor will not be fully consummated until the eschaton. Jesus said, the poor you will always have with you (Matt 26:11a). This is not an excuse for escapism, however. The fulfillment of the pneumatic vision of Jesus in Luke 4 in which he came to proclaim the year of the Lord's favor is only fully realized in the future, but the Holy Spirit is actualizing this potential even today. Salvation, healing, restoration and freedom all happen today as the Holy Spirit directs the cosmos toward fulfillment in Jesus. These instances give tastes and visions of this reality and hope for it to be holistically realized in the here and now in as many areas of our world as possible. In this section, we demonstrate how the eschatological vision which the Holy Spirit is actualizing among all flesh connects with a holistic Pneumatology of poverty. In this discussion, we will particularly explore the cosmic and prophetic nature of eschatology, the urban element in eschatology, and how this moves us with hope to holistically address urban poverty in the United States and beyond. This section will be slightly briefer than past sections because the eschatological vision of salvation for the poor has driven each previous section.

In Luke 4:18–19, Jesus concludes his pneumatic proclamation describing that he has come, empowered by the Spirit, to proclaim the year of the Lord's favor. This statement had a clear connection with the liberative day of Jubilee in the book of Leviticus. It had clear economic and spiritual

---

93. Coffey, "Method of Third Article Theology," 27–28.
94. McDonough, "Leibniz's Philosophy of Physics."

implications for the hearers. In Jesus's ministry we see Zacchaeus's encounter with Jesus empower him to live out such Jubilee practices, giving half of what he owned to the poor and cancelling the debts of and repaying those he had cheated (Luke 19:1–9). Because of this Jubilee act demonstrating the year of the Lord's favor, Jesus proclaimed, "Today, salvation has come to this house" (Luke 19:10). Jesus also encouraged a ruler who believed he had followed all the law that the one thing he lacked was to follow these jubilee practices by selling all he had and giving it to the poor. (Luke 18:18–30). There are different visions throughout Scripture of what the Holy Spirit's role would be and exactly what this year of the Lord's favor would look like. Usually it harkens back to the Genesis stories and sees the Holy Spirit as recreating the world much in the same way the Spirit was present and active in the beginning. Steven M. Studebaker in his article, "Soteriology: A Story of the Spirit," connects the eschatological vision with how the Holy Spirit was involved in new creation and redemption going to a barren land and making it a land of abundance (Isa 32:15; 42:5–7).[95] He sees a similar motif in Ezekiel's use of pneumatological images to describe Yahweh's fulfillment of the promise to restore the people of Israel (Ezek 36–37).[96]

These eschatological visions paint a picture of what salvation should look like in our world and what it will one day look like consummated. Perhaps the clearest picture of this in Scripture is in Revelation 21, John's vision of the new heaven and the new earth. Central to the vision is the new Jerusalem, an urban city that comes from heaven and becomes God's dwelling place among the people on earth so there is no separation between God and his people. Every tear will be wiped away with no more death or pain. Verses 6–21 give an in-depth description of the city before John describes that there is no need for a temple in the city, nor for sun or moon because God provides everything these would have provided before. And there is a final declaration that the nations will walk by this light and fill the new city. There is even an indication that the meal will be central to the eschatological kingdom, making Eucharist a prophetic vision of this newness (Rev 19:9). This is how the Holy Spirit is making everything new (Rev 21:5).

Numerous important elements for a holistic Pneumatology of urban poverty arise from this scriptural survey. First, eschatological Pneumatology brings out the element of cosmic salvation. It emphasizes the interconnectedness of human beings with one another, with the environment, and their mutual redemption (Isa 11:69; 65:25). Particularly central to the eschatological vision are those who have been left out and defenseless including the

---

95. Studebaker, "Soteriology," 236.
96. Studebaker, "Soteriology," 240–41.

poor, the environment, and even martyrs (Rev 6:9). It is God's final saving and vindication of the people of God who yearn for divine intervention in their experiences of persecution, oppression and alienation.[97] Miroslav Volf sees this as not just reconciliation between God and humanity but between humans and themselves, in particular between victims and victimizers.[98] We might extend this idea to include those implicit in the oppression of the poor and the poor themselves. Again, this becomes a holistic salvation that is envisioned for all of humanity, rich and poor. Even the language of the description of the new city being made of precious metals and gems invokes a God for whom wealth is of no issue and there is no more want. Such a vision should engender hope and motivation to partner with the Holy Spirit in the actualization of this potential vision in the here and now. In the same way, the Holy Spirit led Jesus to begin to work toward such a vision in his own life through the numerous teachings and miracles we have recounted, the Spirit that has been poured out on all flesh is inviting us to do the same. It works today as a prophetic vision to engender hope for the people of God in the church and among the poor. As Helene Slessarev-Jamir mentions, such a prophetic voice is not just future telling but a new story for those who are currently suffering.[99]

Second, there is a distinct urban element in the eschatological vision given to John in Revelation when under the power of the Holy Spirit. This city is a place without need or want. It is a place of reconciliation where God is in the midst of the people, a place of belonging. This is very different than the urban settings we explored in chapter 2. It is interesting that even when garden imagery is mentioned in the beginning of Revelation 22, which harkens back to the Garden of Eden at creation, that the river that once ran through the garden with the tree of life on its banks now runs "down the middle of the great street of the city" (Rev 22:2). Such imagery gives hope that God has not given up on cities. That while "White flight" is a real phenomenon, God has not fled even the most dilapidated neighborhoods, but includes them in an eschatological vision of hope. Just as theologians point out that heaven is not an escape from this world but a renewing of this world, neither is it an escape from the inner-city, but it's very hope.

Third, the eschatological vision should move us to address poverty well beyond our own neighborhoods, gender, race, and even beyond the United States. While our focus in this thesis has been on the United States as our most immediate context, poverty is an even greater pandemic

---

97. Yong, *Spirit Poured Out*, 96.
98. Volf, "Final Reconciliation," 91–113.
99. Slessarev-Jamir, *Prophetic Activism*, 35–38.

world-wide. The vision of the pneumatological kingdom is one of every tribe and tongue, gender, socioeconomic class fully whole and healed, including the relationships between them. While many of these relationships are still strained in our present-day context, the Spirit, through baptism, is at work forming a new community. While our initial strategy to address poverty is local, personalized and community based, a Spirit-empowered community cannot just stay inward focused but reaches out beyond itself to the other. The vision of the Spirit is for the healing of every nation. Susan Holman purports the importance of encouraging an empathetic Christian. Such a Christian is "mindful of one's on place in the global community. Experiencing the global community will affect how we think about Christian responses to contemporary human need."[100] Participation in the global community gives us better insight intellectually and emotionally to respond to the needs around us, so it should not be forsaken. This is equally true for both the poor and the rich. The functional world of the poor is often even smaller, but it must be broadened to truly see the eschatological vision of God and the way forward even in one's own community. This may begin with engaging other communities of poverty within the United States, or even cosmopolitans engaging the poor, but it must eventually become even broader among the nations. Likewise, any global work should move toward empathy for one's local community.

This section on eschatology has focused on hope and vision. We outlined many of the practicals in the other sections, but as we have mentioned, all of these sections are interrelated. In partnering with the Spirit, however, the Spirit empowers us to actualize this potential vision for the poor in today's world. One of the ways we actualize it is by being globally minded and allowing this sensing of the world around us to inform our practices locally. We must also speak out this prophetic vision so that it engenders hope in our world for the salvation of the poor, the urban city and for us all.

CONCLUSION

We have outlined a holistic pneumatological approach to urban poverty using the pneumatic proclamation of Jesus of good news for the poor. This led us to identify the pneumatological metaphor of salvation as a means to talk about the Spirit's holistic work among the poor. In talking about the Spirit as savior, baptizer, healer, and entelechy of the eschatological kingdom, we have developed a robust theology of salvation for the poor addressing the whole person, the community, and the multidimensionality of salvation. We

---

100. Holman, *God Knows There's Need*, 40.

have proposed a number of applications, but primarily proposed a response to poverty that includes a decentralized system in the form of one-on-one life coaching meetings as a dynamic pneumatological response to the intricacies of poverty within an individual and a community. In our unpacking of personal salvation, we saw the need to focus on the individual but within a local community setting of civil society, particularly the family. We saw that both the rich and the poor need salvation and that our approach should be personalized to each person which is best accomplished through face to face interaction through whole-life coaching. This coaching can and should be done through all three major sectors of our society in the United States: the government (though on a local level), religion and business.

We also suggested the Eucharist as a practice that happens in daily life and in specific ceremonies where holistic healing is sought for its participants. In the Eucharist is the very presence of Jesus through the power of the Spirit. It is a prophetic eschatological vision of the wholeness the Holy Spirit is actualizing in the present. This gift of presence through the Spirit-created community that lives out hospitality and *koinonia* is a healing balm for social division caused by poverty. One other way besides Eucharist to live out this presence is through small group settings where life is shared with one another and the community helps one another move forward in life. Small groups are a compliment and possible vehicle to the one-on-one coaching. We also proposed that a pneumatological approach to poverty must be globally minded, allowing intercultural experiences and dialogue to inform local responses and vice versa. Finally, the Spirit who is actualizing this vision in our very midst engenders hope that there is another way and we can partner with the Spirit in this new vision for reality.

Conclusion

This study argues that a pneumatological approach to urban poverty can be developed by means of a Renewal four-fold gospel model, which complements a christological focus. The result is a nuanced response to urban poverty that holistically addresses the individual, the community, and the internal and external causes and repercussions of poverty. We began by exploring both the face and the underside of urban poverty in the United States. We saw poverty is as a complex reality that affects a wide array of races, ages, genders and family compositions. Poverty, while primarily measured by economic factors also has social, psychological and spiritual factors that both cause poverty and are also affected by poverty on individual and communal levels. Such a complex and subtle problem calls for an equally personalized response which we have attempted to provide a theological basis for through a holistic pneumatological response to urban poverty.

After exploring urban poverty sociologically, we surveyed a number of theological responses to poverty including Evangelical, ecumenical and Renewal responses. We saw that while they all provided helpful elements, none of them addressed the problem pneumatologically or holistically, including Renewal which has traditionally had a strong pneumatological emphasis. The fact that Renewal has grown among the poor so prolifically, particularly globally, caused us to ask whether or not Pneumatology could be a good resource for responding to urban poverty. We therefore turned to exploring Pneumatology, including its scope, challenges, and potential to underlie a more dynamic and holistic approach to urban poverty.

Following Amos Yong's pneumatological imagination, we identified the pneumatic metaphor of salvation as an entry way into talking about urban poverty pneumatologically. We used a pneumatological reading of the Pentecostal four-fold gospel which envisioned the Spirit as savior, baptizer, healer and entelechy of the eschatological Kingdom. The same Spirit who empowered Christ to proclaim good news to the poor in Luke 4:18–19 is the same Spirit that empowers the church today to respond to the poor with a dynamic salvation in their own local context. Our approach is holistic, dealing with the entire person and society which affects poverty. It is also nuanced to fit each person's particular situation rather than be a one size fits all response to poverty. In particular, we proposed an individual, whole life coaching that addresses each person and the whole person. Such a response should be run through a partnership of all three of the major sectors of society—government, civil and religious—to provide the necessary resources.

The significance of this work is multi-fold. The hope is that scholarship will see the resources a holistic Pneumatology has to offer theology and how they are unique and important compared to traditional theistic or christocentric paradigms. If we truly hold to a Trinitarianism in which God is uniquely three yet wholly one, then there should also be an important place for the Spirit in any theological reflection, even something like a social action among the urban poor.

A second significance of this study is demonstrating the central place Renewal Studies has taken in the pneumatological revolution. Many of the scholars doing the most constructive work on the Holy Spirit lie in Renewal traditions that consider themselves people of the Spirit, but their work has greater implications than just a proper Pneumatology or topics like spiritual gifts.

Third, by looking at the topic of urban poverty from a completely different perspective, I hope that new motivations and methods will arise that will propel increased engagement with poverty and other social justice issues. In particular, my own Pentecostal tradition, as well as the larger Renewal movement, has often been labeled quietistic concerning social issues and the poor. It has been shown by Miller and Yamamori in their sociological study, *Global Pentecostalism: The New Face of Christian Social Engagement*, that this quietistic charge is largely unfounded.[1] Their work is empirical, but I hope that this study will put some theological meat behind their claims by demonstrating that Renewal Studies and its Pneumatology has great resources for a theology of social action. With this, I hope that Renewalists who have been engaging in social action for the poor see that it is not untrue to their own theological and historical roots. It is not just a fad to be picked up from other traditions, but it is true to the Renewal identity of a people of the Spirit. Hopefully, this will also encourage those Renewalists who are deserving of the term quietistic to see that their tradition and emphasis on the Spirit should motivate them and give them ample resources to begin engaging in social action.

---

1. Miller and Yamamori, *Global Pentecostalism*, 212.

While I believe much progress has been made toward a holistic Pneumatology of poverty, there is always work to be done on poverty. As Jesus said, "The poor you will always have with you" (Matt 26:11a). We started with a sociological survey and the next step is to turn back to sociology to see how these proposals best live themselves out in society and in policy that truly makes a difference in the world. We have taken steps in this direction, but a complete proposal is beyond the scope of this thesis. Another area of further research is to take the beginning of my pneumatological work on poverty and to expand it. We used the four-fold gospel as a contained structure in which to explore the possibility of a holistic pneumatological approach. Now that is has been substantiated that such an approach holds great promise, there are further pneumatological themes to explore. Finally, I think that the pneumatological potential we have uncovered should inspire more pneumatological studies within the realm of social action. We have seen works on creation care and now poverty, but there are so many other broken areas of our world that the Holy Spirit can bring salvation to from gender and race relations, to sex trafficking and matters of life including corporal punishment and abortion. The Holy Spirit responds to the whole person and that same Spirit is at work in every one of these atrocities already, but there are theological gems to uncover to help us respond in step with the Spirit.

Bibliography

"About the International House of Prayer." International House of Prayer. http://www.ihopkc.org/about.

"About the Rock Thrift Store." Rock Church. http://rockthriftstore.com/about.

Alfaro, Sammy. *Divino Compañero: Toward a Hispanic Pentecostal Christology*. Princeton Theological Monograph Series 147. Eugene, OR: Pickwick, 2010.

Althouse, Peter. *Spirit of the Last Days: Pentecostal Eschatology in Conversation with Jürgen Moltmann*. Journal of Pentecostal Theology Supplemental Series 25. London: T. & T. Clark, 2003.

Altmeyer, Arthur J. "Social Welfare in the United States." Social Security Administration. https://www.ssa.gov/history/aja964.html.

Anderson, Allan. "Varieties, Taxonomies, and Definitions." In *Studying Global Pentecostalism: Theories and Methods*, edited by Allan Anderson, et al., 13–29. Berkeley, CA: University of California Press, 2010.

Bacik, James J. *Catholic Spirituality: Its History and Challenge*. New York: Paulist, 2002.

Baldwin, Marjorie L., and Chung Choe. "Re-Examining the Models Used to Estimate Disability-Related Wage Discrimination." *Applied Economics* 46.12 (2014) 1393–1408.

Barth, Karl. *Church Dogmatics*. Vol. 1/1 Translated by G. Bromiley and T. Torrance. Edinburgh: T. & T. Clark, 1975.

Bartleman, Frank. *Azusa Street*. Plainfield, NJ: Logos International, 1980.

Bass, Stephen. *Reducing Poverty and Sustaining the Environment: The Politics of Local Engagement*. London: Earthscan, 2005.

Baum, Fran E., et al. "Changes Not for the Fainthearted: Reorienting Health Care Systems Toward Health Equity Through Action on the Social Determinants of Health." *American Journal of Public Health* 99.11 (2009) 1967–74.

Bean, Lydia. "Compassionate Conservatives? Evangelicals, Economic Conservatism, and National Identity." *Journal for the Scientific Study of Religion* 53.1 (2014) 164–86.

Bebbington, David. *Evangelicalism in Modern Britain: A History from 1730s to the 1980s*. London: Unwin Hyman, 1989.

Beckett, Katherine, and Steven Kelly Herbert. *Banished: The New Social Control in Urban America*. Studies in Crime and Public Policy. New York: Oxford University Press, 2011.

Bell, E. N. "The Baptized Body of Christ." *Christian Evangel*, June 14, 1919.

Bendroth, Margaret Lamberts. "Evangelicals, Family, and Modernity." In *American Religions and the Family: How Faith Traditions Cope with Modernization and*

Democracy, edited by David Clairmont and Don Browning, 56–69. New York: Columbia University Press, 2007.

Bennett, Dennis J. *Nine O'Clock in the Morning*. Plainfield, NJ: Logos International, 1970.

Blumhofer, Edith Waldvogel. *Aimee Semple McPherson: Everybody's Sister*. Library of Religious Biography. Grand Rapids: Eerdmans, 1993.

Boff, Clodovis. *Theology and Praxis: Epistemological Foundations*. Translated by Robert R. Barr. Maryknoll, NY: Orbis, 1987.

Boff, Leonardo. *Church: Charism and Power—Liberation Theology and the Institutional Church*. New York: Crossroad, 1985.

———. *Trinity and Society*. Translated by Paul Burns. Maryknoll, NY: Orbis, 1988.

Boff, Leonardo, and Clodovis Boff. *Introducing Liberation Theology*. Maryknoll, NY: Orbis, 1987.

Bultmann, Rudolf. *The History of the Synoptic Tradition*. Rev. ed. New York: Harper & Row, 1968.

Burdick, John. "Struggling Against the Devil: Pentecostalism and Social Movements in Urban Brazil." In *Rethinking Protestantism in Latin America*, edited by Virginia Garrard-Burnett and David Stoll, 20–44. Philadelphia: Temple University Press, 1993.

Burgess, Stanley M. "Christianity: Historical Setting." In *The Wiley-Blackwell Companion to Religion and Social Justice*, edited by Michael D. Palmer and Stanley M. Burgess, 46–60. Wiley-Blackwell Companions to Religion. Malden, MA: Wiley-Blackwell, 2012.

Cadorette, Curt. *Liberation Theology: An Introductory Reader*. Eugene, OR: Wipf & Stock, 2004.

Campolo, Tony, and Walter Rauschenbusch. "Response: A Response by an Evangelical." In *Christianity and the Social Crisis in the Twenty-First Century: The Classic That Woke Up the Church*, edited by Paul Rauschenbusch, 39–80. New York: Harper Collins, 2007.

Cannon, Katie G. *Katie's Canon: Womanism and the Soul of the Black Community*. New York: Continuum, 1995.

Cartledge, Mark J. "Can Theology Be 'Practical'? Part II: A Reflection on Renewal Methodology and the Practice of Research." *Journal of Contemporary Ministry* 3 (2017) 18–34.

———. *Charismatic Glossolalia: An Empirical-Theological Study*. Aldershot, England: Ashgate, 2002.

———. "The Early Pentecostal Theology of Confidence Magazine (1908–1926): A Version of the Five-Fold Gospel?" *Journal of the European Pentecostal Theological Association* 28.2 (2008) 117–30.

Castelo, Daniel. *Pneumatology: A Guide for the Perplexed*. London: Bloomsbury; T. & T. Clark, 2015.

Cawthorne, Alexandra. "The Straight Facts on Women in Poverty." *Center for American Progress*, October 8, 2008. https://www.americanprogress.org/issues/women/reports/2008/10/08/5103/the-straight-facts-on-women-in-poverty.

Center on Policy Initiatives. "Poverty, Earnings, and Income in the City of San Diego 2014." *Center on Policy Initiatives*, September 24, 2015. https://d3n8a8pro7vhmx.cloudfront.net/onlinecpi/pages/1201/attachments/original/1449176087/poverty_report_2015.pdf?1449176087.

Chan, Simon. "Asian Pentecostalism, Social Concern and the Ethics of Conformism." *Transformation* 11.1 (1994) 29–32.

———. *Pentecostal Theology and the Christian Spiritual Tradition*. Sheffield: Sheffield Academic, 2001.

Christenson, Larry. *A Charismatic Approach to Social Action*. Minneapolis, MN: Bethany Fellowship, 1974.

Cleary, Edward L. *The Rise of Charismatic Catholicism in Latin America*. Gainesville, FL: University Press of Florida, 2011.

Clifton, Shane. "Preaching the 'Full Gospel' in the Context of Global Environment Crises." In *The Spirit Renews the Face of the Earth: Pentecostal Forays in Science and Theology of Creation*, edited by Amos Yong, 117–34. Eugene, OR: Pickwick, 2009.

Coffey, David. "The Method of Third Article Theology." In *Third Article Theology: A Pneumatological Dogmatics*, edited by Myk Habets, 21–36. Minneapolis: Fortress, 2016.

Cohn, Scott. "America's Most Affordable States to Call Home." *CNBC*, June 24, 2015. http://www.cnbc.com/2015/06/24/americas-cheapest-states-to-live-in-2015.html?slide=11.

Collins, A. P. "A Plea for Unity." *Christian Evangel*, June 29, 1918.

Collins, Billie Jean, ed. *The SBL Handbook of Style: For Biblical Studies and Related Disciplines*. 2nd ed. Atlanta, GA: SBL, 2014.

Comblin, José. "The Holy Spirit." In *Mysterium Liberationis: Fundamental Concepts of Liberation Theology*, edited by Ignacio Ellacuría and Jon Sobrino, xv, 752. Translated by Robert R. Barr. Maryknoll, NY: Orbis, 1993.

———. *The Holy Spirit and Liberation*. Translated by Paul Burns. Maryknoll, NY: Orbis, 1989.

Cone, James H. "Black Theology and the Black Church: Where Do We Go From Here?" *CrossCurrents* 27.2 (1977) 147–56.

———. *Black Theology and Black Power*. New York: Seabury, 1969.

———. *A Black Theology of Liberation*. C. Eric Lincoln Series in Black Religion. Philadelphia: Lippincott, 1970.

———. *God of the Oppressed*. New York: Seabury, 1975.

———. *The Spirituals and the Blues*. New York: Seabury, 1972.

Cook, William. "Evangelical Reflections on the Church of the Poor." *Missiology* 11.1 (1983) 47–53.

Culpepper, R. Alan, and Gail R. O'Day. *The Gospel of Luke, the Gospel of John*. Vol. 9 of *The New Interpreter's Bible*. Nashville, TN: Abingdon, 1995.

Cunningham, Lawrence, and Keith J. Egan. *Christian Spirituality: Themes from the Tradition*. New York: Paulist, 1996.

Curtis, Susan. *A Consuming Faith: The Social Gospel and Modern American Culture*. Columbia, MO: University of Missouri Press, 2001.

Dabney, D. Lyle. "Naming the Spirit: Towards a Pneumatology of the Cross." In *Starting with the Spirit*, edited by Australian Theological Forum, 28–50. The Task of Theology Today 2. London, England: SCM, 2002.

———. "Saul's Armor: The Problem and the Promise of Pentecostal Theology Today." *Pneuma* 23.1 (2001) 115–46.

Dabney, D. Lyle, and Bradford E. Hinze, eds. *Advents of the Spirit: An Introduction to the Current Study of Pneumatology*. Marquette Studies in Theology. Milwaukee, WI: Marquette University Press, 2001.

Daly, Mary, and Hilary Silver. "Social Exclusion and Social Capital: A Comparison and Critique." *Theory and Society* 37.6 (2008) 537–66.

Daneel, M. L. "Earthkeeping in Missiological Perspective: An African Challenge." *Mission Studies* 13.1–2 (1996) 130–88.

Danielson, Dan. "Charismatic Renewal and Social Concern." *Post American* 4.2 (1975) 24–25.

Dayton, Donald W. "Pentecostal/Charismatic Renewal and Social Change: A Western Perspective." *Transformation* 5.4 (1988) 7–13.

———. *Theological Roots of Pentecostalism*. Grand Rapids, MI: Francis Asbury, 1987.

De Jesús, Wilfredo. Interview with Brandon Kertson. Personal interview. Anaheim, CA, June 1, 2016.

Del Colle, Ralph. *Christ and the Spirit: Spirit-Christology in Trinitarian Perspective*. New York: Oxford University Press, 1994.

Dempster, Murray W. "Christian Social Concern in Pentecostal Perspective: Reformulating Pentecostal Eschatology." *Journal of Pentecostal Theology* 1.2 (1993) 51–64.

———. "Eschatology, Spirit Baptism, and Inclusiveness: An Exploration into the Hallmarks of a Pentecostal Social Ethic." In *Perspectives in Pentecostal Eschatologies*, edited by Peter Althouse, 155–88. Eugene, OR: Pickwick, 2010.

———. "Pentecostal Social Concern and the Biblical Mandate of Social Justice." *Pneuma* 9.2 (1987) 129–53.

DeNavas-Walt, Carmen, and Bernadette D. Proctor. *Income and Poverty in the United States 2014*. US Census Bureau P60-252. Washington, DC: US Government Printing Office, 2015. https://www.census.gov/content/dam/Census/library/publications/2015/demo/p60-252.pdf.

DeNavas-Walt, Carmen, et al. *Income, Poverty, and Health Coverage in the United States 2009*. US Census Bureau P60-238. Washington DC: US Government Printing Office, 2010. https://www.census.gov/prod/2010pubs/p60-238.pdf.

DeYoung, Curtis Paul. "Christianity: Contemporary Expressions." In *The Wiley-Blackwell Companion to Religion and Social Justice*, edited by Michael D. Palmer and Stanley M. Burgess, 61–76. Wiley-Blackwell Companions to Religion. Malden, MA: Wiley-Blackwell, 2012.

Dreyer, Elizabeth. "Resources for a Renewed Life in the Spirit and Pneumatology: Medieval Mystics and Saints." Paper presented at Advent of the Spirit: Orientations in Pneumatology (Symposium), Marquette University, Milwaukee, WI, April 17–19, 1998.

Du Bois, W. E. B. *The Souls of Black Folk*. New York: Dover, 1994.

Dunn, James D. G. *Baptism in the Holy Spirit*. London: SCM, 1970.

———. *Jesus and the Spirit: A Study of the Religious and Charismatic Experience of Jesus and the First Christians as Reflected in the New Testament*. Philadelphia, PA: Westminster, 1975.

Dunnavant, Anthony L. "David Lipscomb and the 'Preferential Option for the Poor' Among Post-Bellum Church of Christ." In *Poverty and Ecclesiology: Nineteenth-Century Evangelicals in the Light of Liberation Theology*, edited by Anthony L. Dunnavant, 27–50. Collegeville, MN: Liturgical, 1992.

Edin, K. J., and H. L. Shaefer. *$2.00 a Day: Living on Almost Nothing in America*. Boston, MA: Houghton Mifflin Harcourt, 2015.

Edwards, Wendy J. Deichmann. "Manifest Destiny, the Social Gospel and the Coming Kingdom: Josiah Strong's Program of Global Reform 1885–1916." In *Perspectives on the Social Gospel: Papers from the Inaugural Social Gospel Conference at Colgate Rochester Divinity School*, edited by Christopher Hodge Evans, 81–116. Texts and Studies in the Social Gospel 3. Lewiston, NY: Edwin Mellen, 1999.

Ehrenreich, Barbara. *Nickel and Dimed: On (Not) Getting by in America*. 10th Anniversary ed. New York: Henry Holt, 2011.

Eide, Arne H., and Benedicte Ingstad. *Disability and Poverty: A Global Challenge*. Bristol, England: Policy, 2011.

Elowsky, Joel C. *We Believe in the Holy Spirit*. Ancient Christian Doctrine. Downers Grove, IL: IVP Academic, 2009.

Ely, Richard T. *Social Aspects of Christianity, and Other Essays*. New York: T. Y. Crowell, 1889.

Emling, Shelley. "These 12 Everyday Words Used to Have Completely Different Meanings." *Huffington Post*, February 26, 2014. http://www.huffingtonpost.com/2014/02/26/words-that-have-changed-meaning_n_4847343.html.

"Entelechy." Encyclopedia Britannica. July 20, 1998. https://www.britannica.com/topic/entelechy.

Esler, Philip Francis. *The Early Christian World*. Vol. 1. London: Routledge, 2004.

Ettlinger, Gerard H. "The Holy Spirit in the Theology of the Second Ecumenical Synod and in the Undivided Church." *The Greek Orthodox Theological Review* 27.4 (1982) 431–40.

"Expatisan's Cost of Living Map of North America." Expatisan. May 25, 2016. https://www.expatistan.com/cost-of-living/index/north-america.

Fleisher, Mark. "Coping with Macro-Structural Adversity: Chronic Poverty, Female Youth Gangs, and Cultural Resilience in a US African-American Urban Community." *Journal of Contingencies & Crisis Management* 17.4 (2009) 274–84.

Flory, Richard W., and Donald E. Miller. "The Dream Center: Spirit-Infused and Socially Engaged Urban Ministry." *PentecoStudies* 11.1 (2012) 9–26.

Floyd-Thomas, Stacey M., and Anthony B. Pinn. *Liberation Theologies in the United States: An Introduction*. New York: NYU Press, 2010.

Freston, Paul. "Charismatic Evangelicals in Latin America: Mission and Politics on the Frontiers of Protestant Growth." In *Charismatic Christianity: Sociological Perspectives*, edited by Stephen Hunt, et al., 184–204. New York: St. Martin's, 1997.

Frodsham, Stanley H. "Sunday School Lesson from a Pentecostal Viewpoint." *Christian Evangel*, July 12, 1919.

Gasaway, Brantley W., ed. *Progressive Evangelicals and the Pursuit of Social Justice*. Chapel Hill, NC: University of North Carolina Press, 2014.

Gause, R. H. *Living in the Spirit: The Way of Salvation*. Cleveland, TN: Pathway, 1980.

Gebara, Ivone. *Longing for Running Water: Ecofeminism and Liberation*. Minneapolis, MN: Fortress, 1999.

Gelpi, Donald L. *Charism and Sacrament: A Theology of Christian Conversion*. New York: Paulist, 1976.

———. *The Conversion Experience: A Reflective Process for RCIA Participants and Others*. New York: Paulist, 1998.

General Council of the Assemblies of God. *Minutes of the General Council of the Assemblies of God*. St. Louis, MO, October 1–7, 1916. n.p. Online. https://

pentecostalarchives.org/digitalPublications/USA/Assemblies%20of%20God%20USA/Minutes%20General%20Council/Unregistered/1916/FPHC/1916.pdf.

Glaeser, Edward L., et al. "Why Do the Poor Live in Cities? The Role of Public Transportation." *Journal of Urban Economics* 63.1 (2008) 1–24.

Goodman, Lisa A., et al. "Homelessness as Psychological Trauma: Broadening Perspectives." *American Psychologist* 46.11 (1991) 1219–25.

Gorter, Herman, et al. *Non-Leninist Marxism: Writings on the Workers Councils*. St. Petersburg, FL: Red and Black, 2007.

Greaves, Stuart. *False Justice: Unveiling the Truth about Social Justice*. Shippensburg, PA: Destiny Image, 2012.

Greenawalt, D. S., et al. "Posttraumatic Stress Disorder and Odds of Major Invasive Procedures among US Veterans Affairs Patients." *Journal of Psychosomatic Research* 75.4 (2013) 386–93.

Greggs, Tom. "Communio Ecclesiology: The Spirit's Work of Salvation in the Life of the Church." In *Third Article Theology: A Pneumatological Dogmatics*, edited by Myk Habets, 347–66. Minneapolis, MN: Fortress, 2016.

Grundmann, Christoffer H. "Inviting the Spirit to Fight the Spirits?: Pneumatological Challenges for Missions in Healing and Exorcism." *International Review of Mission* 94.372 (2005) 51–73.

Gushee, David P. *A New Evangelical Manifesto: A Kingdom Vision for the Common Good*. St Louis, MO: Chalice, 2012.

———. "Rebuilding Marriage and the Family." In *Toward a Just and Caring Society: Christian Responses to Poverty in America*, edited by David P. Gushee, 499–530. Grand Rapids, MI: Baker, 1999.

———, ed. *Toward a Just and Caring Society: Christian Responses to Poverty in America*. Grand Rapids, MI: Baker, 1999.

Gutiérrez, Gustavo. *A Theology of Liberation: History, Politics, and Salvation*. Translated by Sister Idina Caridad and John Eagleson. Maryknoll, NY: Orbis, 1973.

———. *We Drink From Our Own Wells: The Spiritual Journey of a People*. Translated by Matthew J. O'Connell. Maryknoll, NY: Orbis, 1984.

Habets, Myk. *The Anointed Son: A Trinitarian Spirit Christology*. Princeton Theological Monograph Series. Eugene, OR: Pickwick, 2010.

———. *Ecumenical Perspectives on the Filioque for the Twenty-First Century*. T. & T. Clark Theology. London: Bloomsbury Academic, 2015.

Haight, Roger. *Jesus, Symbol of God*. Maryknoll, NY: Orbis, 1999.

Hall, Taylor L., et al. "Postincarceration Policies and Prisoner Reentry: Implications for Policies and Programs Aimed at Reducing Recidivism and Poverty." *Journal of Poverty* 20.1 (2016) 56–72.

Hallgrimsdottir, Helga Kristin, and Cecilia Benoit. "From Wage Slaves to Wage Workers: Cultural Opportunity Structures and the Evolution of the Wage Demands of the Knights of Labor and the American Federation of Labor, 1880–1900." *Social Forces* 85.3 (2007) 1393–411.

Halteman, James. "The Market System, the Poor, and Economic Theory." In *A New Evangelical Manifesto: A Kingdom Vision for the Common Good*, edited by David P. Gushee, 72–111. St. Louis, MO: Chalice, 2012.

Hayes, Diana L. *Standing in the Shoes My Mother Made: A Womanist Theology*. Minneapolis, MN: Fortress, 2011.

Heller, Wendy. "Poverty: The Most Challenging Condition of Prisoner Release." *Georgetown Journal on Poverty Law & Policy* 13.2 (2006) 219–47.
Heltberg, Rasmus. "Malnutrition, Poverty, and Economic Growth." Supplement, *Health Economics* 18.s1.1 (2009) 77–88.
Hendel, Kurt K. "The Care of the Poor: An Evangelical Perspective." *Currents in Theology and Mission* 15.6 (1988) 526–32.
Hocken, Peter. "The Catholic Charismatic Renewal." In *The Century of the Holy Spirit: 100 Years of Pentecostal and Charismatic Renewal, 1901–2001*, edited by Vinson Synan, 209–232. Nashville, TN: Thomas Nelson, 2001.
Hollenweger, Walter J. "Pentecostals and the Charismatic Movement." In *Study of Spirituality*, edited by Cheslyn Jones, et al., 549–54. New York: Oxford University Press, 1986.
———. *The Pentecostals: The Charismatic Movement in the Churches*. Minneapolis, MN: Augsburg, 1972.
———. "Two Extraordinary Pentecostal Ecumenists: The Letters of Donald Gee and David Du Plessis." *The Ecumenical Review* 52.3 (2000) 391–402.
Holman, Susan R. *God Knows There's Need: Christian Responses to Poverty*. New York: Oxford University Press, 2009.
Holzer, Harry J., et al. "The Economic Costs of Childhood Poverty in the United States." *Journal of Children and Poverty* 14.1 (2008) 41–61.
Hopkins, Charles Howard. *The Rise of the Social Gospel in American Protestantism, 1865–1915*. Yale Studies in Religious Education 14. New Haven, CT: Yale University Press, 1940.
Horn, Jonathan. "The Salary You Need to Buy a Home Here." *San Diego Union-Tribune*, May 22, 2014. https://www.sandiegouniontribune.com/business/real-estate/sdut-hsh-home-affordability-median-income-mortgage-2014may22-htmlstory.html.
Hunter, Harold D. *Spirit-Baptism: A Pentecostal Alternative*. Lanham, MD: University Press of America, 1983.
Hunter, Joel C. *A New Kind of Conservative*. Ventura, CA: Regal, 2008.
Iceland, John. *Poverty in America: A Handbook*. 3rd ed. Berkeley, CA: University of California Press, 2013.
Jacobsen, Douglas G. *A Reader in Pentecostal Theology: Voices from the First Generation*. Bloomington, IN: Indiana University Press, 2006.
James, Jonathan D. *McDonaldisation, Masala McGospel, and Om Economics: Televangelism in Contemporary India*. New Delhi, India: SAGE, 2010.
Jennings, James. *Understanding the Nature of Poverty in Urban America*. Westport, CT: Praeger, 1994.
Jensen, David Hadley. *The Lord and Giver of Life: Perspectives on Constructive Pneumatology*. Louisville, KY: Westminster John Knox, 2008.
Johnson, Elizabeth A. *She Who Is: The Mystery of God in Feminist Theological Discourse*. New York: Crossroad, 1992.
Johnson, Todd M. "The Global Demographics of the Pentecostal and Charismatic Renewal." *Society* 46.6 (2009) 479–83.
Kahan, Michael B. "Urban Poverty." In *Poverty in the United States: An Encyclopedia of History, Politics, and Policy*, edited by Gwendolyn Mink and Alice O'Connor, 738–42. Santa Barbara, CA: ABC-CLIO, 2004.

Kamsteeg, Frans. "Pentecostalism and Political Awakening in Pinochet's Chile and Beyond." In *Latin American Religion in Motion*, edited by Christian Smith and Joshua Prokopy, 187–204. New York: Routledge, 1999.

Kärkkäinen, Veli-Matti. *Ad Ultimum Terrae: Evangelization, Proselytism, and Common Witness in the Roman Catholic-Pentecostal Dialogue (1990–1997)*. New York: P. Lang, 1999.

———. "Are Pentecostals Oblivious to Social Justice? Theological and Ecumenical Perspectives." *Missiology* 29.4 (2001) 417–31.

———. "Evangelization, Proselytism, and Common Witness: Roman Catholic-Pentecostal Dialogue on Mission, 1990–1997." *International Bulletin of Missionary Research* 25.1 (2001) 16–22.

———. "Mission, Spirit and Eschatology: An Outline of a Pentecostal-Charismatic Theology of Mission." *Mission Studies* 16.1 (1999) 73–94.

———. *Pneumatology: The Holy Spirit in Ecumenical, International, and Contextual Perspective*. Grand Rapids, MI: Baker Academic, 2002.

———. "Spirituality as a Resource for Social Justice: Reflections from the Catholic-Pentecostal Dialogue." *Asian Journal of Pentecostal Studies* 6.1 (2003) 83–96.

———. *Spiritus Ubi Vult Spirat: Pneumatology in Roman Catholic-Pentecostal Dialogue (1972–1989)*. Helsinki: Luther-Agricola-Society, 1998.

Katz, Michael B. *The Price of Citizenship: Redefining the American Welfare State*. New York: Holt, 2001.

Kaun, Ali. "Generosity Multiplied." Rock Church. April 23, 2015. https://www.sdrock.com/stories/generositymultiplied.

Kertson, Brandon. "Pneumatology in Latin American Liberation Theology." In *Pentecostals and Charismatics in Latin America and Latino Communities*, edited by Néstor Medina and Samuel Alfaro, 85–99. Malden, MA: Wiley-Blackwell, 2015.

———. "Spirit Baptism in the Pentecostal Evangel 1918–1922: Static or Dynamic?" *Pneuma* 37.2 (2015) 244–61.

Kostlevy, William C. "Benjamin Titus Roberts and the 'Preferential Option for the Poor' in the Early Free Methodist Church." In *Poverty and Ecclesiology: Nineteenth-Century Evangelicals in the Light of Liberation Theology*, edited by Anthony L. Dunnavant, 51–67. Collegeville, MN: Liturgical, 1992.

———. "Culture, Class and Gender in the Progressive Era: The Social Thought of the Free Methodist Church During the Age of Gladden, Strong and Rauschenbusch." In *Perspectives on the Social Gospel: Papers from the Inaugural Social Gospel Conference at Colgate Rochester Divinity School*, edited by Christopher Hodge Evans, 157–82. Texts and Studies in the Social Gospel 3. Lewiston, NY: Edwin Mellen, 1999.

Lampe, G. W. H. *God as Spirit*. The Bampton Lectures. Oxford: Clarendon, 1977.

Land, Steven J. *Pentecostal Spirituality: A Passion for the Kingdom*. Journal of Pentecostal Theology Supplement Series 1. Sheffield: Sheffield Academic, 1993.

Lonergan, Bernard J. F. *Method in Theology*. New York: Herder & Herder, 1972.

Long, James P. "Miles McPherson: The Rock Church, San Diego." *Outreach Magazine*, November 3, 2009. http://www.outreachmagazine.com/interviews/3353-miles-mcpherson-rock-church-san-diego.html.

Luker, Ralph E. "Interpreting the Social Gospel: Reflections on Two Generations of Historiography." In *Perspectives on the Social Gospel: Papers from the Inaugural Social Gospel Conference at Colgate Rochester Divinity School*, edited by Christopher

Hodge Evans, 1–14. Texts and Studies in the Social Gospel 3. Lewiston, NY: Edwin Mellen, 1999.

Lyon, David. *Jesus in Disneyland: Religion in Postmodern Times.* Cambridge: Polity; Blackwell, 2000.

Macchia, Frank D. *Baptized in the Spirit: A Global Pentecostal Theology.* Grand Rapids, MI: Zondervan, 2006.

———. *Spirituality and Social Liberation: The Message of the Blumhardts in the Light of Wuerttemberg Pietism.* Pietist and Wesleyan Studies 4. Metuchen, NJ: Scarecrow, 1993.

Margolies, Luise. "The Paradoxical Growth of Pentecostalism." In *Perspectives on Pentecostalism Case Studies from the Caribbeans and Latin America*, edited by Stephen D. Glazier, 1–5. Lanham, MD: University Press America, 1980.

Markham, Paul N. "A Theology That 'Works.'" In *A New Evangelical Manifesto: A Kingdom Vision for the Common Good*, edited by David P. Gushee, 42–49. St Louis, MO: Chalice, 2012.

Martin, Ralph. "Interview with Ralph Martin." *Post American* 4.2 (1975) 8–14.

Mason, John D. "The Good City: Inner-City Poverty and Metropolitan Responsibility." In *Toward a Just and Caring Society: Christian Responses to Poverty in America*, edited by David P. Gushee, 340–95. Grand Rapids, MI: Baker, 1999.

Mayer, Susan E. *What Money Can't Buy: Family Income and Children's Life Chances.* Cambridge, MA: Harvard University Press, 1998.

McCracken, Grant. "Culture and Consumption: A Theoretical Account of the Structure and Movement of the Cultural Meaning of Consumer Goods." *Journal of Consumer Research* 13.1 (1986) 71–84.

McDonnell, Kilian. *The Other Hand of God: The Holy Spirit as the Universal Touch and Goal.* Collegeville, MN: Liturgical, 2003.

———. *Presence, Power, Praise: Documents on the Charismatic Renewal.* 3 vols. Collegeville, MN: Liturgical, 1980.

McDonnell, Kilian, and George T. Montague. *Christian Initiation and Baptism in the Holy Spirit: Evidence from the First Eight Centuries.* 2nd rev. ed. Collegeville, MN: Liturgical, 1994.

McDonough, Jeffrey K. "Leibniz's Philosophy of Physics." Stanford Encyclopedia of Philosophy. Mar 7, 2014. https://plato.stanford.edu/archives/spr2014/entries/leibniz-physics.

McFague, Sallie. *The Body of God: An Ecological Theology.* Minneapolis, MN: Fortress, 1993.

McGinn, Bernard. *Apocalyptic Spirituality: Treatises and Letters of Lactantius, Adso of Montier-En-Der, Joachim of Fiore, the Franciscan Spirituals, Savonarola.* The Classics of Western Spirituality. New York: Paulist, 1979.

Meikle, Sheilah. "The Urban Context and Poor People." In *Urban Livelihoods: A People-Centred Approach to Reducing Poverty*, edited by Tony Lloyd-Jones and Carole Rakodi, 37–51. London; Sterling, VA: Earthscan, 2002.

"Mental Health, Poverty, and Development." World Health Organization. http://www.who.int/mental_health/policy/development/en.

Menzies, Robert P. *Empowered for Witness: The Spirit in Luke-Acts.* New York: T. & T. Clark, 2004.

Miller, Donald E., and Tetsunao Yamamori. *Global Pentecostalism: The New Face of Christian Social Engagement.* Berkeley, CA: University of California Press, 2007.

"Ministries." Rock Church. http://www.sdrock.com/ministries.

Mink, Gwendolyn, and Alice O'Connor. *Poverty in the United States: An Encyclopedia of History, Politics, and Policy*. Santa Barbara, CA: ABC-CLIO, 2004.

Mittelstadt, Martin William. *Reading Luke-Acts in the Pentecostal Tradition*. Cleveland, TN: CPT, 2010.

Mladenovska-Tešija, Julijana. "Crucified as a Necessity: The Relevance of Moltmann's Theology for Evangelical Believers and Their Social Commitment." *Raspeti Kao Nužnost: Relevantnost Moltmannove Teologije Za Evanđeoske Vjernike I Njihov Društveni Angažman* 8.1 (2014) 7–24.

Moberg, David O. *The Great Reversal: Evangelism versus Social Concern*. Philadelphia, PA: J. B. Lippincott, 1972.

Moltmann, Jürgen. *The Church in the Power of the Spirit: A Contribution of Messianic Ecclesiology*. London: SCM, 1977.

———. *The Spirit of Life: A Universal Affirmation*. Minneapolis, MN: Fortress, 1992.

———. *The Trinity and the Kingdom: The Doctrine of God*. San Francisco: Harper & Row, 1981.

Monsma, George N. "Income Distribution in the United States." In *Toward a Just and Caring Society: Christian Responses to Poverty in America*, edited by David P. Gushee, 162–94. Grand Rapids, MI: Baker, 1999.

Monsma, Stephen V. "Evangelicals and Poverty." In *Is the Good Book Good Enough?: Evangelical Perspectives on Public Policy*, edited by David K. Ryden, 41–55. Lanham, MD: Lexington, 2011.

———. "Poverty, Civil Society and the Public Policy Impasse." In *Toward a Just and Caring Society: Christian Responses to Poverty in America*, edited by David P. Gushee, 46–71. Grand Rapids, MI: Baker, 1999.

Moore, Rick D. *God Saves: Lessons from the Elisha Stories*. Sheffield: JSOT, 1990.

Moore, Stephen D. *Poststructural-Ism and the New Testament: Derrida and Foucault at the Foot of the Cross*. Minneapolis, MN: Fortress, 1994.

Mott, Stephen. "Economic Justice: A Biblical Paradigm." In *A New Evangelical Manifesto: A Kingdom Vision for the Common Good*, edited by David P. Gushee, 15–45. St Louis, MO: Chalice, 2012.

Mouw, Richard J. "Thinking About the Poor: What Evangelicals Can Learn from the Bishops." In *Prophetic Visions and Economic Realities: Protestants, Jews, and Catholics Confront the Bishops' Letter on the Economy*, edited by Charles R. Strain, 20–34. Grand Rapids, MI: Eerdmans, 1989.

Müller-Fahrenholz, Geiko. *God's Spirit: Transforming a World in Crisis*. Geneva: WCC, 1995.

Nelson, Janet R. "Walter Rauschenbusch and the Social Gospel: A Hopeful Theology for the Twenty-First-Century Economy." *Cross Currents* 59.4 (2009) 442–56.

Nestler, Erich. "Was Montanism a Heresy?" *Pneuma* 6.1 (1984) 67–78.

Neumann, Peter D. *Pentecostal Experience: An Ecumenical Encounter*. Eugene, OR: Pickwick, 2012.

Newman, Paul W. *Spirit Christology: Recovering the Biblical Paradigm of Christian Faith*. Lanham, MD: University Press of America, 1987.

Nichols, Christopher M., and Nancy C. Unger. *A Companion to the Gilded Age and Progressive Era*. Malden, MA: Wiley, 2017.

Noll, Mark A. *The Rise of Evangelicalism: The Age of Edwards, Whitefield and the Wesleys*. History of Evangelicalism. Leicester: Intervarsity, 2004.

Noss, Amanda. *Household Income: 2013*. US Census Bureau ACSBR/13-02. Washington, DC: US Government Printing Office, 2014. https://www.nj.gov/labor/lpa/acs/2013/acsbr13-02.pdf.

Omenyo, Cephas. "A Comparative Analysis of the Development Intervention of Protestant and Charismatic/Pentecostal Organizations in Ghana." *Svensk Missionstidskrift* 94.1 (2006) 5–22.

Orshansky, Mollie. *The Measure of Poverty: Technical Paper I, Documentation of Background Information and Rationale for Current Poverty Matrix*. Washington, DC: Department of Health, Education, and Welfare, 1977.

Pagano, Nan. "Charismatic Social Action/Church of the Redeemer at Lantrip School: Common Life." *Sojourners* 5.1 (1976) 24–28.

Pannenberg, Wolfhart. *Systematic Theology*. 3 vols. Grand Rapids, MI: Eerdmans, 1991.

Patel, Vikram, et al. "Women, Poverty and Common Mental Disorders in Four Restructuring Societies." *Social Science & Medicine* 49.11 (1999) 1461–71.

Pearce, Diana M. "The Statistical Measure of Poverty." In *Poverty in the United States: An Encyclopedia of History, Politics, and Policy*, edited by Gwendolyn Mink and Alice O'Connor, 565–67. Santa Barbara, CA: ABC-CLIO, 2004.

Petersen, Douglas. *Not by Might, Nor by Power: A Pentecostal Theology of Social Concern in Latin America*. Oxford: Regnum, 1996.

Pew Forum on Religion and Public Life. "Global Christianity: A Report on the Size and Distribution of the World's Christian Population." Pew Research Center. December 19, 2011. https://www.pewforum.org/2011/12/19/global-christianity-exec.

Pilgrim, Walter E. *Good News to the Poor: Wealth and Poverty in Luke-Acts*. Minneapolis, MN: Augsburg, 1981.

Pinnock, Clark H. "Charismatic Renewal for the Radical Church." *Post American* 4.2 (1975) 16–21.

———. *Flame of Love: A Theology of the Holy Spirit*. Downers Grove, IL: InterVarsity, 1996.

Pinson, William M. *Applying the Gospel: Suggestions for Christian Social Action in a Local Church*. Nashville, TN: Broadman, 1975.

Rambo, Lewis R. *Understanding Religious Conversion*. New Haven, CT: Yale University Press, 1993.

Rauschenbusch, Walter. *Christianity and the Social Crisis*. New York: Macmillan, 1907.

———. *Christianizing the Social Order*. New York: Macmillan, 1912.

———. *The Social Principles of Jesus*. New York: Association, 1916.

———. *A Theology for the Social Gospel*. New York: Macmillan, 1917.

Ravallion, Martin, et al. "Dollar a Day Revisited." Policy Research Working Paper. Washington, DC: World Bank, 2008.

Reynolds, Blair. *Toward a Process Pneumatology*. London; Selinsgrove: Susquehanna University Press, 1990.

Robeck, Cecil M., Jr. *The Azusa Street Mission and Revival: The Birth of the Global Pentecostal Movement*. Nashville, TN: Nelson Reference & Electronic, 2006.

———. "The Social Concern of Early American Pentecostalism." In *Pentecost, Mission and Ecumenism*, edited by Walter J. Hollenweger and J. A. B. Jongeneel, 97–106. Frankfurt: Peter Lang, 1992.

Robeck, Cecil M., Jr., and Amos Yong, eds. *The Cambridge Companion to Pentecostalism*. Cambridge: Cambridge University Press, 2014.

Roberts, Alexander, and James Donaldson. *Ante-Nicene Fathers*. Grand Rapids, MI: Eerdmans, 1950.

Roth, S. John. *The Blind, the Lame, and the Poor: Character Types in Luke-Acts*. Sheffield: Sheffield Academic, 1997.

Saracco, Norberto. "Charismatic Renewal and Social Change: A Historical Analysis from a Third World Perspective." *Transformation* 5.4 (1988) 14–18.

———. "The Holy Spirit and the Church's Mission of Healing." *International Review of Mission* 93.370–71 (2004) 413–20.

Schaff, Philip, ed. *Nicene and Post-Nicene Fathers*. Peabody, MA: Hendrickson, 1994.

Schmemann, Alexander. *For the Life of the World: Sacraments and Orthodoxy*. 2nd rev. and expanded ed. Crestwood, NY: St. Vladimir's Seminary Press, 1982.

Schoonenberg, Piet J. A. M. *Der Geist, das Wort und der Sohn: Eine Geist-Christologie*. Regensburg, Germany: F. Pustet, 1992.

Scotland, Nigel. *Charismatics and the Next Millennium: Do They Have A Future?* London: Hoddern & Stoughton, 1995.

Segundo, Juan Luis. *Liberation of Theology*. Translated by John Drury. Maryknoll, NY: Orbis, 1976.

Short, Kathleen S. *Experimental Poverty Measures: 1999*. US Census Bureau P60-216. Washington, DC: US Government Printing Office, 2001. https://www.census.gov/prod/2001pubs/p60-216.pdf.

———. "Who Is Poor? A New Look with the Supplemental Poverty Measure." Paper presented at the Allied Social Science Associations, Society of Government Economists Conference, Denver, CO, January 6–9, 2011. https://www.census.gov/content/dam/Census/library/working-papers/2011/demo/sge-short.pdf.

Shriver, Donald W., Jr. "Introduction." In *A Theology for the Social Gospel*, by Walter Rauschenbusch, xi–xxv. New York: Macmillan, 1917.

Sider, Ronald J. *Evangelism and Social Action: Uniting the Church to Heal a Lost and Broken World*. London: Hodder & Stoughton, 1993.

———. *Just Generosity: A New Vision for Overcoming Poverty in America*. Grand Rapids, MI: Baker, 1999.

———. *Just Politics: A Guide for Christian Engagement*. Grand Rapids, MI: Brazos, 2012.

———. *Rich Christians in an Age of Hunger: Moving from Affluence to Generosity*. 5th ed. Nashville, TN: Thomas Nelson, 2005.

———. *The Scandal of the Evangelical Conscience: Why Are Christians Living Just Like the Rest of the World?* Grand Rapids, MI: Baker, 2005.

Siecienski, A. Edward. *The Filioque: History of a Doctrinal Controversy*. Oxford: Oxford University Press, 2010.

Silver, Hilary. "Culture, Politics, and National Discourses of the New Urban Poverty." In *Urban Poverty and the Underclass: A Reader*, edited by Enzo Mingione, 105–38. Studies in Urban and Social Change 19. Cambridge, MA: Blackwell, 1996.

Slaper, Timothy. "Redefining Progress: Economic Indicators and the Shalom of God." In *Toward a Just and Caring Society: Christian Responses to Poverty in America*, edited by David P. Gushee, 195–227. Grand Rapids, MI: Baker, 1999.

Slessarev-Jamir, Helene. *Prophetic Activism: Progressive Religious Justice Movements in Contemporary America*. Religion and Social Transformation. New York: New York University Press, 2011.

Smiley, Tavis, and Cornel West. *The Rich and the Rest of Us: A Poverty Manifesto*. New York: Smiley, 2012.

Sobrino, Jon. "Spirituality and the Following of Jesus." In *Mysterium Liberationis: Fundamental Concepts of Liberation Theology*, edited by Ignacio Ellacuría and Jon Sobrino, translated by Robert R. Barr, 677–701. Maryknoll, NY: Orbis, 1993.

———. *Spirituality of Liberation: Toward Political Holiness*. Translated by Robert R. Barr. Maryknoll, NY: Orbis, 1988.

———. "Systematic Christology: Jesus Christ, the Absolute Mediator of the Reign of God." In *Mysterium Liberationis*, edited by Ignacio Ellacuría and Jon Sobrino, translated by Robert R. Barr, 440–61. Maryknoll, NY: Orbis, 1993.

———. *The True Church and the Poor*. Maryknoll, NY: Orbis, 1984.

Solivan, Samuel. *Spirit, Pathos, and Liberation: Toward an Hispanic Pentecostal Theology*. Journal of Pentecostal Theology Supplement. Sheffield: Sheffield Academic, 1998.

Stephanou, Eusebius A. "Charismata in the Early Church Fathers." *The Greek Orthodox Theological Review* 21.2 (1976) 125–46.

Stephenson, Christopher A. *Types of Pentecostal Theology: Method, System, Spirit*. New York: Oxford University Press, 2013.

Steward, Joshua. "SD Income Rises, But High Poverty Persists." *San Diego Union-Tribune*, September 17, 2014. https://www.sandiegouniontribune.com/news/politics/sdut-census-income-poverty-recession-healthcare-2015sep17-htmlstory.html.

Strong, Josiah. *Our Country*. The John Harvard Library. Cambridge: Belknap Press of Harvard University Press, 1963.

Strong, Josiah, and Congregational Home Missionary Society. *Our Country: Its Possible Future and Its Present Crisis*. New York: Baker & Taylor, 1885.

Stronstad, Roger. *The Charismatic Theology of St. Luke*. Peabody, MA: Hendrickson, 1984.

Studebaker, Steven M. "Creation Care as 'Keeping in Step with the Spirit.'" In *A Liberating Spirit: Pentecostals and Social Action in North America*, edited by Michael Wilkinson and Steven M. Studebaker, 248–64. Pentecostals, Peacemaking, and Social Justice Series 2. Eugene, OR: Pickwick, 2010.

———. "Soteriology: A Story of the Spirit." In *Third Article Theology: A Pneumatological Dogmatics*, edited by Myk Habets, 233–49. Minneapolis, MN: Fortress, 2016.

Suenens, Léon Joseph, and Hélder Câmara. *Charismatic Renewal and Social Action: A Dialogue*. Malines Document 3. Ann Arbor, MI: Servant, 1979.

Sullivan, Andi Thomas. "Those Suffering From Preventable Diseases." In *A New Evangelical Manifesto: A Kingdom Vision For the Common Good*, edited by David P. Gushee, 85–93. St Louis, MO: Chalice, 2012.

Sutton, Matthew Avery. *Aimee Semple McPherson and the Resurrection of Christian America*. Cambridge, MA: Harvard University Press, 2007.

Suurmond, Jean-Jacques. *The Ethical Influence of the Spirit of God: An Exegetical and Theological Study with Special Reference to 1 Corinthians, Romans 7:14–8:30, and the Johannine Literature*. PhD diss., Fuller Theological Seminary, 1983.

Swoboda, A. J. *Tongues and Trees: Towards a Pentecostal Ecological Theology*. Journal of Pentecostal Theology Supplement Series 40. Blandford Forum, Dorset, UK: Deo, 2013.

Synan, Vinson. *The Century of the Holy Spirit: 100 Years of Pentecostal and Charismatic Renewal, 1901–2001*. Nashville, TN: Thomas Nelson, 2001.

———. *The Holiness-Pentecostal Movement in the United States*. Grand Rapids, MI: Eerdmans, 1971.

———. *The Holiness-Pentecostal Tradition: Charismatic Movements in the Twentieth Century*. 2nd ed. Grand Rapids, MI: Eerdmans, 1997.

Tallman, Matthew. "Pentecostal Ecology: A Theological Paradigm for Pentecostal Environmentalism." In *The Spirit Renews the Face of the Earth: Pentecostal Forays in Science and Theology of Creation*, edited by Amos Yong, 135–54. Eugene, OR: Pickwick, 2009.

Thomas, John Christopher. *Footwashing in John 13 and the Johannine Community*. Sheffield: Sheffield Academic, 1991.

———. "The Spirit, Healing and Mission: An Overview of the Biblical Canon." *International Review of Mission* 93.370–71 (2004) 421–42.

Tigges, Leann M., et al. "Social Isolation of the Urban Poor: Race, Class, and Neighborhood Effects on Social Resources." *The Sociological Quarterly* 39.1 (1998) 53–77.

Trawick, Robert C. "Called to a New Ethic: Walter Rauschenbusch and the Resuscitation of Vocation." In *Perspectives on the Social Gospel: Papers from the Inaugural Social Gospel Conference at Colgate Rochester Divinity School*, edited by Christopher Hodge Evans, 139–56. Texts and Studies in the Social Gospel 3. Lewiston, NY: Edwin Mellen, 1999.

Varkey, Wilson. *Role of the Holy Spirit in Protestant Systematic Theology: A Comparative Study between Karl Barth, Jürgen Moltmann, and Wolfhart Pannenberg*. Carlisle, England: Langham Monographs, 2011.

Venkatesh, Sudhir Alladi. *Off the Books: The Underground Economy of the Urban Poor*. Cambridge, MA: Harvard University Press, 2006.

Vigil, José-María. "The Option for the Poor Is an Option for Justice, and Not Preferential: A New Theological-Systematic Framework for the Preferential Option." *Voices from the Third Word* 1.27 (2004) 7–21.

Villafañe, Eldin. *The Liberating Spirit: Toward an Hispanic American Pentecostal Social Ethic*. Grand Rapids, MI: Eerdmans, 1993.

Volf, Miroslav. "The Final Reconciliation: Reflections on a Social Dimension of the Eschatological Transition." *Modern Theology* 16.1 (2000) 91–113.

———. "Materiality of Salvation: An Investigation in the Soteriologies of Liberation and Pentecostal Theologies." *Journal of Ecumenical Studies* 26.3 (1989) 447–67.

Vondey, Wolfgang. *Pentecostalism: A Guide for the Perplexed*. Guides for the Perplexed. London: Bloomsbury; T. & T. Clark, 2013.

———. *People of Bread: Rediscovering Ecclesiology*. New York: Paulist, 2008.

Wagner, David. *The Poorhouse: America's Forgotten Institution*. Lanham, MD: Rowman & Littlefield, 2005.

Wallis, Jim. *Faith Works: Lessons From the Life of an Activist Preacher*. New York: Random House, 2000.

———. *God's Politics: Why the Right Gets It Wrong and the Left Doesn't Get It*. New York: HarperCollins, 2005.

———. *The Soul of Politics: A Practical and Prophetic Vision for Social Change*. Maryknoll, NY: Orbis, 1994.

Warren, Rick. "Wilfredo De Jesús: Pastor, 48." *Time*, April 29, 2013. http://time100.time.com/2013/04/18/time-100/slide/wilfredo-de-jesus.

Warrior, Robert Allen. "Canaanites, Cowboys, and Indians." *Union Seminary Quarterly Review* 59.1–2 (2005) 1–8.

Weitzman, Beth C., and Carolyn A Berry. "Health Status and Health Care Utilization Among New York City Home Attendants: An Illustration of the Needs of Working Poor, Immigrant Women." *Women & Health* 19.2–3 (1992) 87.

Welker, Michael. *God the Spirit*. Translated by John F Hoffmeyer. Minneapolis, MN: Fortress, 1994.

Wessels, Francois G. "Charismatic Christian Congregations and Social Justice: A South African Perspective." *Missionalia* 25.3 (1997) 360–74.

West, Cornel. *Prophesy Deliverance!: An Afro-American Revolutionary Christianity*. Philadelphia, PA: Westminster, 1982.

Wiles, Maurice, and Mark Santer. *Documents in Early Christian Thought*. Cambridge: Cambridge University Press, 1987.

Wilkinson, Michael, and Steven M. Studebaker. *A Liberating Spirit: Pentecostals and Social Action in North America*. Pentecostals, Peacemaking, and Social Justice Series 2. Eugene, OR: Pickwick, 2010.

Wilson, William J. *The Truly Disadvantaged: The Inner City, the Underclass, and Public Policy*. Chicago: University of Chicago Press, 1987.

———. *When Work Disappears: The World of the New Urban Poor*. New York: Knopf, 1996.

Wink, Walter. *Engaging the Powers: Discernment and Resistance in a World of Domination*. Vol. 3 of *The Powers*. Minneapolis, MN: Fortress, 1992.

———. *Unmasking the Powers: The Invisible Forces That Determine Human Existence*. Vol. 2 of *The Powers*. Philadelphia: Fortress, 1986.

———. *When the Powers Fall: Reconciliation in the Healing of Nations*. Vol. 4 of *The Powers*. Minneapolis, MN: Fortress, 1998.

Witherington, Ben, III. "Salvation and Health in Christian Antiquity: The Soteriology of Luke-Acts in Its First-Century Setting." In *The Acts of the Apostles: A Socio-Rhetorical Commentary*, edited by Ben Witherington III, 821–43. Grand Rapids, MI: Eerdmans, 1998.

Wolterstorff, Nicholas. *Justice in Love*. Emory University Studies in Law and Religion. Grand Rapids, MI: Eerdmans, 2011.

World Council of Churches. *Baptism, Eucharist, and Ministry*. Faith and Order Paper 111. Geneva: World Council of Churches, 1982.

Yamamura, Kei. "Development of the Doctrine of the Holy Spirit in Patristic Philosophy: St Basil and St Gregory of Nyssa." *St Vladimir's Theological Quarterly* 18.1 (1974) 3–21.

Yong, Amos. *The Bible, Disability, and the Church: A New Vision of the People of God*. Grand Rapids, MI: Eerdmans, 2011.

———. *In the Days of Caesar: Pentecostalism and Political Theology*. The Cadbury Lectures 2009. Grand Rapids, MI: Eerdmans, 2010.

———. "Sons and Daughters, Young and Old: Toward a Pentecostal Theology of the Family." *PentecoStudies: An Interdisciplinary Journal for Research on the Pentecostal and Charismatic Movements* 10.2 (2012) 147–73.

———. *The Spirit of Creation: Modern Science and Divine Action in the Pentecostal-Charismatic Imagination*. Grand Rapids, MI: Eerdmans, 2011.

———. *The Spirit Poured Out on All Flesh: Pentecostalism and the Possibility of Global Theology*. Grand Rapids, MI: Baker Academic, 2005.

———. *Spirit-Word-Community: Theological Hermeneutics in Trinitarian Perspective*. Burlington, VT: Ashgate, 2002.

www.ingramcontent.com/pod-product-compliance
Lightning Source LLC
Chambersburg PA
CBHW062024220426
43662CB00010B/1471